APOCALYPSE

IN

SIGHT

The Significance of the Revelation

for the 21st Century

Roger Chambers B.Sc., M.Sc.

Apocalypse in Sight:
The significance of the Revelation for the 21st century
Copyright © 2010 Roger A. Chambers
All rights reserved

ISBN 978-1-4457-0566-8

Graphics used for the book cover and as illustrations are
Copyright © 2008 David Miles
and are reproduced by kind permission

Bible quotations, except where stated otherwise,
are from the Revised English Bible
Copyright © 1989 Oxford University Press & Cambridge University Press
and are reproduced by kind permission

CONTENTS

Preface	ix

1. Approaching the Revelation — 1
    1.1 The Main Problem — 1
    1.2 How the Message is Conveyed — 1
    1.3 Symbols and Meanings — 2
    1.4 Symbols as Consistent Biblical "Codes" — 3
    1.5 Structure of Revelation and Pointers from Earlier Prophecies — 5
    1.6 Summary of the Approach — 8

2. Establishing the Context (Rev. Ch. 1) — 9
    2.1 A Revelation to John (Rev. 1 v. 1) — 9
    2.2 How Rev. Ch. 1 Sets the Scene — 11
    2.3 The Authority of the Message — 14
    2.4 Summary of Rev. Ch. 1 — 16

3. The Seven Letters (Rev. Ch. 2 & 3) — 17
    3.1 Linking with Revelation Chapter 1 — 17
    3.2 Structure and Content of the Letters — 17
    3.3 Facing Problems – Then and Now — 18
    3.4 The Letters to Ephesus and Smyrna — 19
    3.5 The Letters to Pergamum and Thyatira — 21
    3.6 The letters to Sardis, Philadelphia, and Laodicea — 23
    3.7 The Promises in the Letters — 25
    3.8 Summary of Main Points in the Messages — 27

4. Understanding the Letters (Rev. 2 & 3 cont.) — 28
    4.1 Looking for Patterns in the Letters — 28
    4.2 Comparing the Churches — 28
    4.3 Churches Viewed as a Progression — 30

4.4 The Significance of the Number Seven	31
4.5 Summarising the Significance of the Seven Letters	32

5. The Throne of God (Rev. Ch. 4)   33

5.1 Introducing a New Vision – a View into Heaven	33
5.2 Comparison with Earlier Visions	34
5.3 The 24 Elders (Rev. Ch. 4 v. 4)	37
5.4 Throne Vision as Climax to Letters	39

6. The Lamb and the Scroll (Rev. Ch. 5)   41

6.1 The Scroll	41
6.2 The Lamb	42
6.3 The Lamb can Unseal the Scroll	43

7. The Message behind the Seven Seals (Rev. Ch. 6)   45

7.1 Introduction – the Four Horsemen of the Apocalypse	45
7.2 The 1st seal (Rev. 6 v. 1-2)	46
7.3 The 2nd Seal (Rev. 6 v. 3-4)	48
7.4 The 3rd Seal (Rev. 6 v. 5-6)	49
7.5 The Oil and the Wine (Rev. 6 v. 6)	50
7.6 The 4th Seal (Rev. 6 v. 7-8)	51
7.7 Summary of the Four Horses	52
7.8 The 5th Seal (Rev. 6 v. 9-11)	52
7.9 The 6th Seal (Rev. 6 v. 12-17)	54
7.10 The 7th Seal (Rev. 8 v. 1)	55
7.11 The End of the Seals – The Day of Wrath	56
7.12 Summary of the Seven Seals	57

8. The 144,000 & The Multitude (Rev. Ch. 7)   59

8.1 Holding Back the Winds (Rev. 7 v. 1-3)	59
8.2 Sealing the 144,000 (Rev. 7 v. 3-4)	60
8.3 Sealed out of Twelve Tribes (Rev. 7 v. 5-8)	61

8.4 The Great Multitude (Rev. 7 v. 9-17)	62
8.5 Binding and Freeing the Four Angels	63

9. The Seven Trumpets (Rev. Chs 8, 9 & 11 v. 14-19)   65

9.1 The Meaning of Trumpets	65
9.2 Preparing the Trumpets (Rev. 8 v. 2-6)	65
9.3 The First Trumpet Judgement (Rev. 8 v. 7)	67
9.4 The Second Trumpet Judgement (Rev. 8 v. 8-9)	67
9.5 The Third Trumpet Judgement (Rev. 8 v. 10-11)	68
9.6 The Fourth Trumpet Judgement (Rev. 8 v. 12)	69
9.7 Prelude to the Three Woes – the Eagle (Rev. 8 v. 13)	70
9.8 The First Woe or Fifth Trumpet (Rev. 9 v. 1-12)	71
9.9 The Second Woe or Sixth Trumpet (Rev. 9 v. 13-21)	74
9.10 The Third Woe or Seventh Trumpet (Rev. 11 v. 14-19)	76
9.11 Summary of the Seven Trumpets	77

10. The Rainbow Angel (Rev. Ch. 10)   79

10.1 The Angel and the Message	79
10.2 The Little Scroll	80

11. The Two Witnesses (Rev. Ch. 11 v. 1-13)   82

11.1 Jewish Aspects of the Witnesses	82
11.2 A Period of Witness	83
11.3 The Climax of the Trumpet Interlude	85

12. Half-Way Review   87

12.1 Summary of Revelation Chapters 1-11	87
12.2 A Peep at Revelation Chapters 12-22	90

13. The "First Fruit" (Rev. Ch. 12)   92

13.1 Introduction	92
13.2 The Woman (Rev. 12 v. 1-2)	92

v

13.3 The Man-Child and his Relatives	93
13.4 The Dragon / Serpent Symbol	96
13.5 Representing Empires in Daniel and Revelation	96
13.6 The Action Takes Place in Heaven	99
13.7 The "Firstfruits" of God's Harvest	99
13.8 The Struggle Continues	100
13.9 Eagle's Wings and the Dragon's River	102

14. The Two Beasts (Rev. Ch. 13) — 105

14.1 Introduction – Reminder of Earth & Sea Symbols	105
14.2 Beast of the Sea – Background	105
14.3 Transition from Dragon to Sea Beast	106
14.4 Sea Beast in Action	108
14.5 Beast of the Earth – Rev. 13 v 11-15	110
14.6 Earth Beast in Action	111
14.7 Mark and Number of the Beast – Rev. 13 v. 16-18	113

15. The Seven Angels & the Harvest (Rev. Ch. 14) — 115

15.1 The 144,000 – Rev. 14 v. 1-5	115
15.2 The Seven Angels – Rev. 14 v. 6-20	117
15.3 The Wheat Harvest – Rev. 14 v. 14-16	118
15.4 The Grape Harvest – Rev. 14 v. 17-20	120
15.5 Summary of Rev. Chs 12-14: Firstfruits to Harvest	122

16. The Seven Last Plagues (Rev. Chs 15, 16) — 124

16.1 A Vision of Heaven (Rev. Ch. 15)	124
16.2 Number Seven: Cycle and Completion	125
16.3 The First Bowl (Rev. 16 v. 1, 2)	127
16.4 The Second Bowl (Rev. 16 v. 3)	128
16.5 The Third Bowl (Rev. 16 v. 4-7)	128
16.6 The Fourth Bowl (Rev. 16 v. 8, 9)	129
16.7 The Fifth Bowl (Rev. 16 v. 10, 11)	129
16.8 The Sixth Bowl (Rev. 16 v. 12-16)	131

16.9 Nature of the Frog Spirits	133
16.10 The Seventh Bowl (Rev. 16 v. 17-21)	135
16.11 Summary Chart – Bowls (Vials) in Context	137

17. The Fall of Babylon (Rev. Chs 17 to 19 v. 10)   139

17.1 The Two Symbols for Babylon	139
17.2 Babylon the Harlot	139
17.3 The Beast	141
17.4 Harlot / Beast Interaction	144
17.5 The City of Babylon and the Euphrates	145
17.6 Babylon Fallen (Rev. Ch. 18)	148
17.7 Lessons for Believers	149
17.8 The Lamb's Wedding and Bride (Rev. 19 v. 1-8)	150
17.9 A Footnote to the Wedding Feast (Rev. 19 v 9-10)	151
17.10 Chart of Chs. 17 & 18 in Wider Context	152

18. The Kingdom and The End (Rev. 19 v. 11 to Rev. 22)   154

18.1 The Last Battle (Rev. 19 v. 11-21)	154
18.2 Overthrow of the Enemy	156
18.3 The Saints in Glory (Rev. 20 v. 4-6)	158
18.4 The Dragon Bound and Freed (Rev. 20 v. 1-3, 7-10)	159
18.5 The Second Death (Rev. 20 v. 11-15)	161
18.6 The End (Rev. 21 v. 1-8)	162
18.7 Vision of the Bride (Rev. 21 v. 9 to 22 v. 5)	164
18.8 The City as a Temple	166
18.9 The Two Women – a Summary	168
18.10 Epilogue (Rev. 22 v. 6-21)	169
18.11 Final Summary Charts	173

19. Postscript: The Events of Christ's Return   176

19.1 Gentile and Jewish Perspectives on the Return of Jesus	176
19.2 Prophecies that Set the Context	177
19.3 Prophecies of War Against Jerusalem	179

19.4 Identifying Israel's Enemies	181
19.5 Recap of the Final Battle in Revelation	183
19.6 Merging the Apocalyptic View with Other Bible Prophecies	184

Appendix A: Symbol Glossary   **189**

Appendix B: Alternative Ways to Approach the Revelation   **212**

PREFACE

The exposition of the Revelation presented here is the fruit of a long-standing personal interest in the book. That interest was given a sharper focus several years ago when a few members of my home church in North London decided to get together informally to study the book in detail. The style of study adopted was quite simple. Starting at the beginning, we read just a short section of text at a time and discussed it until we had at least some candidate interpretations of what it might mean. We generally did not allow ourselves to look ahead to later passages, but tried to concentrate on the portion of text currently being studied. However we did allow ourselves to refer back to previous work in order to reuse interpretations already agreed, or to choose between earlier, unresolved alternatives where later material cast extra light on the topic. If we ended a study session with any issues not resolved, then we took them away with us for personal study and meditation, and resumed the discussion at the next session. When we reached the end we went back to the beginning for a second pass through the text to consolidate our findings and resolve any outstanding issues.

The guiding principle we tried to follow was to let scripture interpret scripture. Although we had access to a number of different works of exposition and reference, we tended to use them mainly as prompts for fresh ideas if our own efforts were getting "bogged down". As part of our study strategy we decided not use any particular work as a regular guide or "set book" for our studies but always tried to be guided first and foremost by the Bible's own words. We also did not start with any pre-existing theories about the structure or key messages of the book. Although the text below does contain references to patterns and some charts outlining the structure of the Revelation, these emerged during and after the study as we tried to summarize our growing understanding of the book.

Altogether our studies ran on a regular monthly basis over a three-year period. Following this there was a period of wider dissemination of our findings through formal presentations of part or whole of the material to other groups, and through discussions and feedback with individuals. One particularly helpful step forward was an invitation to present all the material to one of our churches at two study weekends. Up to this point none of the original study-group members had made any significant notes of our findings. So, under time pressure as the invited presenter, I produced a large set of presentation material for use at the study weekends. Subsequently I used this material to form the backbone of the present text, supplemented by further reflections and research.

The title I have chosen makes a deliberately ambiguous play on the word "sight". Firstly, based on the experiences of the initial study group and the method of interpretation that the group developed, I have tried to present a way of tackling the complexities of the Revelation by focussing on the very visual style in which its messages are conveyed. Secondly, taking the modern usage of "apocalypse" to denote world-shaking events, I wanted to highlight that the messages uncovered by this approach are very relevant to the world of the 21st century, and that the climactic events leading up to the return of Christ may be coming into view much faster than many are expecting.

The large volume of existing expositions of the Revelation, put forward by so many knowledgeable Bible scholars, could easily have inhibited me from trying to add to the number, if I had not found an approach to the book that has proved to be so rewarding. I have been so excited and stimulated by the way that Biblical precedents can be used to identify the meanings of symbolic language and act as keys to unlock the message of the Revelation, that I have felt impelled to offer the ideas to a wider public. I do not put the approach forward with the intention of presenting it as the only right way of viewing this fascinating but complex part of the Bible, and I certainly do not expect everyone to agree with me. The views expressed here are purely personal and have no backing or sponsorship from any particular church or fellowship. I present them in the hope that you, the reader, might be encouraged to visit the Revelation with a newly awakened interest and with a few new ideas that may help you to make up your own mind about its message and its relevance to the times in which we live.

Finally, I would like to offer my grateful thanks to all those who have given support, help, and feedback during the years that it has taken to develop these ideas and get them into print. The full list of such supporters is too long to include here but particular thanks are due to:
- Margery McGregor
    - for hosting and chairing the original study sessions
- Bill Davison, Paul Hayes and Tony Moore
    - for editorial support and proofreading feedback
- Arthur Haythorn
    - whose quiet enthusiasm and persistent but gently expressed desire to see a finished text spurred me on, more than once, to renewed efforts when my progress had slowed or stopped
- David Miles
    - for his kind permission to use his Apocalyptic Images as illustrations which make a valuable addition to a book which lays so much emphasis on the visual elements of the Revelation (though this permission should not, in itself, be taken to imply his endorsement of the content of the book).

1. APPROACHING THE REVELATION

1.1 The Main Problem

The Revelation is full of vivid visual images. As the book progresses John conveys to us the sense of how he was swept along through a kaleidoscope of shifting scenes, some glorious, some frightening, and some puzzling. This gives the book a very dramatic impact and a sense of mystery, but it also presents the reader with a major problem – how to make narrative sense of such a pictorial presentation. As we start the exposition in Revelation chapter 1, we will be looking for guidance on how to approach the book, both from the text itself, and from precedents in earlier scriptures.

1.2 How the Message is Conveyed

The special, visual nature of this book is hinted at right at the start by the wording of verse 1: "This is the revelation of Jesus Christ, which God gave him so that he might show his servants what must soon take place". It is interesting that in describing the transmission of the message from Jesus, a word such as "tell" is not used. Many of the Old Testament (OT) prophets relate how the word of God came to them in verbal form, e.g. "the word of the Lord, spoken through the prophet Haggai." (Hag. 1 v. 1). At the opening of the Revelation the word "show" (translated as "signify" in the King James Version (KJV)) is used. This is from the Greek verb "semaino" which is closely related to the noun "semeion" meaning sign, miracle, or token. The verb form, meaning "to signify" is only used in five other places in the New Testament, and three of these are in the Gospel of John referring to use by Christ of indirect or symbolic language. Thus the word chosen in the first verse of the Revelation conveys a sense of transmitting a message visually and conveying its meaning indirectly by symbols or allegories. This is reinforced in verse 2 by John saying that he is "telling all that he saw" (and not what he heard).

So right from the start we are led to expect a book making heavy use of visual imagery. This initial impression is confirmed if we analyse the way John conveys how he received the content of the book. We can do this by comparing times when he indicates that he saw, or was shown, some visual scene or action, with the times when he indicates that he heard, or was told, some form of verbal communication. Looking at the total number of such indications across the whole book, we find that approximately sixty percent of them refer to visual communication while only about forty percent relate to speech and words. Also, many of the incidents of verbal messages are given relevance and context by attributing them to beings taking part in one of the visual scenes. On reflection, we should not be surprised at the strong visual element in the Revelation, since Christ, during his earthly ministry, also made considerable use of visual imagery in conveying so much of his teaching in the form of parables.

1.3 Symbols and Meanings

Presenting a message rich in visual imagery has some benefits and some problems. A key strength is the impact and memorability of the message, which was particularly valuable in times before literacy was widespread in the general population. A key problem is that it is not always obvious what the images mean, because typically the object being portrayed represents some other object or idea, e.g. Jesus' use of grains of wheat to represent the gospel message, wheat plants to represent believers, and weeds to represent unbelievers (Matt. 13 v. 36-43). When one object is used to represent another in this way it becomes a symbol or a metaphor.

Even though symbolic language is common in Bible prophecy, the disciples were concerned that Jesus' use of parables might obscure the clarity of his teaching. His answer to their query as to why he taught the people in that way was a little surprising. He said, "To you it has been granted to know the secrets of the kingdom of heaven, but not to them.... That is why I speak to them in parables; for they look without seeing, and listen without hearing or understanding." (Matt. 13 v. 11, 13 and quoting Is. 6 v. 9-10). So biblical symbols are not aimed at the casually curious but are intended to be understood by those with a sincere desire to learn and believe. The greater effort required to reach an understanding is also likely to make the message more highly valued once it has been understood.

That still leaves us with the problem of finding meanings for the symbols in the Revelation. Some symbols are given meaning in the text; for example the seven lamps described in chapter 1 v. 12 are explained in v. 20 as representing the seven churches (previously identified by name in v.11). However many of the images in the book are not explained, and perhaps the most fundamental problem of exposition lies in deciding the basis on which to interpret these symbols. Back in Daniel's day, Nebuchadnezzar was obviously aware of how easy it is to attribute subjective meanings to symbols when he decided not to tell his wise men what he had seen in his dream, but to insist that if they had the insight to know the meaning they should also be able to perceive the content of the dream (Dan. 2 v. 8-9). We have at least been shown the images in the visions conveyed to John, but the wealth of different meanings put forward by various writers over many years shows something of the magnitude of the problem of interpretation.

Probably one of the most common pitfalls in interpreting the imagery of the Revelation is to try to map each symbol directly on to some significant person, place, or event in history. This approach has two major drawbacks: the first is that there are many differing views of history and of what is significant in it; the second, and perhaps the more serious, is that the human view of what is important in history does not necessarily reflect what God sees as important in the unfolding of his purpose with the world.

1.4 Symbols as Consistent Biblical "Codes"

A very important claim made at the start of the Revelation, is that it came to John, via Christ, from God. This fits with so many other similar claims for divine inspiration made elsewhere in the books of the Bible. If we believe these claims then there are certain foundation assumptions that we can make about the message. If the whole is the work of the divine mind, then we can expect consistency and coherence, not just within the book or within the New Testament, but right across Old and New Testaments. After all, Christ himself frequently quoted the Old Testament as a basis for his own teaching, and to explain all that was to happen to him. With this assurance of coherence we can have confidence that biblical signs and symbols, like any other part of the message, are likely to have consistent meanings. So the foundation principle of our interpretation should be to try to let scripture interpret scripture wherever possible.

Thus our approach to the Revelation should be to examine the images occurring in each vision and first of all to try to find similar symbols elsewhere in the scriptures. We should not pick and choose, but try to find as many occurrences as possible in the hope of finding at least one or two that have clear explanations. Failing that, we should look for meanings that fit all, or the majority, of occurrences in a way that is compatible with their context and is consistent with the overall message. Only after we have found meanings for symbols from earlier biblical precedents should we attempt to interpret the meaning intended in the Revelation, and only then apply it to the world and its history or its future. The approach is rather like decoding pictograms or hieroglyphs on ancient inscriptions; once a clear meaning is found in one context, we can apply it to other uses of the same symbol in new contexts. So a key element of our approach is to proceed symbol by symbol, attaching meanings on the basis of scriptural precedent.

In the visions of the Revelation the individual symbols often occur in groups to form some kind of static picture or narrative scene. The meanings of the individual symbols and the way they are combined or interact provide many clues to the overall meaning of each picture or scene. As we view these clusters of symbols, a further aspect of our interpretative approach also needs to be considered. That is how we are to decide, once the meaning of a scene starts to emerge, whether we are to apply that meaning to a single event, or to take it as a general principle applying as a kind of pattern across a whole series or cycle of future events. For this aspect of interpretation it is harder to lay down very firm rules, but we can establish some general guidelines as follows:

- look for help in the text itself; e.g. when the seven bowls or vials are being introduced (Rev. 15 v. 1) it says that "with them the wrath of God was completed", which is a strong pointer that this refers to a single episode or period, and not to a general principle or pattern
- look for scriptural precedents; that is, look at earlier uses of the same symbol or passages which relate to the same idea or concept, and see whether a general or specific local point is being made; e.g. Christ's parable of the sower (for which we will show parallels in Rev. Ch. 6, when we investigate the seven seals) refers to the effects of preaching in general, not to a specific event, and so is likely to be the basis for a "pattern"
- look at the context of the symbol and its place in the emerging structure of the book; e.g. a section presenting a sequence of specific events, such as the seven vials or bowls depicting the seven last plagues, is unlikely to introduce a major new pattern as one of its component elements, since this would disrupt the flow and make it harder to follow the main sequence of events.

So, the overall approach we have taken is one characterized by understanding individual symbols by scriptural precedent, combining their meanings to explain the pictures or scenes in the book, and then trying to determine whether those scenes relate to specific events or, where appropriate, represent wider reaching patterns with general application.

1.5 Structure of Revelation and Pointers from Earlier Prophecies

The idea of exploring symbols in the context of the poetic and prophetic imagery of the rest of the Bible, and then grouping them into pictures or scenes, provides us with a way of allowing the meaning of different sections of the Revelation to emerge on a small scale. That still leaves the problem of trying to understand the structure or logical flow of the whole book. This is not easy or obvious, as the narrative seems to be very episodic, at least on a first reading.

It is tempting to make assumptions about the structure of the book based on personal preferences or the influence of other expositors whose work has proved helpful, but it is very dangerous. The symbolic nature of the text all too easily allows the detailed interpretation to be slanted, sometimes unconsciously, to fit the structural assumptions. I believe it is much preferable to try to keep an open mind and to allow the relationships between the different visions emerge gradually as we begin to develop an understanding of their possible meanings. Fortunately there are various narrative devices that help to divide the text into sections and to show the relationships between sections. So, for example, a sudden change of scene often marks the start of a new section, while a build-up to a climax, such as Christ being revealed in his regal glory, will often conclude a section. Also structural devices, such as grouping events or scenes into sets of seven, often denote larger scale divisions of the text, while multiple references to the same event or symbol can indicate links between sections.

As well as these textual prompts there are some scriptural precedents for how important topics were conveyed to earlier prophets and recorded as written structures. We often find in biblical prophecy that a group of successive prophetic utterances, using different images or symbols, may actually serve to reinforce a common underlying message or to present the same event from different viewpoints. Thus when a set of apparently different prophetic visions are related in the biblical text as a sequence it does not always imply that they will be fulfilled as a sequence of separate events. This will become clearer if we look at some examples.

First let us look at some of the prophecies given to Daniel, a book with many parallels in the Revelation. If we look at his visions about the sequence of empires that were to rule over the Middle East, we find that one historical event, i.e. the Greeks taking over power from the Persians, is shown in three different visions. In Nebuchadnezzar's dream of the great image, it is shown as a bronze belly and thighs following the chest and arms of silver (Dan. 2). In Daniel's own dream of the "beasts" it is shown as the leopard following the bear (Dan. 7), and in his next vision of the animals in conflict on the banks of the Euphrates, it is shown as the ram being defeated by the he-goat (Dan. 8). These three separate dreams, which use different imagery and contain different details, all relate to the same point of interpretation, namely that Persia will be conquered by Greece.

Daniel's case is not unique. We see a similar occurrence of complementary visions if we turn to experiences of Joseph. In two of his own dreams (Gen. 37) he had the dream about the "sheaves", and then the one about the "sun, moon and stars". Although these were two separate dreams, they had a single fulfilment in his rise to power in Egypt. Then something similar happened when Joseph interpreted his fellow-prisoners' dreams in Egypt (Gen. 40). He interpreted the butler's dream and the baker's dream; in this case there were two dreams with differing detail, but they referred to different strands of events that were fulfilled on the same day. Finally when Joseph interpreted Pharaoh's dreams about the coming years of plenty and famine (Gen. 41), there was the "cows" dream and the "ears of wheat" dream. These were two different dreams, which naturally had to be related in sequence, but they both referred to the same fulfilment occurring across one period of time. As Joseph says (Gen. 41 v 25) "Pharaoh's dreams are both the same; God has told Pharaoh what he is about to do".

It is particularly interesting in this context to note the words in Gen. 41 v. 32, "that Pharaoh has dreamed this twice means that God is firmly resolved on this plan, and very soon he will put it into effect". In other words, if God is intent on some aspect of his purpose and intends to implement his plan soon, then it is likely that he will give more than one warning via his chosen prophet. So, when we read in Rev. 1 v. 1 of God's intention "that he might show his servants what must soon take place", we might expect, from the precedent set in Genesis, that the visions which follow are likely to contain some elements of repeated or complimentary visions.

Thus the visions have to be related in sequence, because no one can have two at once, and words like "then...." and "then I saw...." are used to describe the vision sequence. However, we do not have to expect that the events predicted by the sequence of visions will necessarily unfold in sequence. So, following the precedents above, we should be on the lookout for occasions when different visions might be covering the same event. Such duplication might serve to add different details, to view the events from a different perspective, or simply to stress the importance of the message, as was the case with Pharaoh's dreams.

1.6 Summary of the Approach

In this opening chapter I have tried to establish some principles of interpretation. The overriding intention is to try to use scripture to interpret scripture. In this book of visual images and symbols we can use earlier scriptures to find precedents for attaching meanings to symbols and so find help in understanding how the symbols relate to each other as they are combined to depict the pictures and scenes that make up the apocalyptic visions. Once we begin to grasp the import of these scenes, we can start to make sense of the flow of the narrative and start to understand the overall structure of the whole book.

In looking for guidance on how to understand the flow of the narrative, we took pointers from earlier prophetic writings. There we found that a sequence of visions need not represent a sequence of events, but may represent complementary views of the same event or period of history.

2. ESTABLISHING THE CONTEXT (Rev. Ch. 1)

2.1 A Revelation to John (Rev. 1 v. 1)

The recipient of these portentous visions is simply identified as "John". The lack of any more detailed identification suggests that this John is noteworthy and easily identifiable in the early church, so a natural assumption is that this is John the apostle and gospel writer. This seems to be confirmed by the way the writer alludes to himself as a servant of Jesus (v. 1) and as a preacher who had given personal witness to Jesus (v. 9). The earliest traditions in church history, dating from the second century A.D., support the view that the John of the Revelation is the same as John the apostle. Other ideas have been expressed since, but the historical evidence seems to uphold the earlier opinion.

As a vision of the future and of the "time of the end", the role of the Revelation in the New Testament has much in common with that of the book of Daniel in the Old Testament. That being so, it is very interesting to compare John, assuming he is the apostle, with Daniel. A brief comparison of key characteristics is shown in Table 1 below.

Table 1: Similarities of John and Daniel

Characteristic	John	Daniel
Eminent in Jewish Matters	Pillar of the church in Jerusalem (Gal. 2 v. 9)	Young Jewish noble (Dan. 1 v. 3, 6) and prophet
Lived at the end of a Jewish epoch	Approaching the Jewish dispersion (AD 70-100)	Entering captivity in Babylon – end of kingship
Exiled from Israel	To Patmos	To Babylon
Beloved of God	4 times as "agapao" (John 13 v. 23; 19 v. 26; 21 v. 7; 21 v. 20) 1 time as "phileo" (Jn. 20 v. 2)	3 times (Dan. 9 v. 23; 10 v. 11; 10 v. 19)
Devout, prayerful	In the Spirit on the Lord's day (Rev. 1 v. 10)	Entered chamber to pray 3 times a day, even in danger (Dan. 6 v. 10)

If John is so like Daniel then perhaps we are being prompted to look for similarities in the purport of the messages they received from God. Essentially, the message that Daniel needed to understand was that the Jews had lost their position as an independent nation and as the active witnesses of the true God, and that gentile powers were now to dominate their land and their temple for a period, i.e. during the Babylonian exile. If John had to learn a similar message to that given to Daniel, then we can already start to form a working hypothesis about it. That is, that the Jews have lost, or will shortly lose, their political identity (in the Roman dispersion) and that they will also lose their role as the primary guardians of God's word, with the mainly gentile Christians taking on the main preaching role. Thus the time of Christ's absence will, both politically and spiritually, be "Gentile times". If this is so then the Revelation can be viewed as a complementary amplification of Christ's earlier "Olivet prophecy", expanding the brief reference to "the day of the Gentiles" in Luke 21 v. 24 into a more comprehensive message for a Gentile Christian audience.

Also, given these similarities between John and Daniel we can perhaps make a more speculative inference. It is likely that in the matter of worship, the attitude of the exiled John was like that of Daniel as recorded in Dan. 6 v. 10 when he opened his window to pray towards Jerusalem three times a day. It is also probable that both were very mindful of Solomon's prayer at the dedication of the temple (2 Chron. 6 v. 36-39, particularly v. 38), asking God to hear when exiles turn towards the temple in Jerusalem to offer their petitions. Thus John may well have been facing Jerusalem as he prayed on the Lord's day (Rev. 1 v. 10). If we look at Patmos, Jerusalem, and the seven churches of Asia Minor on a map, then we see that, from Patmos, Jerusalem lies approximately to the south-east, while the seven churches lie a little west of north. If we now picture John facing Jerusalem from Patmos, where do the churches lie? They lie behind his left shoulder! So when Jesus, standing amongst the lamp-stands (churches), speaks to John, he records that "I heard *behind me* a loud voice......" (Rev. 1 v. 10). Without this geographical context, there is no obvious reason for this specific direction of the voice being mentioned.

If this perception is true, then, by the physical movement, John is being graphically directed to turn away from a Jewish focus and is being prompted to look towards the emerging gentile church as the centre for future worship and preaching. It reinforces the gentile, not Jewish, orientation of the message.

2.2 How Rev. Ch. 1 Sets the Scene

At the beginning of any book we expect to be given some idea of the background or context within which its message is being presented, and the Revelation does not disappoint us in this. We have already seen that the early verses give us a brief identification of the messenger, John, and his personal circumstances. We have also been given a broad hint about the symbolic nature of the visions. In the remainder of chapter 1 we find that, besides the figure of Jesus himself, one other image is given great prominence, that is a selected group of seven of the early churches in Asia Minor.

The seven churches are made the addressees of the opening greeting (Rev. 1 v. 4), and John is further specifically commissioned to send the completed book to them in verse 11, where they are each identified by name. Then in the first vision after the opening commission and greetings, Jesus is represented as a radiant figure standing amongst them. The churches themselves are depicted as seven golden lamp-stands (Rev. 1 v. 13, 20), and their "angels" are shown as seven stars in his hand (Rev. 1 v. 16, 20). Since the original Greek for "angel" carries a root meaning of messenger or agent, it seems likely that these represent the elders of the churches who were entrusted with conveying and teaching the gospel message to the flocks in their care.

In the content of this vision there seems to be some support for our earlier hypothesis, about John facing Jerusalem during prayer and turning towards the voice heard "behind me" (v. 12). By the vision John is being graphically directed to look away from Jerusalem, the historic centre of the worship of God at a physical temple, and to look towards the new gentile church. Even if we cannot be totally sure about where John was facing initially, there is a clear emphasis in the text on the importance of the new, gentile churches of Asia

Minor as the new focus of John's attention and the addressees of his message.

Figure 1: Christ among the Lamp stands (Rev. 1 v 13)

Even the choice of imagery in this vision is significant. The golden, seven-branched lamp-stand was a significant item in the furnishing of the tabernacle, and a set of ten similar stands was used in the temple. These were the only source of illumination during the hours of darkness in these sacred centres of Jewish worship and the priests tended them as part of their sacred duties. In symbol they represent the illuminating power of God's word in a world darkened by sin (see **Gold**, **Lamp-stand**, and **Oil** in the symbol glossary). Now this image is being transferred to the gentile churches, which are portrayed in this vision as seven individual lamp-stands attended by a figure representing the glorified Christ. What a strong echo this is of Christ's words to the woman at Sychar. When she asked him whether it was right to worship at the main Samaritan shrine or at the temple in Jerusalem, he replied, "The time is coming when you will worship the Father neither on this mountain nor in Jerusalem..... but the time is coming, indeed it is already here, when true worshippers will worship the Father in spirit and in truth" (John 4 v. 21-23). Surely it is exactly this change of focus, from the literal temple in Jerusalem to the dispersed worship in the hearts of true believers, that is being so vividly illustrated in this vision. Also, how fitting it is that the messenger was not one of the authors of the three synoptic gospels, but the one who framed his gospel narrative round the cycle of the Jewish feasts prescribed under the Mosaic Law, and who showed how Jesus so perfectly fulfilled the types and symbols of that ritual. With this fulfilment, the time had come for believers to move on from literal obedience to the ritual of the Mosaic Law, to trying to live every aspect of life under the influence of the spirit and truth, which the law enshrined.

Thus it seems to be emerging from this first chapter that the Revelation is a message to the new, predominantly gentile church, being conveyed via a strongly Jewish apostle. The alternatives, of either a Jewish message through a Jewish apostle, or a gentile message through a gentile apostle, would both have carried severe risks of worsening the tensions and divisions between Jews and Gentiles in the early church. As it is, it seems that through God's wisdom, the use of a pillar of the early Jewish church to address mainly gentile issues would achieve maximum credibility and cohesive force across both wings of the community of believers.

2.3 The Authority of the Message

Another aspect of this opening chapter is the stress placed on the authority behind the message. Already in the first verse we see the claim for its origins with God and its transmission from Christ via an angel. The onward communication of this by John is referred to in the second verse as both the word of God and the testimony of Jesus – rather like his last will and testament in which he leaves his treasures to his heirs, and to which John is the witness.

The next few verses go on to stress the uniqueness of Christ and the central position he holds in the purpose of God. In verses 5 to 7 his death, resurrection, and future return as king over the whole world are briefly indicated, together with his role as the loving saviour who will raise his faithful followers to most elevated positions. At that time those who have ignored or rejected his claims will regret their failure with true remorse. Verse 7 in particular stresses Christ's second coming, with obvious references to the words of the angels at the ascension (Acts 1 v. 9-11) and the prophecy of Zechariah (Ch. 12 v. 10), this being a topic that will be examined more fully later.

This very brief summary of the gospel is bracketed by the greeting in verse 5 and the stamp of divine authority in verse 8 which both seem to be invoking the special name of God. That takes us right back to Moses at the burning bush, when God was commissioning him to go to his people in Egypt. When Moses asked God what name he should give when the people asked who had sent him, he was told to say, "I am that I am. Tell them 'I am' has sent you" (Ex. 3 v. 14). Hebrew scholars explain that the verb "I am" is used there in a tense conveying continuing action. This is fittingly rendered here as "the one who was, and is, and is to come", in other words the God who is eternal, before all and beyond all, or as rendered again here, the Alpha and the Omega (the first and last letters of the Greek alphabet).

Also the main graphic vision in this chapter, which John sees when he turns towards the voice heard behind him, reveals an image of Christ in glory (verses 10 to 20). This was prefigured in the Transfiguration (e.g. Luke 9 v. 29), but has become Christ's true state since he ascended to sit at his Father's right hand (e.g. Heb. 1 v. 13; Heb. 2 v. 9). This vision shares some of the imagery of earlier biblical visions of the Glory of God; also see **Glory** in the symbol glossary. In this vision, some of the notable features are:

- The figure is "like a man", obviously Jesus, who is referred to as "the Son of man" so many times in the gospels.
- The visible flesh of his face and feet, not covered by the long garment, are radiant, and the eyes are like fire. This is not just to represent glory, but also carries significant symbolic importance as part of the imagery associated with the concept of "light".
- From his mouth there comes "a two-edged sword". From a mouth we normally expect words, but the words of Christ carry particular power, e.g.:
    - "The word I have spoken will be his judge on the last day" (John 12 v. 48).
    - "The word of God is alive and active. It cuts more keenly than any two-edged sword; ... it discriminates among the purposes and thoughts of the heart." (Heb. 4 v. 12).
- He identifies himself as one who is raised from the dead and is now immortal, and as one to whom ultimate judgement over life and death has been committed. This links to the description of Jesus in verses 5 to 7.
- As one who even in his mortality revealed the Father to us (John 14 v. 9-10), the glorified Christ now reveals him so perfectly, and shares his purpose so fully, that he takes on his title of First and Last. He yields pre-eminence to no one, except the one who conferred this honour on him (Eph. 1 v. 20-22; Heb. 2. v 5-9).

Like the vision of the Lord seen by Paul on the road to Damascus, a striking feature of this vision is its radiance. Given the significance of light (see **Light** in the symbol glossary) as a symbol for that which is spiritually enlightening, and the linked symbol of the sword from the mouth as the word of God, we surely have in this vision a striking reference to the opening of John's gospel. Here, in a symbolic image, is the word that came from God, the true light that gives light to everyone. Here is the word made flesh, now radiant in glory.

2.4 Summary of Rev. Ch. 1

From the content of the chapter there seems to be strong evidence that the Revelation is directed towards gentile times and the largely gentile Christian church. The message has powerful authority, since it originates from God and is sent to John by the ascended and glorified Christ.

The visual impact of the first main vision centres on light as an image for the word of God. The use of this imagery at the opening of the Revelation seems to point strongly to its being a fulfilment of Simeon's prophetic words, when the infant Jesus was taken to the temple, of Christ being "... a light that will bring revelation to the Gentiles" (Luke 2 v. 32). Also the churches to which the book is addressed are portrayed as lamp-stands. These, being of human origin, are naturally not as bright as the sun-like radiance emanating from Christ, but their function is to project light into what otherwise would be darkness, i.e. to obey Christ's injunction to go into the world and preach the gospel. With this as a key theme in the introductory chapter, we might expect some of the following visions to deal with the successes or problems that the church might expect to encounter in carrying out its light-bringing task. It will be helpful to bear this in mind in examining subsequent chapters of the Revelation.

3. THE SEVEN LETTERS (Rev. Chs 2 & 3)

3.1 Linking with Revelation Chapter 1

As we move into chapter 2 we must remind ourselves that the chapter and verse divisions in our Bibles are not part of the original text, but are later additions made for convenience of reference. In the present case, there is no break in the narrative at this point. Rather we are still in the vision of Christ amongst the lamp-stands. The seven letters are the direct messages from the glorified Christ to each of the churches among whom he is standing. This is borne out in the wording of the greeting at the beginning of each letter.

3.2 Structure and Content of the Letters

Chapters 2 and 3 of the Revelation contain a sequence of seven letters, each specifically addressed to one of the churches identified by name in chapter 1 v. 11. Each of the letters follows the same structure, i.e.:

- The address, which gives the name of the church to receive the message.
- The greeting, which identifies the sender (Jesus) by highlighting some aspect of the vision of the glorified Christ in Rev. 1 v. 12-20.
- The message to that church, which contains praise, or warning, or both.
- A refrain, "he who has an ear, let him hear...", which is very significant because it indicates that the message is for all hearers with spiritual perception, not just for the church being specifically addressed in the letter.
    - This carries a strong echo of Jesus' use of a very similar phrase when he used symbolic language in his parables to teach the people during his ministry (e.g. Matt. 11 v. 15; 13 v. 9, 43). Then he was asking his hearers not just to listen to the story but also to perceive the underlying spiritual message,

and that same appeal is being made to those who read the Revelation.
- A promise, "to anyone who is victorious", which points to some aspect of future salvation. The promises use various symbols of resurrection, immortality, and glory, many of which are used again later as the book unfolds.

3.3 Facing Problems – Then and Now

It is obvious from the Acts of the Apostles and the Epistles that the early church experienced a variety of problems as pagans turned to Christ. Two of the seven churches addressed in the Revelation have their own, or a shared, New Testament epistle. The church at Ephesus had the epistle to Ephesians, and the church at Laodicea, which was near Colossae, was directed to share the epistle to the Colossians (Col. 4 v. 16).

From these and the other epistles we see that the types of problem experienced in the early church included struggles against the influence of external forces, problems with internal divisions and leadership, and personal problems with human relationships and morals. The external influences included Roman political domination which at times extended to persecution of Christians; Greco-Roman culture with its worldly philosophy, pantheism and pagan ritual; and local Jewish communities which often opposed the preaching of Christ as Messiah.

The internal problems developed as the original generation of apostles and eyewitnesses to Christ began to die out. In their place new converts sought to take over, sometimes with impure motives such as monetary profit or personal ambition, and sometimes promoting divergent views.

The personal problems were those of attempting to be an ambassador for Christ, by striving to live by the Christian ideal of purity, and of trying to love one's neighbour, while surrounded by a culture in which life was often short and day-to-day survival was an overriding priority for most people.

Many of the problems experienced by the early church are the same as, or have parallels with, those experienced by all believers, such as enduring temptation or trials, holding on firmly to the faith, and maintaining enthusiasm. In addressing such problems, the seven letters have great exhortatory value to all believers. It is a wonderful aspect of these visions that the seven letters were addressed to real churches, contemporary with the writer, and addressed real problems with words of comfort, guidance or reproof that still apply to believers today.

Many works of exposition of the Revelation put the letters in their fullest context by drawing on historical and archaeological sources to describe the way of life in the seven cities. As a key aim of this book is to draw out lessons for the modern reader, such details will only be touched on relatively briefly. Most of the detail covered will be related to parts of the text that are less obvious because they use some form of symbolic or "coded" language.

3.4 The Letters to Ephesus and Smyrna

In the greeting in the first letter, to Ephesus, Christ is identified as the one walking amongst the lamp-stands, as seen earlier in the vision. Amongst the problems facing this church was that of being in a city which was a major centre for the worship of Artemis, or Diana, (Acts Ch. 19), so that Paul in his epistle (Eph. Ch. 2) had to remind them that they had been called out of their previous pagan state to a new and more rewarding life in Christ. We also read in Paul's letter to Timothy (1 Tim. 1 v. 3) that Paul had left him in Ephesus "... to instruct certain people to give up teaching erroneous doctrines", so that was obviously another problem they faced.

A less obvious problem, although it is one that they seem to be overcoming, is that concerning the practices of the "Nicolaitans" (Rev. 2 v. 6). A possible clue is given by the underlying meaning of the Greek word used here, which means "conqueror of the people". This may be an allusion to a trend towards the emergence of a "priest" class within the church that sought to rule over the flock as an exercise of power rather than providing a humble offering of service. Such problems were known elsewhere, like the case of Diotrephes (3 John v. 9), and were quite contrary to Jesus' instructions that greatness in the church should come from service rather than position and status (Matt. 23 v. 8-10).

The second letter, to Smyrna, carries a greeting from the "first and last" who has risen from the dead – both references to titles or attributes of Christ used in chapter one. One of this church's main problems is the opposition of a "Synagogue of Satan" (Rev. 2 v. 9). The word "Satan" in Greek, as in earlier Hebrew, simply means an opponent or enemy (see **Satan** in the symbol glossary). In this case the enemy is described as a body of people who claim to be Jews, but are not. Using the word "synagogue" to identify the enemy points fairly directly at local Jewish communities who reject Jesus as the fulfilment of the promises to the patriarchs, deny him being their Messiah, and actively persecute any Christians active in their area. Paul met such communities many times in his preaching work (e.g. Acts 13 v. 45, 50). Smyrna seems to have such a Jewish community, and the warning is that they, or others possibly stirred up by the Jews, will soon be increasing their persecutions of the church. The duration of this persecution is described as "ten days". This seems most likely to be a symbolic time period, indicating a relatively short period. The use of the number ten in scripture can be associated with assessing or measuring human actions; possibly derived from the hand being used as a metaphor for action and the hands having ten digits (see **Ten** in the symbol glossary). For example, in the OT the standards for assessing human actions are summarised in the Ten Commandments, and in the NT the ten virgins represent the body of believers being tested for fitness to enter their Lord's wedding feast. In the case of Smyrna, it may be being used to indicate that the coming persecution is not to be feared as a divine punishment, but rather is a short period of testing that can be endured and overcome with God's help, leaving the church stronger. It may carry echoes of the time when Daniel's conscience led him to propose that he should only eat vegetables so as to avoid the unclean foods at the Babylonian court. At the end of a test period of ten days Daniel had prospered better than any of those on the court diet (Dan. 1 v. 12-15).

3.5 The Letters to Pergamum and Thyatira

The third letter, to Pergamum, carries a greeting from the one with the two-edged sword, another reference to the vision of Christ among the lamp-stands. They are said to be "where Satan is enthroned" and "where Satan has his home" (Rev. 2 v. 13). There is strong historical and archaeological evidence to indicate that Pergamum, or Pergamon in its modern spelling, was the site of the largest acropolis outside Greece, and contained major temples dedicated to some of the best known pagan gods. Many significant archaeological finds from this site, including a sculptured frieze and statues representing many of the gods, can still be seen today at the Pergamon museum in Berlin. Significant centres of pagan worship often opposed Christians, as was the case with the worshippers of Artemis at Ephesus (Acts 19 v. 23-40) and their opposition to Paul. The language of the third letter indicates that similar opposition had already occurred at Smyrna, leading to martyrdom for some of the believers, thus making the pagans a dangerous adversary (or "Satan") due to the strength of their opposition to the faith.

The letter indicates that the church at Pergamum had held fast to its faith through these troubles, but was facing further threats from within. The first problem concerns some in the church who followed Balaam's ways in encouraging participation in pagan cult practices. This refers to the time when the Jews were completing the exodus and were about to enter the Promised Land. Balak the leader of Moab, one of the peoples in Israel's way, saw the threat they presented and offered a great reward to the prophet Balaam if he would come and curse Israel (Num. Chs. 22-24). When God inspired Balaam to bless his people, rather than curse them, it seems that he still sought to get the reward by bringing about the people's downfall by more underhand ways. The people were invited to join in worship to the local pagan god, the Baal of Peor (Num. Ch. 25). We can infer that this was the work of Balaam from the specific mention of his execution when he was captured later among the Midianites (Num. 31. v. 8). The name of Balaam is thus associated with someone who knows God's way but tries to pollute or destroy it by the introduction of false teaching. It is not surprising that Pergamum was vulnerable to such a threat, as one very human reaction to persecution is to try to be assimilated into the local culture so as not to be noticed so easily by the persecutors.

The second internal problem at Pergamum was that some were accepting the Nicolaitan teaching that was also troubling Ephesus. If, as discussed earlier, this was the trend towards the development of a priestly class within the church, then it is likely that Pergamum would have been fertile ground for such a movement. Firstly, in a major centre of pagan worship, the local culture and social structure would naturally accept the role of priests as having important status and influence. Secondly, during a time of persecution and stress, the church would be very grateful for the guidance and encouragement of strong leaders. The combination of these two factors could easily lead to strong elders being accorded, and accepting, more power and status by the believers than that advised by the teachings of Christ.

The fourth letter, to Thyatira, carries a greeting from "the son of God" and makes reference to the radiant eyes and feet of the figure standing among the churches. One of their main problems was that they tolerated a self-proclaimed prophetess referred to as "Jezebel" (Rev. 2 v. 20). This is another Old Testament reference, concerning the foreign queen of evil king Ahab (1 Kings 16 v. 31; 18 v. 4; etc.). She led him astray into the idolatrous ways she brought from her home country, and encouraged him to abandon the strong moral code of the Mosaic Law, by arranging Naboth's death to allow Ahab to posses his vineyard. Thus the reference to Jezebel obviously symbolizes the subversive influence of worldly and false religions working from within, at the heart of what should be a believing community. The reference to her teachings as "the deep secrets of Satan" (Rev. 2 v. 24) really means "the deep secrets of the adversary" (see **Satan** in the symbol glossary). In this case, as indicated by the reference to Jezebel, the adversary consists of those who advocate the thinking and practices of the world. This may be an indication of the beginnings of Gnostic heresies within the church. The Gnostics, like many of the Greek mystery religions, initiated followers into their teachings through a series of stages, with their greatest secrets or mysteries only being revealed to, and closely guarded by, a small inner circle. This is possibly what is being referred to in the letter as the "deep secrets". Also the

Gnostics taught that if the spirit was truly illuminated via their teachings, then the flesh could be indulged without restraint. These characteristics of Gnostic teaching make the use of the symbol of Jezebel very apt.

3.6 The letters to Sardis, Philadelphia, and Laodicea

The last three letters contain fewer difficult symbols. The letter to Sardis carries a greeting from the "one who has (or holds) the seven spirits of God and the seven stars", a reference to the start of the vision which emphasises how Christ knows what is in the heart of each church and its elders. The problem with Sardis is obviously that they are resting on an earlier good reputation, but are in fact losing their vigour and possibly their faith. Two key images are used. The first is of death, referring to the outcome of sins when not covered by forgiveness because of the loss or absence of faith. Paul uses this image to describe the condition of the Ephesians before they came to Christ (Eph. 2 v. 1) "you once were dead because of your sins". The second, complementary image is of white garments, a symbol going right back to the clothing of the Levitical priests, and indicating a covering for our mortality and our sinful inclinations by a divinely provided righteousness. God confers this gift through his forgiveness and mercy to those who have and keep their faith in him. Its ultimate expression is the granting of eternal life to the faithful at the resurrection, and in this context Paul uses the image of human nakedness being clothed with a heavenly covering (2 Cor. 5 v. 1-3).

In the greeting of the sixth letter, to Philadelphia, the phrases identifying Jesus are not quite direct quotes from chapter one. However, the phrase "the Holy One" summarises very well the image of the glorified Christ, and the phrase "the True One" is very close to "the faithful witness" from verse 5 of chapter one. The main imagery of the letter is of doors and keys. Christ called himself the door of the sheepfold (John 10 v. 7) to illustrate how the only way into his kingdom was by going "through" him, which is done symbolically in baptism. After his ascension, it was the duty of the church to invite or guide people through this door, and in giving Peter this commission, Christ uses the image of passing over the keys (Matt. 16 v. 19). In several epistles, Paul takes up the symbol of an open door to describe profitable opportunities for preaching (e.g. 1 Cor. 16 v. 9 KJV).

The letter to Philadelphia also uses the image of the "Synagogue of Satan" which was discussed in looking at the letter to Smyrna. The added detail here is that these opponents of the church will eventually be made to recognize that it is the Christian believers who "are my beloved people" (Rev. 3 v. 9). This reinforces the interpretation that these enemies are a local Jewish community as they would normally be the ones laying claim to be God's chosen people.

The final letter, to Laodicea, carries a greeting from "the Amen" (i.e. the end or Omega), "the faithful and true witness" (see Ch. 1 v. 5), and "the source of God's creation". This latter phrase refers to the key role of Christ as the primary agent of salvation in God's purpose of creating a special people for himself. As access to this creative process is via the gospel, the phrase captures the import of the start of the vision, where a radiant Christ stands at the heart of the churches and inspires them to pass on the light as effective lamp stands. Unfortunately in the case of Laodicea this commission was not being well executed. Using images of wealth, clothing, and sight or understanding, the letter contrasts the church's good standing in the literal, material meaning of these things with its poverty in their spiritual counterparts, i.e. their lack of spiritual wealth in the form of valuable gospel knowledge, spiritual clothing by divinely provided righteousness, and spiritual sight as insight into the true nature of their own condition.

Another image used in the letter, that of hot, cold and lukewarm water, draws on geographical features local to the city, as there were in the vicinity hot springs, typically judged to be curative, and cold springs that would be very refreshing. As a body of believers, the church should have had both of these properties, of being able to offer both cure and refreshment to the spiritually troubled. Unfortunately they were able to do neither. The strong note of encouragement arising from this last and potentially depressing letter is that, despite all their weaknesses and faults, the church is not being cut off; but its members, like those of all the other churches, are promised places in Christ's kingdom if they open their hearts more fully to him.

3.7 The Promises in the Letters

A great encouragement to be drawn from all seven of the letters is that no church, no matter how severe the criticisms against it, is left without hope. All are offered a reward, if they will hear the message addressed to them and respond to it in faith. The promises to the seven churches are all different but all refer in some way to the granting of immortal life and entry into Christ's kingdom.

The promise to Ephesus is to eat from the tree of life. This is a vision of Eden restored, a new access to the tree of life from which Adam and Eve were barred on their expulsion from the garden (Gen. 3 v. 22-24). It promises a removal of the effects of the curse brought about in response to Adam's sin, and depicts the ultimate fulfilment of the promise implicit in the divine provision of a covering for sin by the shedding of innocent blood (Gen. 3 v. 21).

The believers at Smyrna are promised that they will not suffer a second death. This anticipates the vision, at the end of chapter 20, of the final destruction of all evil and even death itself at the end of the millennial era. Being spared from that destruction implies that immortality and entry to Christ's kingdom have already been conferred at the start of the millennium. These issues will be covered in more detail in the commentary on chapters 19 and 20.

For the church at Pergamum, the promise is of being given some of the hidden manna and a new name on a white stone. The hidden manna refers to the pot of manna that Aaron was told to put in the Ark of the Covenant (Ex. 16 v. 33). This represents a divinely provided source of life in a desert place where there would otherwise be only death – a good image of God's promise of salvation. As for the new name, in scriptural use a name often captures the essence or essential nature of the thing being named. The new name promised here seems to convey the change of nature that will occur at the resurrection. Having the name written on a stone strikes echoes of God's finger writing the commandments on the stone tables given to Moses, especially since these were also put in the ark. This also strikes echoes of having God's law written on our hearts to effect the change in our natures (see Jer. 31 v. 33-34). The stone being white portrays the pure and righteous nature of what is being given.

The promise to the church at Thyatira is twofold. Firstly the believers are promised a place of power in having future rulership over the nations of the earth. This is couched in terms of ruling the nations with a rod of iron, which relates directly to the messianic promises of Psalm 2, which are applied to Christ himself later in Revelation (Rev. 12 v. 5; Rev. 19 v. 15). The second part of the promise is to be given the morning star. This is the last of the heavenly bodies still visible as the sky brightens with the rising sun. The image involved is that of Christ at his return being the rising sun, bringing the light of the kingdom to the earth and replacing or extinguishing all other lights except that of the faithful who will share his glory (see **Heavenly Bodies** in the symbol glossary). These promises to Thyatira are very similar to the simpler and more explicit promise made to the believers at Laodicea that they will sit on Jesus' throne.

The faithful in Sardis are promised white garments. These correspond to the linen clothes of the Levitical priests and the garments often described as the clothing of angels, both symbolizing purity and righteousness (see **White** in the symbol glossary). This represents the fulfilment of the desire expressed by Paul to be "clothed" by being "absorbed into life immortal" at the coming of Christ (2 Cor. 5 v. 1-4). This image is used again, with a specific explanation of being "the righteous deeds of God's people", in the section describing the start of the millennium in Rev. 19 v. 7-8. There is also a related promise of having a name retained in the Book of Life; an image of being recorded and remembered by God in order to have new life conferred in the resurrection (see also Malachi 3 v. 16-18).

The believers at Philadelphia are promised that they will be permanent pillars in the temple of God. This is very like the language used by Peter (1 Pet. 2 v. 4-7) likening believers to living stones being built into a spiritual house. The finished temple, like that built by Solomon, is a place for God's name to dwell; and so the promise continues by saying that the believers will carry the names of God, of Christ, and of the New Jerusalem. This forms a forward reference to Rev. Ch. 21, which depicts the purified saints as the holy city in which God and Christ dwell.

3.8 Summary of Main Points in the Messages

To get some idea of the range of messages sent to the different churches, it is useful to step back from the detail and try to draw out the main two or three points of praise or reproof addressed to each church. Making a fairly subjective assessment of the significance of the points in the letters, it is possible to draw up a summary as shown in Table 2 below.

Table 2: Key Points from the Seven Letters

Church	Praise	Reproof
Ephesus (Ch. 2 v. 1-7)	- Patient endurance - Testing falsehood - Hate Nicolaitans	- Loss of first love
Smyrna (Ch. 2 v. 8-11)	- Endurance of poverty - Endurance of persecution	- (None)
Pergamum (Ch. 2 v. 12-17)	- Endurance of difficulties	- Pagan tendencies - Follow Nicolaitans
Thyatira (Ch. 2 v. 18-29)	- Good qualities - Increasing works	- Tolerate Jezebel
Sardis (Ch. 3 v. 1-6)	- Some still pure	- Church is dying
Philadelphia (Ch. 3 v. 7-13)	- Continuing to work - Patient endurance in faith	- (None)
Laodicea (Ch. 3 v. 14-22)	- (None)	- Lukewarm - Spiritually blind - Materialism

Summarizing the contents of two chapters into one simple table enables us to get a much clearer oversight of the main thrust of the seven letters, and on the basis of this summary we can start to look for some shape or pattern that will guide us to a deeper understanding of these letters.

4. UNDERSTANDING THE LETTERS (Rev. 2 & 3 Cont.)

4.1 Looking for Patterns in the Letters

Having considered the seven letters individually, it has been possible to interpret some of the key symbols used, and to understand something of the spiritual condition of each of the churches. This provides a basis for further analysis of the churches as a group to see if any pattern can be detected that will enhance our understanding. One question that springs to mind is why these particular churches were selected to be in this very special list of seven? We might also wonder if the choice of just seven churches has any particular significance. Finding some kind of pattern might help us to answer these questions, and the summary table drawn up at the end of the last chapter provides a suitable basis for doing some simple analysis.

4.2 Comparing the Churches

A striking feature of the table summarising the content of the seven letters is the wide range of variation in the amount of praise and reproof contained in each letter. One way of seeing if that variation follows any pattern is to count the number of main points made to each church, allocating one positive point for each main item of praise, and one negative point for each main item of reproof. This is not to imply that divine judgment involves any dry, legalistic counting and balancing of good works and sins, as that would totally discount the greatness of God's love and mercy. Rather, counting is a basic skill that allows our human minds to bring some order to a complex world.

The simple count is of limited value as the total number of points raised about each church varies from 2 to 4, making it difficult to compare the scores in this form. However, a more directly comparable measure can be obtained by converting the raw scores to percentages, i.e. expressing the positive and negative points totals for each church as a percentage of the total points addressed to that church. These calculations result in the table of scores shown below.

Table 3: Key Points Expressed as Scores

Church Addressed	+ve points	-ve points	% +ve	% -ve
Ephesus	3	1	75	25
Smyrna	2	0	100	0
Pergamum	1	2	40	60
Thyatira	2	1	60	40
Sardis	1	1	50	50
Philadelphia	2	0	100	0
Laodicea	0	3	0	100

A simple comparison table can now be derived by dropping the raw scores and keeping only the positive percentage scores. The negative percentages can also be dropped, as they are just the complementary values of the positive scores. One final change to the presentation helps to draw out the underlying pattern, that is to list the churches in the order of their positive (praise) percentage score. This gives the ranked table shown below.

Table 4: Churches Ranked by "Praise Score"

Church Addressed	% +ve
Philadelphia	100
Smyrna	100
Ephesus	75
Thyatira	60
Sardis	50
Pergamum	40
Laodicea	0

From this simple scoring process we can see a pattern emerging. Presenting the various churches in a graded list shows that they form a spectrum of spiritual quality. Since people and their communities rarely stand still, we can take our analysis one step further to try to find connections between the steps.

4.3 Churches Viewed as a Progression

Taking the scores of the churches, and interpreting them in the light of the comments made in each letter, we can reorder the list again to form a possible life cycle for spiritual development. For a starting point, we can take one of the middle-ranking churches, about which the tone of the comments is quite positive, and consider it to be in a growth phase.

The **_growth_** phase seems to fit Thyatira, which receives comments that it has good qualities, is increasing in works, but still has some problems to overcome.

Then, **_maturity_** would be the next natural phase in the cycle, and two churches, which both receive only praise, seem to fit here. There is Philadelphia, which is continuing to work and enduring in faith, and Smyrna, which is enduring despite poverty and persecution. From such a high point, things can only start to decline.

So, **_declining_** seems to be the next phase, and this fits two churches to different degrees. First Ephesus, which receives mostly praise, has started to decline because although it is approved for being patient, and for testing and hating falsehood, it has most significantly lost its first love. Beyond this, Sardis, with equal praise and reproof, has only some who are still pure; but underneath the surface appearance Sardis is described as dying. A growth cycle like this is not irreversible, and declining churches can recover, but without correction decline tends to accelerate.

Thus, **_sinking_** seems to be the final stage, again fitting two churches to different degrees. For Pergamum there is some approval for enduring in difficulty, but this is outweighed by some serious criticism for major problems. Finally, Laodicea gets nothing but reproof for being lukewarm, blind, and materialistic, though even here the hope of regaining lost ground is still held out. Indeed a promise of great reward is held out to those who stay faithful in all of the churches in the list.

Since the scoring system used in this analysis is very basic, we cannot be dogmatic about the exact position of any of the churches in this cycle. However the idea of a cycle of spiritual development and decline is very useful because it helps us to recognize that the situations described are not unique to Asia Minor, or even just to the 1st Century. Rather they are experienced by many churches and movements and can be seen to have occurred in many different places at many different times. So perhaps we have an answer to one of our earlier questions about why these particular seven churches were selected. It now seems that they were selected as very typical examples of the problems, strengths, and weaknesses that would affect the spiritual growth and decline of individuals, churches, and whole religious movements throughout the Christian era.

4.4 The Significance of the Number Seven

We now return to another question we asked earlier. Does the choice of seven churches have any particular significance? Following our principles we must try to answer this from within the Bible and this is done in detail under *Seven* in the symbol glossary, which shows that the number relates to ideas of carrying to completion or reaching an end, and also of doing this repeatedly in a cycle or repeating pattern.

The actual geographical location of the seven chosen cities also contributes to this idea of circularity. If we look at a map of Asia Minor, particularly a historical map of Roman times, we see that the cities lie on a roughly circular route. They were connected by what is believed to have been a Roman post road. A messenger leaving John on Patmos would have crossed by sea to the nearest city on the list, Ephesus (or its port Miletus), and from there, travelling clockwise round the circle, would have visited each of the named cities in turn. This would have followed the sequence of cities in the order that the letters are addressed in the Revelation. From the last city, Laodicea, it would only have been a relatively short journey on to the start of the circle at Ephesus and thence by ship back to Patmos to report on the completed task. Even if this journey was not in fact undertaken, the layout and presentation of the letters in this sequence, with instructions to have the whole message delivered, seems to reinforce the idea of the letters, and the messages they contain, forming some sort of a cycle.

4.5 Summarising the Significance of the Seven Letters

The seven letters were written to seven real churches to address real problems that those churches were experiencing. However their messages are also addressed to "those who have ears to hear", and so may be taken to have a more general application. Starting with the idea of a spectrum of spiritual quality we have discovered that the range of the messages spans a whole cycle of spiritual development and decline. When we combine this with the ideas of cycles and circles that arise from other Biblical uses of the number seven, we see a major pattern emerging; namely that the seven letters represent a cycle of the development of faith within the church and its members. This cycle of faith is one that recurs in many places over varying time-spans. Its exhortations, warnings and promises apply to believers living throughout the whole of the Christian era.

5. THE THRONE OF GOD (Rev. Ch. 4)

5.1 Introducing a New Vision – a View into Heaven

In our study of the Revelation so far, chapters 1 to 3, after a few verses of introduction, have just covered one extended vision of Christ amongst the lamp-stands (the churches of Asia Minor) and his messages to them. With the opening of chapter 4 we are introduced to a new vision. John sees a door in heaven and is invited to come up and be told of future events (Rev. 4 v. 1). To understand what this shift of perspective means, we must try to get clear what the scriptures mean by "heaven" and in what sense it is "up" or "above".

A Biblical background to these ideas is presented under **Heaven** in the symbol glossary. In brief, heaven refers to the presence, or sphere of action, of God. Since God is omniscient and omnipresent, this is not physically located somewhere in our three-dimensional, spatial universe. It is more like a parallel, spiritual dimension with which we can be in contact in any physical location. The idea of it being elevated, or "up" above us, conveys the spiritual elevation of a God whose ways and thoughts are so much above ours (as in Is. 55 v. 8-9).

When the focus of John's attention is drawn up to this elevated realm, he sees a vision of awe-inspiring power. In the vision he sees a radiant being seated on a heavenly throne. The idea of a throne is common to most civilizations as a symbol of ruling authority, like that of kings or emperors. This throne is in "heaven", with its scriptural connotations of the spiritual realm, which contains all that belongs to, and responds to, God. It is thus a symbol of supreme power, above all earthly rule, both secular and religious. So it is fitting that the figure on the throne is addressed as being "God the sovereign Lord of all, who was, and is, and is to come" (Rev. 4 v. 8), in other words God, the almighty and eternal. John is not the only prophet to be granted such a vision, and it is interesting to see how many of the visions in earlier books of the Bible use similar imagery to portray God's glory (also see **Glory** in the symbol glossary).

5.2 Comparison with Earlier Visions

The vision of glory in Revelation chapter 4 is similar to other prophets' visions as recorded in the Old Testament, but it is perhaps the most detailed. Key elements of the vision are:

- It is elevated or heavenly – this is an indication of the spiritual superiority of God, as discussed above.
- It focuses on a throne – this is a symbol of royal power and authority.
- It contains winged creatures – these appear to be "cherubim" like the figures modelled in gold on the lid of the ark of the covenant or engraved on the walls of Solomon's temple, which appear to be used to mark or emphasize the boundary between the holy and the temporal – see **Cherubim** in the symbol glossary.
- It shows creatures with four faces – this is a particular feature of cherubim, see above.
- The living creatures have many eyes – this is a symbol of God's omniscience, his ability to see everywhere, under all circumstances, even into human hearts and minds.
- Fire or smoke are present – a symbol conveying the idea of heat, or more generally a source of energy or power, and thus portraying God as a creative and active power; as He also revealed himself to Moses in the burning bush, or to other faithful on the occasions when a sacrifice was consumed without a light being set to the wood beneath it.
- A sea of crystal lies before the throne – a possible symbol for spiritual cleansing and the conferring of immortality to the redeemed – see **Crystal Sea** in the symbol glossary.
- There is a rainbow brightness – the rainbow was the sign of God's covenant, in Noah's day, that he would never again bring an overwhelming flood on the earth; more generally it represents God's promise to forgive and spare those who believe in him as Noah did, and is thus a sign of his offer of salvation.
- Other worshippers are present – a portrayal of God's aim of drawing mankind to him, to know him, and ultimately to share in his glory.

The crosses in Table 5 below show the occurrence of these details in other major visions of the glory of God.

Table 5: Elements of "Heaven" Revealed to Different Prophets

Feature	Rev. 4	Ezek. 1 & 10	Dan. 7 v 9	Is. 6 v 1
Lifted up	+	+		+
A Throne	+	+	+	+
Winged Creatures	+	+		+
4 Faces	+	+		
Eyes	+	+		
Fire / Smoke	+	+	+	+
Crystal Sea	+	+		
Rainbow Brightness	+	+		
Others who Worship	+		+	
On the Throne	God, Almighty & Eternal	Glory of the Lord	Ancient of Days	The Lord
Approaches Throne	The Lamb	Ezekiel, called "Son of Man"	One like a Son of Man	Isaiah, called "Son of Man"

In summary then, the vision revealed in Revelation chapter 4 is one of the Bible's most comprehensive representations of God in his Glory and shares many details with similar visions revealed to some of the great prophets in the Old Testament. As we will see in chapter 5, this glorious throne is approached by Christ who now shares the same glory. Thus it is natural that John's earlier vision of the glorified Christ standing amongst lamp-stands (Rev. Ch. 1) also used some of the same symbols.

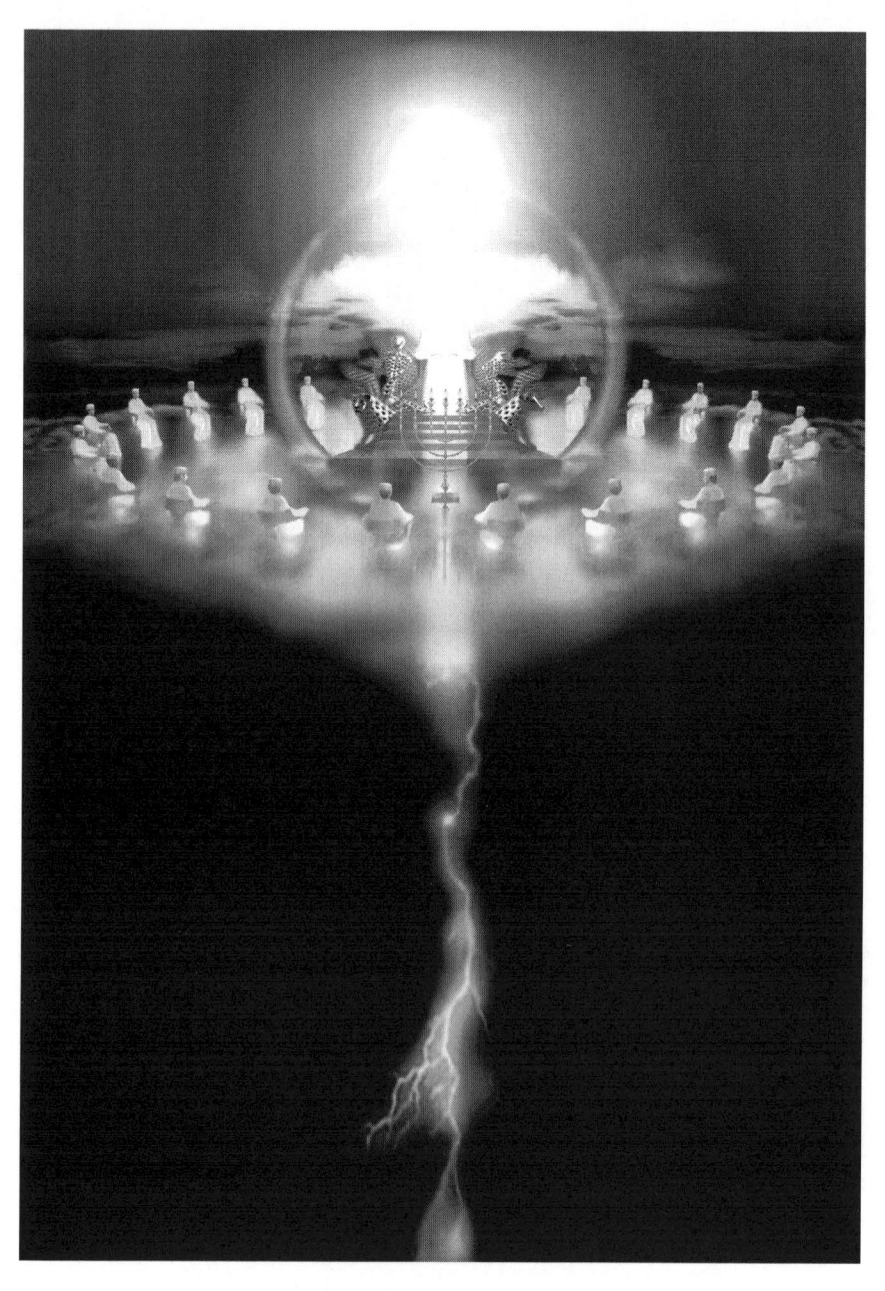

Figure 2: The Throne in Heaven (Rev. 4 v 2)

5.3 The 24 Elders (Rev. Ch. 4 v. 4)

One detail in this vision of God in glory warrants a little further investigation; that is the group of elders surrounding the throne (Rev. 4 v. 4). They are only described briefly, but the details revealed are deeply symbolic and give us some strong clues as to the meaning of this group in the vision.

Firstly the elders are described as being in a circle around the throne. This echoes the circle of the seven churches with Christ in their midst, that we looked at in the opening chapters. It could suggest that the elders have something to do with believers, and this suggestion is reinforced by the other details.

The elders are described as wearing white garments (see *White* in the symbol glossary), a colour generally related to purity and righteousness; indeed the Levitical priests were clothed in fine linen (Ex. Ch. 28). The link between white clothing and the faithful is also made very explicitly later in the book (Rev. 7 v. 13).

The white-clothed elders are also depicted with golden crowns, a symbol closely associated with kings but also connected with the high priest who wore a golden plate attached to the front of his hat or turban (Ex. 28 v. 36-38). In symbolic language, Paul refers to the "crown of righteousness" he is awaiting (2 Tim. 4 v. 8 KJV). This image of royal or priestly authority is further extended by the elders in the vision having their own thrones. This carries strong echoes of Christ's words to the disciples when they ask about their reward for leaving everything to follow him, when he says "you will sit on twelve thrones" (Matt. 19 v. 27-28).

So the depiction of the elders in this vision fits closely with Peter's description of the role of the faithful being that of kings and priests (1 Pet. 2 v. 5, 9). A particular point worth noting in connection with this latter reference is Peter's use of tenses. In verse 5 (KJV) the role is something that the faithful are "to be", implying future, promised attainment. However in the second reference in verse 9, the present tense, "are", is used, implying that, within the limitations of our mortality, we should be striving to fill those roles now.

One final detail supporting this interpretation comes from the recorded number of the elders, i.e. 24. Clues from numerology can sometimes be a bit weak but there are firmer grounds for their use when there is explicit use of the numbers elsewhere in scripture. In this case the number 24 is a product of 12 and 2. The number 12 is strongly associated with the concept of election by God, for example in the Old Testament the 12 tribes descended from Jacob the chosen son of promise, and in the New Testament the 12 apostles were called out by Christ to be entrusted with the Gospel. The multiplier, 2, may possibly be related to the 2 covenants under which the process of election has been made, i.e. the covenant through Moses in the O.T. and that through Christ in the N.T. More explicitly the number 24 is that of the divisions or shifts of priests set up by David (1 Chron. 24 v. 3-19).

If we combine the ideas above, and remember that the context of the passage places the elders in heaven with its associated concept of being "raised up", then we can begin to see the elders as representing the faithful given access to the "heavenly places" as presented in the letters of Paul (e.g. Eph. 1 v. 3, and 2 v. 4-6; also Col. 3 v. 1-4). The elders use their access to God to join in the hymn of praise initiated by four living creatures. They are shown as paying homage and singing praise in Rev. 4 v. 9-11. This accords with the later actions of these elders as recorded in Rev. 5 v. 8-11. Here they are depicted as holding harps, an instrument often associated with praise to God (e.g. Ps. 33 v. 1-3; Ps. 71 v. 22-23; etc.), and having bowls of incense, which are equated with the prayers of the saints.

One final detail seems to reinforce this view. When the elders join with the four living creatures to give praise to God (Rev. 4 v. 8-10) the creatures are making their triple cry of "Holy, holy, holy", a cry also made in Isaiah's vision of heaven (Is. 6 v. 3). This cry carries remarkably strong echoes of Ps. 99 where, in the first verse, God is described as being "enthroned on the cherubim", which is exactly what John's vision focuses upon. Then the psalm splits into three short sections, each of which ends by ascribing holiness to God (v. 3, 5, 9), thus making the Psalm a more extended version of "holy, holy, holy". The final parallel is in verses 6 and 7 of the Psalm, which speak of priests and prophets calling to God and being given answers and guidance that they followed – a role prefiguring that of the saints and now being portrayed by the symbol of the twenty-four elders.

Putting all these ideas together, the role of the elders seems to fulfil the promise implicit in the divine action at the crucifixion of Christ when the veil in the temple was torn in two. This symbolised that the way had become open for the believers to have access to God directly through Jesus with no further need for a human priesthood. The believers thus take on the role of priests themselves, offering prayers and praises through their eternal high priest, Christ (see also Heb. 10 v. 19-22). Thus there are good grounds for seeing the 24 elders in chapter 4 as symbolising the way that the living saints have direct access to the presence of God.

5.4 Throne Vision as Climax to Letters

As we have already seen, the seven letters reveal a spectrum of spiritual quality that was already present in the early church. The widespread use of "seven" in scripture to represent repetitions or cycles (see *Seven* in the symbol glossary) seems to indicate that we can expect this variation of spiritual quality, through growth and decline, to be a repeating, cyclic phenomenon in the life of the church throughout the Christian era. Thus the seven letters represent the cycle of faith as it waxes and wanes, through many instances and at many levels, throughout the whole period of Christ's absence.

This cycle of faith will eventually come to an end when Christ returns, coming with divine glory to establish the Kingdom of God on earth. It is thus very fitting that the depiction of the cycle of faith, in chapters 2 & 3, is followed by a representation of the Glory of God in chapter 4. This throne vision points forward to a future culmination of God's purpose, in God's Kingdom, but it also represents the present situation in which the glory and majesty of the presence of God are woven through the fabric of the physical creation as an invisible thread, only perceived by the spiritually minded, through the eye of faith. While waiting for the final revelation of God's glory, the believers may still have access to a more tenuous experience of being part of God's household, through their life of praise and prayer, in fellowship with each other and with Christ, as represented by the role of the 24 elders in the vision of the heavenly throne.

Figure 3: The Lamb receives the Scroll (Rev. 5 v 7)

6. THE LAMB AND THE SCROLL (Rev. Ch. 5)

6.1 The Scroll

The vision of the throne of glory serves not only to conclude the section presenting the cycle of faith through the seven letters, but also acts as an introduction to the next main section. This section contains another "seven", the seven seals which are introduced at the start of chapter 5 as being attached to a scroll held in the right hand of the figure on the throne. A scroll obviously conveys ideas of a written message, like a letter or a book, but in this case it has divine origins, since it is being held out by the visionary figure representing God. There is a very striking echo here of the way God commissions Ezekiel as his prophet by giving him a scroll to eat before being sent to preach to the people (Ez. 2 v. 8 to 3 v. 11). In fact John is also instructed to eat a scroll himself at a later point in the visions (Rev. 10 v. 9), which we will look at in a later section.

The special feature of this scroll, in chapter 5, is that it is sealed; in other words the message has been prepared, but it is not currently accessible to read. This idea of a sealed message is not unique to the Revelation. There are two passages in the Old Testament which cast some light on its meaning. Firstly in Daniel's prophecy, after he has been given the complex and very detailed insight into the events affecting the Middle East from his own day to the time of Christ (in Dan. Ch. 11), he is then instructed to "keep the words secret and seal the book until the time of the end" (Dan. 12 v. 4). This conveys an intention to obscure or conceal these prophesies until a later time when they will be made clear. Secondly, a similar image is used to warn the prophet Isaiah that his message will be ignored or misunderstood by the people to whom he is sent (Is. 29 v. 11-12). He is told that his vision will be "like the words of a sealed book". The nature of this "sealing" or obscurity is that when the scroll is given to those who can read, namely the scribes and religious leaders, they will say "I cannot; it is sealed"; in other words they will not make the effort or take responsibility for opening it. Instead, they would probably prefer to rely on the opinions and traditions of their predecessors as they did in Christ's day. On the other hand Isaiah is told that if he offers the message to those who cannot read, that is the common, uneducated people, they will say "I cannot read". While true, this is really an excuse to hide the fact that they are content to listen to their leaders and will not make the effort to seek out the truth for themselves. So the message that Isaiah is taking to the people will remain a "sealed book", unknown and not understood.

So, there is good reason, both from common sense and scriptural precedent, to see this sealed scroll in Revelation as a hidden message, known by God but not yet openly revealed or widely understood, in other words a mystery.

6.2 The Lamb

After the vision has shown John the sealed scroll in God's hand, it then indicates that there is no one worthy to open it. This causes John great grief, which suggests that the message is one of great value. However, he is consoled by being told that the one who is "the Lion of the tribe of Judah" (see Jacob's blessing of Judah in Gen. 49 v. 9-10), and "the Root of David" (see the messianic prophecy in Is. 11 v. 1, 10), and who "has conquered", can open the scroll (Rev. 5 v. 5). This obviously refers to the raised and immortalised Christ who has won for us the victory over sin (1 Cor. 15 v. 57). This conclusion is reinforced by the visual imagery that is used to represent this worthy being. John sees a lamb near the throne, and though it is seen to be alive it bears the signs or marks of having been killed. This is an obvious reference to the Lamb of God (see **Lamb** in the symbol glossary).

This lamb has seven horns and seven eyes (Rev. 5 v. 6). Now the number seven can be used as a symbol for two concepts, that of a cycle or repeating pattern, and that of fullness or completion, but with both concepts relating to divine origin or purpose (see **Seven** in the symbol glossary). In this case the idea of fullness seems most relevant, because it applies to the risen Christ whose primary mission of salvation has been accomplished. Also, horns in scripture are used as symbols of power (see **Horn** in the symbol glossary), so the lamb having seven horns would indicate complete power, since the risen Christ now sits at the right hand of the omnipotent God. The eye is a natural symbol for vision, or, more spiritually, for insight or perception. Thus the lamb having seven eyes indicates complete insight, since Christ now shares in God's omniscience, and in fact the eyes are explained as being "the seven spirits of God sent to every part of the world".

The Lamb, i.e. Jesus, is seen receiving the sealed scroll from the figure on the throne, i.e. God, and this stimulates the four creatures and the twenty-four elders to join in a new song (Rev. 5 v. 9-10). The phrase "new song" occurs in the first line of Psalms 96 and 98, both of which deal with the Lord's supremacy in bringing his purpose to fruition and establishing rule and judgement over the world. The words of the song refer directly to the salvation that Christ has brought by his sacrifice, and to the hope it brings to the believer of reigning with him as kings and priests (see also 1 Pet. 2 v. 5, 9). This wave of praise then echoes throughout the created world, surely predicting the fulfilment of the words about God's glory filling the earth (e.g. Is. 40 v. 5; Hab. 2 v. 14, etc.).

6.3 The Lamb can Unseal the Scroll

Putting together the thoughts of the two preceding sections, we find that Christ, in some way connected to his victory on the cross, is able to reveal a hidden message or mystery that has great value. If we trace that idea back in scripture we find some illuminating passages in the Epistles. For example in Rom. 16 v. 25-26, the writer says that his gospel, and that of Jesus, accord with the "revelation of that divine secret kept in silence for long ages, but now disclosed". While Paul, in Col. 1 v. 25-27, says that his commission from God is to put God's word into full effect, which is "that secret purpose (KJV "mystery") hidden for long ages... but now disclosed to God's people"; and that this "mystery" relates to the Gentiles sharing the hope of glory. So the mystery is the good news, or gospel, that God's grace is freely available to all men, Gentiles included (e.g. Is. 42 v. 1-7). This valuable message has been hidden in Jewish times (cf. Is. 29 v. 10-14) but has been revealed in Christ and preached by the Church (cf. Is. 29 v. 18-24). Thus, the opening of the sealed scroll indicates the fuller revelation of God's plan of salvation in Jesus, and the start of gospel preaching. So we might justifiably expect that the opening of the seals will reveal some of the results that will arise from the preaching of the gospel and will indicate how the world will react to it. To see if that is so, we will have to examine the next chapter of the Revelation.

7. THE MESSAGE BEHIND THE SEVEN SEALS (Rev. Ch. 6)

7.1 Introduction – the Four Horsemen of the Apocalypse

Having shown the scroll being presented to the one who could open it, in chapter 5, the vision now proceeds to reveal what happens when the scroll is opened.

During the opening of the first four seals different coloured horses are shown as responding to the divine messenger who is talking to John at this point. There are very striking similarities between these horses and those revealed to Zechariah in parts of his vision, not least that in each case the horses are of four different colours, and the colours described are very similar in the two visions.

In Zechariah's vision the horses first appear at the beginning of the prophecy (Zech. 1 v. 8-11, 16) where they are described as having been sent out to patrol the earth (v. 10) and then report back that a state of rest has been achieved (v. 11). The background to Zechariah's prophecy is the period of the return of the Jews to their homeland from Babylonian captivity, under the leadership of their governor Zerubbabel and their high-priest Joshua (see Ezra Ch. 3). The quiet and peace which the horses report may well refer to the relaxation of the oppression that the Jews were suffering and the opportunity they were granted to return to their own land to rebuild the walls of Jerusalem and the temple (e.g. Zech. 1 v. 16, 17).

However the record of the return indicates that the reconstruction work did not go smoothly, and that local opponents appealed to the Persian overlords to stop the rebuilding (e.g. Ezra Ch. 4). In a continuation of the vision (Zech. 6 v. 1-8) the horses appear again, now pulling chariots, and need to go out again to patrol the four points of the compass. The effect particularly noted is that the horses going to the North set God's spirit at rest. With North being the direction of the capital of the Persian Empire, this setting at rest would seem to refer to the overcoming of the opposition of the

Jew's enemies and the renewal of the emperor's mandate to the returned exiles to resume the rebuilding at Jerusalem.

Thus the evidence we have in Zechariah suggests that horses represent forces or influences that are under God's control, that go out more than once, and that "set my Spirit at rest", i.e. assist in the fulfilment of God's declared purpose. Other scriptural uses support this idea that horses are a symbol of power, often kingly power which can convey and carry out the royal will even at long distances from the throne – see **Horses** in the symbol glossary.

In the Western, "Christian", culture the popular idea of "the four horsemen of the Apocalypse" is derived from a very literal view of the vision. This takes the four as personifications of pestilence, war, famine, and death; four scourges common to human experience that can be seen as judgements from God. However this view takes the interpretation out of the context of the opening of a sealed scroll, which has been so particularly established, in chapter 5. As we have seen, the scroll relates to Christ's revelation of the gospel, the good news that salvation is available to all through Christ's sacrifice and the faith of the believer. We must bear this context in mind as we look at each of the four horses.

7.2 The 1st seal (Rev. 6 v. 1-2)

The opening of the first seal reveals a white horse whose rider wears a crown and who goes out to conquer. A similar image is used later in Rev. 19 v. 11-16 where another white horse carries a rider into battle to win a great victory. In fact the interpretation of this later scene is more obvious as it clearly represents the final battle of Christ ("the Word" – Rev. 19 v. 13), accompanied by more riders on white horses who seem to represent angels and the saints ("armies of heaven" – Rev. 19 v. 14), who are all fighting against the powers of the world ("the nations" – Rev. 19 v. 15). As we shall see in more detail later when we reach these chapters, the forces of heaven win a complete victory over their enemies and the vision goes on in chapter 20 to describe the opening of the millennial age.

Figure 4: The Four Horsemen (Rev. Ch. 6)

Thus, remembering that white is the colour of righteousness (see *White* in the symbol glossary), the earlier white horse and its rider (Rev. 6 v. 2) look like a force for good in earlier battles of the righteous against the dark forces of this world. These are not literal battles fought with physical weapons (see *Warfare* in the symbol glossary). Rather they are part of the struggle against darkness and sin, waged by apostles and believers spreading the word in obedience to Christ's commission to go out into the whole world and preach the gospel (Mark 16 v. 15-16). In this struggle they were to win some battles, but would not gain a total victory. That must wait until the final battle at Christ's return, as we will see in Revelation chapter 19.

So the first horseman conveys the idea of the preaching of the word having some success. This is also depicted in Christ's own parable of the sower (Matt. 13 v. 3-23) where the seed that falls on good ground yields a plentiful return of up to a hundred-fold (v. 23).

7.3 The 2nd Seal (Rev. 6 v. 3-4)

When the second seal is opened, a red horse appears. Red is the colour of blood and conveys ideas of mortality and sacrifice or sin, so we can expect the meaning behind this horse to involve conflict, suffering, and death. In fact this is exactly what Christ warned his followers to expect as being a possible outcome of their discipleship (Matt. 10 v. 34-36). Note particularly how in verse 34 of this passage Jesus says that he has come to bring, not peace, "but a sword", and the rider of the red horse is "given a great sword" (Rev. 6 v. 4). Thus while the opening of the first seal shows a picture of gospel preaching having very positive results, this is now tempered by a very contrasting image revealed under the second seal. The rider of the red horse shows how the act of preaching will stir up forces of opposition that may bring martyrdom and death to the preachers. Such opposition can actually be a means of testing the faith of those called to preach, and this is also indicated in the parable of the sower (Matt. 13 v. 3-23) where the seed that falls on stony ground experiences the fierce heat of the sun, which is interpreted as being trials or persecution (v. 20,21). The resulting withering of the sprouting crop warns us that some who initially accept the gospel may lose faith in the face of determined opposition.

7.4 The 3rd Seal (Rev. 6 v. 5-6)

The third of the horses revealed as the seals are opened is black, and the description conveys obvious images of famine. However this need not be referring to a literal famine of scarce food, or more particularly here a scarcity of grain; after all this is a book of symbol. Indeed in scripture grain is quite a common symbol for "the word", and the harvest it yields, as for example in the parables of the Sower, and the Wheat and the Tares (Matt. ch. 13).

In Israel the barley harvest came first as it could be grown from a winter sowing, while the wheat ripened later, developing very rapidly from a spring sowing. Thus it is possible that barley is being used as a symbol for the growth of faith in Israel, i.e. the first crop. Remember how in the dream that Gideon overheard (Judges 7 v. 13) a barley cake represents Gideon's small band of faithful Jews overcoming their enemies with God's help. Also in Christ's first feeding of the multitude, the 5000 (John 6 v. 9), the grain-based food is five barley loaves, and the leftovers yield twelve baskets fragments, twelve being the number of the tribes of Israel. If the barley carried this meaning, then the wheat could be representing the later harvest of gentile believers.

However, trying to distinguish between the two types of grain may be stretching the symbolism too far. We must not let the details obscure the main meaning, that in the context of preaching, as established by the opening of the sealed scroll, the idea of a scarcity of grain is most likely to be a symbol for a scarce harvest of believers in response to the "sowing" of the word. After all, Christ did warn his followers that there would be only a few that found the "narrow gate" that leads to life (Matt. 7 v. 13, 14); and again, in the parable of sower (Matt. 13 v. 3-23) the seed that falls on thorny ground is choked by the weeds and "it proves barren" (v. 22).

7.5 The Oil and the Wine (Rev. 6 v. 6)

The message accompanying this vision of the black horse goes on to limit the impact of the "famine" by saying that the oil and the wine are not to be harmed. Since we have taken the scarcity of grain to have a spiritual meaning, we might expect that oil and wine are also being used in a symbolic way, so as usual we will look for scriptural precedents to suggest likely meanings.

At a practical level, one major use of olive oil in the ancient Middle-Eastern world was as lamp fuel, for example in the lamps on the seven-branched lamp-stand in the tabernacle and later in the temple. So, oil was closely associated with the ability to bring light where it otherwise would be dark, and in the Old Testament this was specifically linked to the ritual service of God. From this idea of literal light-giving it is an easy step to see oil as a symbol for the ability to provide spiritual enlightenment, and this is what we find in the New Testament, for example in the parable of the ten virgins (Matt. 25 v. 1-13). All ten are initially moved to wait to greet the bridegroom, but in his absence it is dark and they need oil to fuel their lamps. The lamps of the five who have insufficient oil go out, and those foolish virgins are unable to find their way to the wedding feast. In other words, oil represents the enlightening power of God's word, and those who would follow Christ need to gather ample personal supplies of its insight and wisdom if they are to find and follow the way that leads to the wedding supper of the Lamb. This message is reinforced by the depiction of the seven churches in Revelation chapter 1 as seven lamp-stands, to portray their role as bodies of believers spreading the light of the gospel in a world of pagan darkness.

Turning to the other symbol in the pair, wine is a widely recognised symbol for the sacrificial blood of Jesus, which he himself uses at the Last Supper when he passes the cup to the disciples with the words "this is my blood... shed for many for the forgiveness of sins" (Matt. 26 v. 27, 28). The wine thus represents divine forgiveness and grace.

There is also another use of oil and wine together in the same passage, in the parable of the Good Samaritan. He pours both into the wounds of the injured man (Luke 10 v. 34). There the practical purpose was that the wine should cleanse, a symbol for forgiveness, and the oil should help to heal, symbolically to promote new life. The two effects are combined in order to save a man from death, a vivid picture of the saving combination of God's word and his love.

Thus the grain shortage of the third seal foretells a scarce harvest of believers from the sowing of the word of the gospel; but also, in the undamaged supply of oil and wine, it tells us that the light of God's word will never be quenched (see John 1 v. 5: "the light shines in the darkness, and the darkness has never mastered it"), and that God's mercy and forgiveness are never constrained (see 1 Tim. 2 v 4).

7.6 The 4th Seal (Rev. 6 v. 7-8)

When the fourth seal is opened we see a pale horse, but the word "pale" is translated from the Greek word "chloros" which can be rendered more literally as "greeny-yellowy". This is the colour of a human corpse, portraying putrefaction and death. This idea is strongly reinforced by the continuing description, which actually states that the rider of this horse is death, closely followed by Hades, the place of the dead. In other words those influenced by this horse and its rider are unlikely to escape an encounter with the grave. They are those who put worldly needs and demands above the call of Christ, those who even in life are the subjects of death, as when Christ said "leave the dead to bury their dead" (Matt. 8 v. 22).

In the context of preaching, this image represents the reaction of indifference and worldliness in which the word cannot take root and grow, so that the hearers never understand and accept the divine offer that can save them from death. In the equivalent section of the parable of sower (Matt. 13 v. 3-23), this is the seed that falls by the wayside and is eaten by the birds so that it cannot bear any fruit. Thus the underlying meaning of this fourth horse and rider forms a natural corollary to the message of the earlier black horse. For if the third seal reveals an image of a scarce harvest of belief, the implication is that the larger number who do not believe will be gathered up in the harvest of death, and this is what the fourth seal portrays. So while the third seal describes the few that find the "narrow gate" that leads to life, the fourth seal describes the "broad way that leads to destruction" (Matt. 7 v. 13, 14).

7.7 Summary of the Four Horses

Contrary to the popular view of the four horsemen of the apocalypse, the first four seals have revealed the four horses as vivid symbolic depictions of the results of the preaching of the word of God throughout the world. As we have seen, the white horse indicates some successes, the red horse shows there will be opposition, the black horse warns that the overall harvest of believers will be scarce, while the pale horse indicates that the unheeding majority will be gathered up in the harvest of death. This grouping of four types of response matches that of Christ's parable of the sower, with success in the good ground (the white horse), the withering consequences of opposition in the stony ground (the red horse), the choking effects of worldly influences in the thorny ground (the black horse), and the total failure in the unreceptive environment of the wayside (the pale horse). This rather bleak picture provides the context for the messages under the remaining seals.

7.8 The 5th Seal (Rev. 6 v. 9-11)

With the opening of the fifth seal we see the souls under the altar who are described as being "those who had been slaughtered for God's word and the testimony they bore". This is clearly an image of persecution, and particularly of martyrdom resulting from violent opposition to the preaching of the gospel, so fitting in with the whole theme of the seals visions.

The imagery of the phrase "souls under the altar" draws heavily on the rituals of animal sacrifice under the Mosaic Law. Blood was to be seen as representing the whole life, or soul, of the creature from which it came. This is what gave blood its significance in sacrificial offerings to God, and was the reason given for prohibiting the human consumption of blood (Lev. 17 v. 10-12). So when an animal was sacrificed to God its blood had to be poured out at the foot of the altar (e.g. Lev. 1 v. 5). In the original wilderness setting of the tabernacle, the altar would have been set up on sand or dry ground, and the poured-out blood would have soaked underneath the altar. When the camp was struck for the Israelites to move on, a deeply bloodstained patch of earth would bear witness to where the altar had stood. So, in a figure, the track of the gospel preachers, as they have wandered through the world, has been punctuated with the bloodstains of their martyrs. Those who live to move on and preach in new areas or new ages look back to draw strength from the martyrs' faith and to take warning from the world's hostility.

As the cycle of preaching and opposition continues to turn, the faithful may start to weary of the struggle and to despair of God ever bringing it to an end. As they wait for the righteous to be recognised and the world's wickedness to be purged, they appeal to God with a cry of "how long?" (v. 10). This is not to be seen as a cry for vengeance or personal vindication, but as an expression of longing for the promised time when the earth will be filled with peace and blessing and with the knowledge of God's ways.

This cry is not unique to the Revelation but is echoed throughout the scriptures when faithful witnesses encounter stubborn opposition. For example when Isaiah responds enthusiastically to the call to carry God's message, he is daunted when he is told how unheeding his hearers will be, and the same cry comes to his lips (Is. 6 v. 8-11). In this case there is also a reply (v. 11-13), but it is one which, while offering great hope in the future "holy seed", also calls for great patience by implying that much time will elapse, during which faithlessness will prevail and bring desolation in its wake.

A similar cry is made by an angel on behalf of God's people when the returned Jewish exiles face the opposition of the surrounding peoples as they try to rebuild Jerusalem (Zech. 1 v. 12). It is interesting to note that this angel appears to be the rider of a red horse, which under the second seal we took to be the horse associated with opposition to God's word. The reply to this cry (v.

13-17) is one of reassurance, confirming God's support for the rebuilding.

The same cry, "how long?" also occurs in several Psalms (e.g. Ps. 13 v. 1; 74 v. 10; 89 v. 46; and 119 v. 84). In the latter case it is noteworthy that in this longest Psalm, which focuses so intently on the word of God, the cry occurs in one of the very few verses not containing "word" or some synonym for it. It is as if the Psalmist lifts up his eyes briefly from the word and immediately sees a world that rejects it and opposes him as a witness to it.

The cry of "how long?" thus represents a universal call of God's faithful servants when faced with a world that refuses to hear and tries to silence the preaching. The divine response to the call is twofold. It contains an appeal for patience, implying that the full outworking of God's plan will take a long time; but this is coupled with a comforting reassurance that God's purpose will prevail in the end and will bring the promised reward to all those who have kept the faith.

7.9 The 6th Seal (Rev. 6 v. 12-17)

After the fifth seal has shown the outcome of the preaching of the word from the viewpoint of the faithful, the sixth seal turns our attention to the outcome as experienced by the largely unheeding masses. The picture for them is of a day of wrath, the arrival of God's judgements on the ungodly for which the faithful were appealing under the fifth seal. The vivid pictorial language of this section includes the shaking of the earth, the mountains and the islands; the removal of the heavens and the heavenly bodies, or their being darkened or turned to blood; and fear among the people of the earth and their leaders over what is coming. This reflects the way God's day of wrath is depicted in several other prophecies (e.g. Joel 2 v. 30 to Joel 3 v 3; Is. 2 v 10-19; and not least in Christ's own Olivet prophecy in Luke 21 v. 25-28).

These images are also used elsewhere in the Revelation and their meanings are explored in detail in the symbol glossary (see entries for **Earth**, **Mountains**, **Islands**, **Heaven**, and **Heavenly Bodies**).

While not denying the possibility of there being some literal fulfilment of these signs, we must always bear in mind that the Revelation is a book of symbol. There is evidence, as argued in the glossary, for seeing these descriptions of violent upheavals in the earth's physical geography as being symbols of major changes in its political geography; that is in the distribution and control of political, military, and commercial power. We will see partial fulfilments of this under the cycle of the seven trumpets (Rev. chs. 8 & 9), but the great day that brings all the cycles to an end is the return of Christ when the kingdoms of this world become his. Thus as the cycle of seven seals nears its end, the way is prepared for a climax in which God's punishments will be carried out on those who resist the preaching of the word.

7.10 The 7th Seal (Rev. 8 v. 1)

The opening of the sixth seal is at the end of chapter 6, but the whole of chapter 7, with its visions of the 144,000 and the great multitude, is interposed before the cycle of the seals is finally concluded. So here we will briefly skip forward to the start of chapter 8 before considering the "interlude" of chapter 7 as the subject of the next main section.

It seems rather surprising at first to find that the climax of the cycle of the seals takes up only one short verse. The main import of that verse is that when the scroll is fully unsealed, that is when the content of the gospel message has been fully revealed to the world, there is silence in heaven. When we look back we see that John was called up to heaven in his vision at the start of Revelation chapter 4. Since then he has heard voices of many of its symbolic inhabitants, including the four living creatures (Rev. 4 v. 8), the twenty-four elders (Rev. 4 v. 11; 5 v. 9), a strong angel (Rev. 5 v. 2), an individual elder (Rev. 5 v. 5), and each of the individual living creatures (Rev. 6 v. 1, 3, 5, 7). Some of these heavenly voices have been praising God or Jesus for their power and their purpose or ability to save; the others have been helping to lead John through the vision of the presenting of the scroll and its unsealing.

By the end of this process, at the point we have reached now, the mystery of the sealed scroll has been fully revealed, God's purpose with the preaching of the gospel has been fully worked out, and the Kingdom has come with Christ fully revealed as its king in divine power and glory. In the sense of Zechariah's prophecy that we looked at in section 7.1, the horses have finally set God's spirit at rest all the way to the four corners of the earth. At this point the whole world can clearly see the climax of God's plan, which previously could only be seen with the eye of faith enlightened by the word of the gospel. Now, in the sense of revealing the gospel message, as has just been depicted in the visions of the seals, there is no more for the inhabitants of heaven to reveal. So now there is silence in heaven.

As we will see in later sections there is still a form of preaching and teaching to be done in the millennial period. Thus heaven will have more messages to convey, so the silence is for only a short period. This short period is represented as half an hour and I do not believe there is any simple way of converting this symbolic period into a literal period that would fit in our current way of reckoning the calendar. However we will consider other short symbolic periods when they are mentioned later in the Revelation and in understanding these we may be able to throw more light on this topic.

7.11 The End of the Seals – The Day of Wrath

The opening of the sixth seal reveals the approach of the day of the Lord's wrath. The final end of the Seals cycle will be the great day of the Lord affecting the whole world, but there have also been other days of the Lord's wrath, which have been lesser days because they have had more limited scope. For example God's punishment of Babylon is described in this way (Is. 13 v. 1, 9), and the description there uses similar language to that in the passage about the sixth seal. For example, we read that on that day the heavenly bodies will be darkened (Is. 13 v. 10-11). Under the entry for ***Heavenly bodies*** in the symbol glossary we equate these bodies with ruling powers. For Babylon these are to be darkened, i.e. the Babylonians are to lose their empire, and even their city.

Not only is the symbolic language used in Isaiah similar to that used for the sixth seal, but also in both cases the meaning is reinforced by the use of more literal explanations for the upheavals being foretold. The passage in Isaiah explains how Babylon will fall (Is. 13 v. 17-19), saying that the empire will be defeated by the attacking Medes. In the case of the sixth seal the disturbing events, whose approach causes such fear, are attributed directly to the "wrath of the Lamb" rather than to any existing earthly power (Rev. 6 v. 15-16), and of course when the great "day of wrath" comes, Christ will return to become a very tangible power in the earth.

Thus, as there have been "lesser" days of wrath in the past, there could be more than one fulfilment of the seals cycle over time, with various days of the Lord's wrath affecting different areas at different times. Ultimately any such repetitions of the cycle will be brought to an end by the one great day that will usher in Christ's return to set up his kingdom on the earth.

7.12 Summary of the Seven Seals

Reviewing what we have seen above, we can start to see how the seals, like the seven letters earlier, form a cycle, which is typical of the use of "seven" in scripture (see ***Seven*** in the symbol glossary). The seven phases or facets of this cycle are:
- active preaching which meets some success (1st seal)
- opposition to the word bringing bloodshed (2nd seal)
- the seed of the word yielding only a meagre harvest of believers (3rd seal)
- many non-believers being conquered by death (4th seal)
- the persecuted saints being called to endure (5th seal)
- the godless eventually being overthrown by God's judgements (6th seal)
- the visible presence of the returned Christ on the Earth removes the need for the cycle of preaching to continue (7th seal).

Specific instances of many of these kinds of experiences can be identified in the history of the early church. However the scriptural precedents for the meanings of the symbols employed in this vision suggest that it has a more universal application as a kind of cyclic pattern, like many of Christ's parables. Indeed the similarities between the message of the first four seals and the parable of the sower highlight this general applicability. Thus the vision of the seven seals represents a pattern or cycle of events that could be repeated many times, in different parts of the world, in different time periods, and history shows that this has been the case. In the fullness of God's purpose, this cycle will come to one great climax when a final overthrow of the world's powers leads to the establishment of the kingdom of God. At that time there will be no more need for the "folly of the gospel" (1 Cor. 1 v. 21) or "foolishness of preaching" (KJV) because Christ will then rule visibly, with all the demonstrable power of God. Thus the seven seals represent the cycle of the results of preaching the gospel throughout the world as it meets with a mixture of faith and unbelief throughout the whole period of Christ's absence.

8. THE 144,000 & THE MULTITUDE (Rev. Ch. 7)

8.1 Holding Back the Winds (Rev. 7 v. 1-3)

Chapter 7 of the Revelation occurs between the opening of the sixth seal (Rev. 6 v. 12-17) and the seventh seal (Rev. 8 v. 1). This seems to imply that the interpretation of the passage relates to the main theme of the seals. However, the text does not follow the pattern of language used for the seals, for instead of saying, "When he (the Lamb) opened the seal...", this section begins with the phrase "After that..." and makes no mention of the scroll or its seals. This strongly suggests that the message is intended to provide additional information that qualifies or extends the meaning of the main cycle. Also, given the place at which it is inserted into the cycle, it is likely that it has particular relevance to the meaning of the sixth and seventh seals.

As we have discovered, the sixth seal deals with a day, or days, of the Lord's wrath, bringing judgement on the world's inhabitants for their neglect or outright rejection of God's word. This may occur many times as the cycle of preaching is repeated in different places at different times, but it eventually becomes the great day of the Lord in which Christ returns to establish God's kingdom on earth, as intimated under the seventh seal.

The vision inserted between the sixth and seventh seals starts with four angels standing at the four corners of the earth and holding back the four winds so that they do not harm the earth, the sea, or the trees. Similar language is used in other prophetic passages when changes in the earth's ruling powers are being foretold. For example in Daniel's vision of the four different beasts, which symbolise the major empires that will influence the affairs of the Middle-East, the turmoil of their rise and fall is introduced by the image of "the Great Sea churned up by the four winds of heaven". Christ himself uses similar language about "the roar and surge of the sea" to describe the violent unrest on earth that will precede his return (Luke 21 v. 25). Also, in Ezekiel's vision of the dry bones, foretelling the re-emergence of a Jewish state, the breath (or spirit) that brings the dead to life comes from the four winds. This has echoes of the passage from Zechariah that we looked at in section 7.1, where the four chariots drawn by different horses are described as going out to the "four winds of heaven" to accomplish God's purpose and set his spirit at rest (Zech. 6 v. 1-8). Thus the image of the four winds blowing can be seen as a symbol of the unseen power of God altering the political landscape by overturning key nations or empires and setting up new ones in their place; a symbol for the power by which "the Most High is sovereign over the realm of humanity" (Dan. 4 v. 25).

This interpretation seems even more likely when we consider the targets of the wind's power. They are being held back from blowing on the earth, the sea, and the trees. These three symbols are used in various places to represent peoples, nations, and empires; and because they are used in this way in several places in the Revelation, the reasoning behind this interpretation has been put in the symbol glossary for ease of reference (see **Earth**, **Sea**, and **Trees**).

If the four winds about to blow on the earth, sea, and trees really represent God's impending judgements on worldly powers, then there is an immediate link with the sixth seal. Under that seal it is exactly this kind of judgement that is foretold, but now, in this additional passage, the judgements are depicted as being held back or suspended. Why the delay? The text indicates that this is to allow the process of sealing the 144,000 to be completed (Rev. 7 v. 3). Let us now look at what this sealing process represents.

8.2 Sealing the 144,000 (Rev. 7 v. 3-4)

Those being sealed are called "his (i.e. God's) servants" (v. 3) and they are being sealed in the forehead, the symbol for the seat of our thinking powers. The seal is "the seal of the living God" (v. 2) carried by an angel ascending from the rising sun, an image with echoes of the images of light in chapter one, with its ideas of Christ as a light to lighten the Gentiles. Thus we have an image of men and women who in their service to God allow their thinking to be enlightened and reshaped by the gospel, like soft wax taking the imprint of a signet ring. This calls to mind the exhortation that believers should not be conformed to this world but to be "transformed by the renewal of your minds" (Rom. 12 v. 2). Thus the image of being sealed by God's seal relates directly to the intended effect of the preaching of God's word. So as preaching is the main theme of the seals cycle, this new vision is very relevant to the context of the opening of the scroll and its seals.

The number of those sealed is given as 144,000. In terms of number symbolism in the scriptures this figure can be expressed very interestingly as (12 x 12) x (10 x 10 x 10). Twelve is a common number symbol for the process of election by God under both the old and new covenants, for example in the twelve tribes of Israel in the Old Testament and the twelve apostles in the New Testament. On the other hand, the number ten is often related to humanity, since our ten fingers and toes have led to the number being central to our system of counting (see *Ten* in the symbol glossary). Spiritually, "ten" carries connotations of human fallibility. So, for example, the summary of the Law of Moses is in the form of the Ten Commandments, and the human inability to keep that law leads to it consigning all to sin (Gal. 3 v. 19-22). The factor ten being present three times, like the dimensions of a cube, may indicate a volume or mass of humanity. Thus the number 144,000 seems to represent the process of God's election of his chosen ones out of the mass of humanity.

8.3 Sealed out of Twelve Tribes (Rev. 7 v. 5-8)

Having indicated a symbolic number for the elect, the passage now allocates this number equally across twelve named tribes from Israel. However on examining the list of names closely we find that the particular group chosen is unique to this passage, for it is neither the list of Jacob's sons nor the tribes that inherited major areas for settlement in the Promised Land. In making lists of the tribes of Israel there are fourteen names to choose from, i.e. the twelve sons of Jacob and the two sons of Joseph. To make a list of twelve, two names are left out. So, in lists of the patriarchs the sons of Joseph are omitted, while in list of the tribes settled in the land, they are included and Joseph and Levi are omitted.

In this new list in the Revelation, the names of Ephraim and Dan are omitted, which results in a list that has no historical precedent. This suggests that the list is symbolic, not representing the historical chosen people of the Jews, but rather symbolising the elect who will be saved by faith. What then is the meaning of the omission of Ephraim and Dan? When we read back over the history of Israel we find that these two tribes were the sites of the two calf idols, set up by Jeroboam at the time of the division of the kingdom into Israel and Judah (1 Kings 12 v. 28, 29). The idols were set up as a largely political act to persuade the northern tribes not to go south to worship at the temple in Jerusalem, in case this weakened their allegiance to the new monarchy in Samaria. This was a major cause of apostasy and helped to turn away many in Israel from worshipping the true God.

Thus 144,000 is not a literal number but a symbolic figure representing those who are God's elect through faith in Christ. Because they are described as those in the process of being sealed, the number may represent the living saints at any one point in time. These saints are living believers who are heirs to the promises to Abraham, Isaac, and Jacob, but heirs by faith (Gal. 3 v. 6-9) who keep that faith steadfastly without turning aside to apostasy. The sealing process goes on alongside the preaching cycle of the seven seals, and forms its desired and intended outcome. However since it is taking place in people's hearts, it is a more private, hidden side of God's purpose, less visible to the observer than the other effects of the cycle. Hence its description as an aside, or parenthesis, to the main description of the seals cycle; but when the cycle reaches its great climax at Christ's return, the elect will receive their reward publicly and become visible to all. This is what the vision moves on to show next.

8.4 The Great Multitude (Rev. 7 v. 9-17)

After the description of the 144,000 the vision widens out to reveal a great multitude that, from what follows, also seems to be made up of the elect. The information that their number is so great as to be innumerable and that they come from all nations are particulars that point back to the promises that God made to the patriarchs about blessing their descendants (e.g. Gen. 22 v. 17, 18). All in this vast crowd wear white robes, which are a symbol of salvation and righteousness. They also carry palm branches, a detail that carries echoes of Christ's triumphal entry into Jerusalem and of the building of booths for the feast of tabernacles; events which foreshadow Christ's triumphal return to the earth to gather his elect into his kingdom. These redeemed ones all joyfully praise God and the Lamb as the source of salvation, joining in with the other beings seen earlier by John in his vision of heaven. It is further explained to John that the multitude are followers of Christ, having been cleansed by his blood, and that they have endured, that is they have not turned away and become apostate (unlike the symbolic tribes of Ephraim and Dan which are omitted from the earlier tribal list of the 144,000).

The state of blessing in which this multitude now exist, with their close fellowship with God and the Lamb and the absence of afflictions, speaks of the fulfilment of their hopes in Christ's kingdom. Thus this part of the vision looks forward to the ingathering of all the saints to be united with Christ in his kingdom, as prophesied in so many places (e.g. Is. 25 v. 6-9). This represents the goal and reward of those who in each generation are sealed as God's elect. Thus the great multitude represents the sum of repeated harvests of 144,000 taken from each passing age. So the vision of the 144,000 links well with the sixth seal, while the broader vision of the great multitude relates to the great climax of the cycle under the seventh seal, and it is very fitting that these additional visions are placed between the sixth and seventh parts of the main seals cycle.

8.5 Binding and Freeing the Four Angels

As we saw earlier, these visions inserted between the last two seals began with the binding or restraining of the four winds, or their controlling angels, in order to hold back the judgements on the earth while the "sealing" of the elect goes on. In the next cycle of seven, the trumpets, the restraint is removed and these bound or restrained angels are released at the start of the sixth trumpet (Rev. 9 v. 13-15). Our later study of that section will show that the sixth trumpet, like the sixth seal, indicates a "day of the Lord" when divine punishments will be inflicted on the ungodly.

As a common element to both cycles the four angels form a link between the Seals and the Trumpets cycles. The point of linkage is at the sixth phase of each cycle where both are depicting a "day of wrath" falling on the unheeding. This link between the preaching activities of the Seals visions and the subsequent punishment events of the Trumpet visions indicates some connection in the timing or triggering of the events. The sequence of preaching, then punishment suggests that the preaching is allowed to continue until it is no longer being heeded and the number of saints is complete or no longer being added to, then, when the word of the gospel is no longer producing any harvest, the punishments will be allowed to fall. Because of the cyclic nature of these "sevens" this may well have partial fulfilments just for particular regions or time periods, as well as having a major, climactic fulfilment at the return of Christ.

As a further detail, anticipating the more detailed study of Revelation chapter nine, it is worth noting that the phrase "at the Euphrates" (Rev. 9 v. 14) seems to be best understood as referring to the location of the release of the angels, not of their "binding", since there is no reference to the river here in chapter seven. As the release of the four angels signifies the start of punishments in the "day of the Lord", this may then give us some clue as to the context in which the triggering events occur which lead up to the final judgement of the world. It would also seem to tie in with the "fall of Babylon" imagery in chapter 17, since ancient Babylon was on the Euphrates, but so as not to confuse the flow of the Revelation narrative these details will be left for interpretation when the relevant chapters are analysed later.

9. THE SEVEN TRUMPETS
(Rev. Chs 8, 9 & 11 v. 14-19)

9.1 The Meaning of Trumpets

Before looking in detail at the vision of the seven trumpets we will look at the use of trumpets elsewhere in the scriptures and also see how they are introduced to John at the start of this section of his visions.

Specific instructions were given to Moses about the use of trumpets by Israel in their wilderness wanderings. These are recorded in Numbers chapter 10 where we find four main uses, namely as a call to remembrance before God at religious feasts (v. 10); to sound the alarm in preparation for battle (v. 9); to summon the congregation, or just their elders, to the tent of meeting to hear messages from God (v. 2-4); and to signal the people to break camp and move on (v. 5-6).

This early use of trumpets has parallels in a later prophecy through Zephaniah about a day of the Lord (Zeph. 1 v. 14-18) that will be a day of judgement in which: the people's sins are called to remembrance; an alarm is sounded over coming destruction; God delivers a message or lesson to his people; and a phase of God's plan ends and events move on in new ways. This day is characterised as "a day of trumpet-blasts" (v. 16), so we can expect this vision of the seven trumpets in the Revelation to have similar connotations.

9.2 Preparing the Trumpets (Rev. 8 v. 2-6)

Before the trumpets are blown, John sees preparations being made in heaven. Seven angels are given the trumpets, indicating that their blowing will symbolise the carrying out of some kind of divine purpose. The nature of that purpose is indicated by the actions of a further angel who offers incense before God. This action fulfils the type established in the ritual of the tabernacle. There the altar of incense stood outside the veil, within which was the Holy of Holies where the Ark of the Testimony stood. On top of the Ark was the mercy seat, above which God appeared to the high priest. These things were the elements of a ritual form of access to God under the old covenant. At Christ's death, the veil in the temple was ripped from top to bottom, symbolising the opening of access to God to all men, not just to priests, through the new covenant in Christ.

These symbols from the tabernacle and temple worship are now, in John's vision, shown in their fulfilment by being translated to heaven itself. An angel offers the incense, not a priest, and the altar stands before God's throne in heaven, not before the ark. The incense rises up as a sweet smoke before God, and "pleasing fragrance" is a term often used of God's recognition of a sacrifice and his acceptance of the one making, or being reconciled, by the sacrifice (e.g. Eph. 5 v. 2). We have already seen this symbol applied to the prayers of the saints, in the vision of the twenty-four elders that we took as a symbol of the saints having access to heaven (Rev. 5 v. 8, as covered in section 5.3). That meaning is explicitly applied again here, as the prayers of the saints are described as being added to the incense (Rev. 8 v. 3-4).

This incense (the symbol) and the prayers (the reality) are now mixed with fire from the heavenly altar. When Isaiah was called to be God's messenger, fire from a heavenly altar was also used to cleanse his lips (Is. 6 v. 6-9) as a symbol for activating or empowering his speech to proclaim the word of God. So, divine fire can be seen as a cleansing and activating agent. Thus, in John's vision, the divine fire indicates that the prayers of saints are acceptable to God and are now to be activated as part of God's purpose. John is also shown where that purpose is directed, as the burning censer is thrown down on to the earth (Rev. 8 v. 5), where it has a violent effect. But to which of the saints' prayers is God responding? Apart from general praise and worship, the only explicit request recorded in the visions so far is the martyrs' appeal to God (Rev. 6 v. 10) in which they pray for God to judge the ungodly. If, as seems likely, it is these prayers that are being made a reality, then this introduction to the seven trumpets tells that they deal with God's judgements on a world of unbelief that has not responded to the preaching of the word. So, just as the cycle of the seven seals has warned us that the world at large would not heed the preaching, the cycle of the trumpets now seems to be spelling out the nature of the consequences that will follow this heedlessness.

9.3 The First Trumpet Judgement (Rev. 8 v. 7)

When the first trumpet is blown we see that it results in punishment falling on the earth. From a study of earth as a symbol (see ***Earth*** in the symbol glossary) we see that it represents the peoples of well-structured, civilised nations. With their superior education, technology and communications, these people have the best chance of having access to the word of God, though they may not necessarily choose to accept it any more readily than others. Also these strengths mean that they are a correspondingly more powerful influence for evil if they reject the word. So, on the principle of responsibility (e.g. Lk. 12 v. 47, 48), when the world starts to sink into godlessness these peoples are the first to be punished.

The language used carries echoes of that used for the days of the Lord's wrath, under the sixth seal, but it has some distinctive features. The specific targets of the destruction are described as trees and grass. Trees are often used as a symbol of eminent nations (see ***Trees*** in the symbol glossary), while grass is used to describe human populations, emphasising their transient nature as "flesh" (e.g. Is. 40 v. 6-8), or their rapid growth under prosperous conditions (e.g. Ps. 72 v. 16 KJV). The destructive agent is fire, which is a natural power in the earth, as in volcanic action, and which also arises spontaneously in growing things, particularly when dry, as in bush fires. Thus the first trumpet shows God's punishments bringing destruction to the peoples of advanced or eminent worldly kingdoms, probably by means of common forces in nature or human conflicts, such as natural disasters and wars.

9.4 The Second Trumpet Judgement (Rev. 8 v. 8-9)

The judgement revealed under the second trumpet is described in language that is dense with symbols, which we need to "decode" a few at a time. The judgement is triggered by the fall of a burning mountain. In the Bible's symbolic language a mountain is often a symbol for a leading worldly power (see **Mountains** in the symbol glossary). In this case the mountain is burning, but this is exactly the fate that has befallen parts of the earth as a result of the punishments under the first trumpet. This mountain is thrown into sea, so losing its altitude or eminence; that is to say it is reduced to a much lowlier condition, like that of the more primitive nations that it once may have dominated. Such less-developed nations are often represented by the image of the sea (see **Sea** in the symbol glossary), but now the falling mountain turns part of the seas to blood (a symbol of mortality and death), killing its inhabitants and wrecking its ships (the symbol and agency of trade and communications).

Putting the plain text together after the initial "decoding", we see that a major nation or empire is overthrown, and reduced to humble status, possibly as a result of divine punishment for godlessness as indicated under the first trumpet judgements. The knock-on effect of this is to bring conflict and ruin to weaker nations and their peoples, most likely to those that have been dependent on the empire as its colonies or its suppliers of basic materials. It is not unique to the Revelation to use the image of a mountain being cast into the sea as a symbol for the fall of an empire. We also find it used of the fall of Babylon (e.g. Jer. 51 v. 24-25, 41-42). In the Revelation vision, the overthrow of a major nation, probably originating as a First Trumpet judgement, brings chaos to lesser nations in Second Trumpet judgements.

9.5 The Third Trumpet Judgement (Rev. 8 v. 10-11)

The judgements following the blowing of the third trumpet also fall primarily upon a watery environment, but now they fall on to the fresh waters of rivers and springs instead of the sea. Fresh water has the natural significance of giving and sustaining life in the hot, dry lands of the Middle East that form the backdrop to so much of the Bible message. As a biblical symbol, fresh water can be taken to represent the influence of the Spirit or the Spirit-inspired Word that brings life where otherwise death reigns (see **Water** in the symbol glossary). Jesus makes powerful use of this symbolism in his discourse with the woman at Sychar (John 4 v. 7-15), where he uses the water in the well as a symbol for the influence of the Spirit. This image can be generalised a little to allow whole systems of waterways to become a symbol representing the wider realm of spiritual life or true religion.

Into these waters falls a star which, following the exposition of **Heavenly Bodies** in the symbol glossary, we can take to represent a ruler or leader of some kind. However this star is not shedding a natural or true light but is "blazing like a torch", that is it has an artificial, man-made light. Also this star has been "cast down", in other words the "leader" has been deposed from his previously elevated or influential position, but even in his fall he exerts an influence over the fresh water, that is over the religious sphere. The effect achieved is to make the water taste of wormwood, a powerfully bitter herb. This herb and other bitter substances, like gall, are sometime referred to as a "root of bitterness", and used in scripture to characterise the pollution of the true worship of God with false teaching or idolatry (e.g. Deut. 29 v. 18-19; Acts. 8 v. 18, 22-23; Heb. 12 v. 15). The effect of the pollution is to cause the death of many people, not literally as in poisoning, but spiritually by diverting them from the paths of truth and salvation.

Putting together the meanings of the symbols used for this third trumpet judgement, we see that God will overthrow leaders who have religious influence, whether they are secular leaders or princes of the Church, if they shed a false light. However, even in their fall they will pollute the waters of the religious world with the bitter wormwood of false or pagan beliefs and lead many to miss the true saving power of the gospel.

9.6 The Fourth Trumpet Judgement (Rev. 8 v. 12)

The judgements described as following the fourth trumpet affect the sun, moon, and stars. These are common scriptural symbols for ruling secular powers (see **Heavenly Bodies** in the symbol glossary). These powers are to be darkened and cease to shine, that is they will lose their ruling authority. In other words, God will punish rulers of nations who use their influence contrary to his purpose, by deposing them or even destroying their kingdoms or empires.

Almost identical language is used to predict the fall of the empire of Babylon (Is. 13 v. 10) and this is then followed by a more literal explanation of how they are to be defeated by the military power of the Medes (Is. 13 v. 17-22). Thus the fourth trumpet is a reminder that "the Most High is sovereign over the realm of humanity" (Dan. 4 v. 25) and will use his power to ensure that his purpose with the world is not thwarted or diverted.

9.7 Prelude to the Three Woes – the Eagle (Rev. 8 v. 13)

We have already seen that groupings of seven are very significant in the Revelation. Now we are starting to see that within a group of seven there can be smaller sub-groupings. One key sub-grouping is a split into an initial four and then a three, as in the seven Seals which started with the four horses before moving on to different images for the last three seals. In general the first four of a seven seem to cover the longer-lasting activities that make up the bulk of the time occupied by an occurrence of the cycle. The fifth element then seems to point towards the closing phases of the cycle, while the sixth heralds some rather more dramatic intervention which will start to bring the cycle to its end, and the seventh element marks the end or even points forward to the state that will follow the end of the cycle and stop further repetitions of it.

So in the present cycle of seven, there is a short gap between the first four and last three trumpets, which is marked by an eagle flying in mid-heaven. An eagle was one of the four faces of the living creatures in the earlier vision of the heavenly throne of glory (Rev. 4 v. 7), and this is often taken as representing the wisdom or insight of the Spirit, because of the great superiority of the vision of birds of prey compared to humans. The eagle is flying in mid-heaven, and we have already seen that heaven often refers to the spiritual realm (see **Heaven** in the symbol glossary). Thus there are strong hints that this eagle voice represents a spiritually discerned warning. Its message stresses the importance and the danger of the latter phases of this cycle of judgements and it may point to there being related messages elsewhere in the spirit-breathed Word of God. If so it would emphasise the importance of using scripture to interpret scripture as a principle of interpretation for the Revelation.

9.8 The First Woe or Fifth Trumpet (Rev. 9 v. 1-12)

The primary symbol used to characterise this fifth judgement is that of a swarm of locusts. This does lead to some problems in interpretation, as there are few other symbolic uses of locusts in the Bible to use as precedents. However there are enough pointers in the supplementary details to help us to understand the primary nature of this judgement.

First, the locusts appear out of clouds of thick smoke, which create darkness, and arise out of the "pit", a typical Biblical word for the grave or the place of death. The darkness of the smoke obscures the sun (verse 2), which as we have seen elsewhere is often used as a symbol for secular ruling powers (see ***Sun*** in the symbol glossary); so the obscuring of the sun could indicate the emergence of significant lawlessness or immorality. This link with the power of evil and death is underlined in verse 11, where the king of this locust swarm is depicted as the "angel" or messenger of the bottomless pit and is called "the destroyer". This power is given additional names taken directly from Hebrew, as Abaddon, and Greek, as Apollyon. The pairing of the pit (Hebrew "sheol") and destruction (Hebrew "abaddon") occurs several times in the poetic books of Proverbs and Job to describe the universal fate and resting place of sinful mankind, for example Proverbs 27 v. 20 "Sheol and Abaddon are insatiable". Also as one characteristic of locusts that the Bible does point out is their ability for concerted action without a king (Prov. 30 v. 27), this "destroyer" seems to refer to mortality or death itself rather than to any literal leader. In other words the locusts are being depicted as the subjects of death, being led by the spirit of death, which is sin. This is quite similar imagery to the harvest of death under the fourth seal (Rev. 6 v. 8).

Some other scriptural references to locusts also help to cast some light on the symbol. In a prophecy about the fall of Assyria, Nahum (3 v. 15-18) likens the governing and merchant classes of the state to locusts, implying that they feed themselves but give nothing back to support the country, so undermining it and leading to its overthrow. Also, in a more dramatic prophecy of future destruction, Joel pictures invading hordes as locusts (Joel 1 v. 4) but associates this punishment with the pervasive drunkenness of the people (v. 5). These usages seem to bear out a connotation of decline or collapse due to moral decline.

Certain details in the text tend to rule out some of the more obvious options for understanding the locust imagery. For example the fact that they are told not to hurt the grass, plants, or trees (Rev. 9 v. 4) makes it very hard to make a literal interpretation of real locusts since such green vegetation would be their natural food. However, given that the scriptures do use trees as symbols for human systems of politico-economic growth and control (see **Trees** in the symbol glossary), then the locusts could represent a force or movement that affects the religious and moral climate without necessarily destroying the secular power structures.

In the same verse (v. 4) the locusts are restrained from hurting any who have been "sealed" by God, i.e. the servants of God or believers (see sections 8.2 and 8.3 above). It is therefore very unlikely that the locusts could represent destroying armies, as these would not be able to distinguish between true believers and faithless or apostate individuals. This would seem to restrict the meaning of the locusts to some kind of force having a detrimental effect in the moral sphere where believers would be protected from its influence.

Some of the other details in the passage give us further clues as to the nature and effect of this morally destructive power. Firstly it has the power to hurt for five months (Rev. 9 v. 5). There is no immediately obvious biblical time period of five months, but when we examine the religious celebrations and festivals instituted under the Mosaic Law we see that they lasted from the Passover in the first month to the atonement in the seventh month. Thus we can understand that the rest of the year, with no major religious festivals, lasted for five months. This was the winter season of death and decay to be followed by the renewal of spring marked by the next Passover. So a period of five months can be seen as a period of spiritual winter with an absence of spiritual fruit and religious observance.

Other details from the text describe various strange attributes of these unusual "locusts" (Rev. 9 v. 7-10). They look and sound like war horses or chariots and are armoured, which conveys violence, aggression, and toughness. They have lions' teeth, which conveys destructiveness and greed, yet they have human faces and women's hair, which indicates an essentially human nature and possibly hints at sensuousness or vanity. Finally they have tails like scorpions with stings which inject a poison that causes lingering sufferings, which seems to indicate that the damage the locusts cause is like an after-effect, or "sting in the tail", rather than an immediate result of an encounter with them.

So, putting together all the findings and clues gathered above, we see that the locusts represent an essentially human force, displaying many of the worst attributes of human nature and bringing about moral decline with its associated sufferings. They thus act like parasitic destroyers, under the leadership or influence of sin and death, to undermine individual lives and society as a whole without at this stage destroying the existing power structures. All this is achieved in a season of spiritual decay, a metaphorical "winter", with those worst affected being the ones with no protection from an active faith in God.

To sum up this section, all the evidence points to the First Woe, arising under the fifth seal, being the moral decline of a society through the rise of decadence. This is a condition in which pleasure is valued over duty, rights are demanded while obligations are ignored, and self-expression is esteemed while self-denial is mocked. All these are typical of the fall of many great powers, not least the Roman Empire.

As a footnote to this conclusion it is interesting to draw a parallel from the biology of the swarming locust, which is at the heart of this symbol. The swarming, or desert, locust (of the species *schistocerca gregaria*) is remarkable for the way in which it changes, physically and behaviourally, as the density of the insects on the ground increases. At low density the species adopts its solitary form with the insects being coloured brown and acting as individuals. As they increase and become more crowded they take on the gregarious form, changing to pink (in the immature insects) or yellow (for the mature ones) and start to behave as a coherent group or swarm. These differences are so striking that for a long time the solitary and gregarious forms were thought to be two different species. If the locust symbol in Revelation represents the growing numbers of individuals in a society that adopt a hedonistic and decadent lifestyle, then the human behaviour can be seen to mimic that of the locusts in a very similar way. Thus a small percentage of decadent individuals can be tolerated without having much impact on the society in which they live. However, above a certain critical density there is increasing pressure for everyone else to conform to this lifestyle and a pervasive atmosphere that tolerates or even encourages progressively more extreme and perverse behaviour. It takes a lot of courage to stand out against such pressures when they become dominant in a society, but a strong and active faith in God is a very powerful support to such resistance.

9.9 The Second Woe or Sixth Trumpet (Rev. 9 v. 13-21)

The sounding of the sixth trumpet marks the beginning of the second woe. There is a link between these events and the sequence of the seven seals. Such a linkage is quite natural as the seals represent the consequences of preaching and the trumpets represent the judgements on those who fail to respond to, or actively oppose, the preaching. The particular link here is that this woe starts with the release of four bound angels (Rev. 9 v. 13-15) which seem to correspond to the four angels that were originally restrained, or "bound", by the divine command at the end of the sixth seal (Rev. 7 v. 1-3). Then they were told not to release their destructive powers on the earth until the "sealing" of the faithful had been completed. This was covered in the earlier sections 8.1 and 8.5. Now that the angels are being released it would seem that there is no longer any significant response to the preaching and the time has come for the destruction to be unleashed on the unheeding. That destruction forms the second woe.

The nature of the woe is portrayed as the release of massed squadrons of cavalry (Rev. 9 v. 16-19). This takes the symbol of horses (see *horses* in the symbol glossary) and makes it more specifically an image of warfare. This is very similar to the language used in Joel to prophesy the overthrow of Israel (e.g. Joel 2 v. 1, 4-5, 11) where the image of the attacking power of cavalry is mixed with images of the destructive power of fire. Joel links this destruction to a "day of the Lord" (Joel 2 v. 1, 2), which we also considered when looking at the sixth Seal (see section 7.9). So also under the sixth trumpet the cavalry riders wear breastplates reflecting the primary colours of flames, red, yellow and blue.

We can also reflect on the additional symbolism of red being the colour of blood, representing mortality and sin. This ties in with the detail (Rev 9 v. 19) that the tails of the cavalry horses are like serpents, which, from the fall of Adam onwards, are used as a symbol for sin. As the tails flow out behind the galloping horses, so degradation and evil often follow in the wake of warfare and often do more damage than the actual fighting. Thus the cavalry of the second woe are fairly literal symbols for real armies in the world, as opposed to the armies of saints represented by the white horse under the first Seal. Using worldly forces as an instrument of divine punishment is quite typical of how God works in history, when He uses one earthly power to punish another, as in the use of the Medes to punish Babylon as prophesied in Is. Ch. 13.

In fact the text may be alluding to the fall of Babylon as an example of God's judgement over a major power that refuses to acknowledge him. The allusion lies in the reference to location at which the four angels of destruction are released, which was "the Great River, the Euphrates" (Rev. 9 v. 14). This was the location of a crucial event that led to the release of the Jews from their captivity in Babylon. It happened in the sixth century BC, when Darius the Mede diverted the Euphrates so that its course through Babylon was dried up, allowing his army to enter along the river bed and overthrow the city and the whole Babylonian empire (Dan. ch. 5). Thus the river Euphrates can be seen as symbolic of a fatal flaw or weakness at the heart of a power that is opposing God. Exploiting such a flaw to bring about the fall of Babylon can be seen as emblematic of God's ability to redeem those who believe in him by striking suddenly and unexpectedly at the heart of the defences of those who resist his purpose. It is therefore apt that this should be referred to in describing the type of sudden overthrow indicated by this second woe.

So far in the first two woes we have found a sequence that is quite common in history, when first a great power enters terminal decline (fifth trumpet or first woe – decadence), and then as it wanes it is finished off by a rising new power with growing military strength (sixth trumpet or second woe – war). However these passages in the Revelation tell us that this is not always an accident of history, but rather, when God intervenes, it becomes part of a pattern of divine control of the course of history.

The description of the second woe goes on to tell us that the survivors of these large conflicts do not repent (Rev. 9 v. 20-21). This can be taken as an indication that the seven trumpets and the woes they contain form a repeating cycle with each occurrence of second woe events in history being an example of *a* day of the Lord, not *the* Day which will herald the second coming of Jesus. A further indication is that the death toll of one third of mankind (Rev. 9 v. 18) indicates less than total destruction and leaves plenty to replenish the earth and enter another cycle in due course. This partial destruction is similar to a quarter of the earth being destroyed in the harvest of death under the fourth Seal (Rev. 6 v. 8), and we also took the pattern of the seven seals to be a repeating cycle.

9.10 The Third Woe or Seventh Trumpet (Rev. 11 v. 14-19)

After the second woe there is an interlude spanning Rev. 10 v. 1 to Rev. 11 v. 13. In these passages we encounter the "Rainbow Angel" and the "Two Witnesses". This interlude between the sixth and seventh trumpets is a similar structural device to the interlude of "The 144,000" and the "Great Multitude" that occurred between the sixth and seventh seals. This new interlude will be explained in the next main sections, 10 and 11, but we will first conclude the current section by looking at the third and last Woe occurring under the seventh Trumpet.

Although called a woe (v. 14), these final events of the trumpet cycle are full of praise and glory. This is because the events mark the transition by which worldly powers and kingdoms become parts of God's Kingdom (Rev. 11 v. 15) and Christ starts his eternal reign on earth. So it is a woe to the unbelieving who lose what they thought they owned, but a joy to the faithful who see their hopes fulfilled.

A great song of praise to celebrate these events is sung by the 24 elders (Rev. 11 v. 16-18). We first encountered the 24 elders in the vision of God's throne in Revelation chapter 4, and in our analysis there we took them to symbolise the living believers' access to the presence of God (see section 5.3). With the coming of Christ the resurrection will have occurred so the elders now represent all the glorified faithful who join together to give praise to God for setting up his Kingdom. They also give thanks for the vindication of the saints and eradication of evil achieved by the punishment of the godless. Thus their words reflect the culmination of the cycle of the seven trumpets that has turned out to be a cycle of punishments by which God holds evil in check and keeps his purpose on track.

In the final verse of the cycle (Rev. 11 v. 19) we see the opening or revelation of God's temple in heaven. This was previously only visible to the eye of faith, as symbolised in the vision of the throne of glory in Revelation chapter 4, where John had to be summoned to "come up here" in order to see the heavenly scene. Now divine glory and power are revealed clearly to everyone on the earth in the appearance of the returned Christ and the presence of all the glorified saints. So, like the end of the cycle of the seven Seals, the final climax of the seven Trumpets is the establishment of God's Kingdom on the earth.

9.11 Summary of the Seven Trumpets

Summarising what we have found in this section we see that the Trumpets form a cycle, as is typical of the symbolic use of the number seven in scripture. This cycle foretells a pattern of events that will unfold in answer to the saints' prayers to bring judgement on the godless for their fierce opposition to the faithful and to all that is good; an opposition that effectively pits them against the very purpose of God himself. The cycle demonstrates the pattern of how the Most High rules in the Kingdoms of Men (Dan. 4 v. 17): by punishing proud, godless nations (first trumpet); by throwing their empires into chaos (second trumpet); by deposing religious leaders (third trumpet); by overturning all rule when it exceeds the bounds set by God (fourth trumpet); by using the inbuilt flaws of human systems to destroy them from within (fifth trumpet); and by using war to destroy empires from without (sixth trumpet). These Trumpet judgements are not the actions of a spiteful or vindictive God, but represent the actions needed to prevent the world sinking totally into darkness and chaos, and to keep it moving towards the great blessings of God's Kingdom on earth (seventh trumpet).

While many key events of this kind occurred in the history of the early church, they were not unique to that period. Further repeats of the pattern have occurred throughout the Christian era. Finally, after many repetitions in various places and at different times, the cycle will be completed by the full revelation of God's royal power, displayed through the appearance and actions of the glorified Christ as he establishes his kingdom on the earth (seventh trumpet). Thus the seven trumpets represent the cycle of God's control of the world.

10. THE RAINBOW ANGEL (Rev. Ch. 10)

10.1 The Angel and the Message

In the previous main section we found that an interlude was introduced between the accounts of the sixth and the seventh trumpets. As we now examine the messages of that interlude in detail we find that it breaks into two different visions, which we will consider in turn.

The first vision in this interlude introduces an angel clothed in a rainbow (Rev. 10 v. 1-3). This angel has several Christ-like attributes. Firstly the way the angel's appearance is described is very similar to the description of the glorified Christ standing among the light-stands in Rev. 1 v. 13-16, and it is bathed in the same kind of "rainbow" glory that surrounds the heavenly throne in Rev. 4 v. 3. Further, it comes down from heaven in a cloud as is prophesied of the returning Christ (Acts 1 v. 9-11), and it bestrides the earth and the sea, which can be understood as having power over the nations (see *Earth* and *Sea* in the symbol glossary). This angel thus seems to characterise or represent the glorified Christ and, as the following verses show, it is coming with some important messages to John. When we read in 1 Peter 1 v. 10-11 that the prophets tried to find out things "to which the spirit of Christ in them pointed", and we remember that the root meaning of "angel" is "messenger", then we can recognise the angel as being a graphic representation of the process of inspiration.

The angel starts by proclaiming two messages for John to hear. The first is a shout like the roar of a lion, and we recall that one of the titles of Christ is "the Lion from the tribe of Judah" (Rev. 5 v. 5). This roar triggers messages in the form of seven thunders (Rev. 10 v. 3-4) but their contents are not explained and John is told to seal up the messages. This has strong echoes of part of Daniel's later visions where he is told to "seal the book until the time of the end" (Dan. 12 v. 4), so there are hints that it may not be appropriate to describe the message of the seven thunders at this point. Later, in section 16.2, we will look at the possibility of this seven-fold message finally being revealed.

Before leaving the thunders it is worth noting the relevance of Psalm 29. The interlude passage we are considering comes within the cycle of the seven trumpets, which we have taken as dealing with God's punishments on the ungodly. Psalm 29 also extols the glory of God and shows both his destructive power and his ultimate triumph that will bring strength and peace to his people. In the psalm "the God of glory thunders" (v. 3) and in this and subsequent verses the phrase "the voice of the Lord" occurs seven times as God unleashes his power and accomplishes his purpose. This is a powerful scriptural precedent that provides us with a strong hint about the message of the seven thunders.

In his second message the "rainbow" angel affirms the certainty of God's purpose (Rev. 10 v. 5-7) and declares that the seventh trumpet heralds the full revelation of God's plan, that is the establishment of God's Kingdom on earth. He goes on to commission John to prophesy further (Rev. 10 v. 8-11) by giving him a little scroll to eat. We will consider that scroll next, but first it is important to note that John is now being commanded more specifically to prophesy about peoples and kings (v. 11). This suggests that the next main parts of the Revelation will be somewhat different in nature from the first part. So far we have seen the unfolding of generic patterns of events but now, as we move on to examine chapters 12 to 22 of the Revelation, we should be prepared to find prophecies more directly linked to specific nations and leaders in history.

10.2 The Little Scroll

As we have just seen, John's new commission to prophesy is accompanied by his being given a little scroll to eat (Rev. 10 v. 8-10). We have already encountered the image of a scroll in the form of the sealed scroll of Revelation chapter 5. We understood that to represent the message of the gospel that was revealed or "unsealed" by the work of Christ. This small scroll is possibly an addendum to that earlier scroll. As noted earlier (section 6.1) there is a very striking echo here of the way God commissions Ezekiel as his prophet by giving him a scroll to eat before being sent to preach to the people (Ez. 2 v. 8 to 3 v. 11). In John's case he finds the taste at first to be sweet. This probably refers to the exhilaration generated by the experience of inspiration, just as Jeremiah finds "joy and happiness" in "eating" the words of God (Jer. 15 v. 16), and the Psalmist finds God's promise "sweeter on my tongue than honey" (Ps. 119 v. 103). However as the message enters John's stomach it becomes bitter, in other words as he digests the message and recognises its import he becomes dismayed. Possibly, like the souls under the altar in the vision of the fifth seal, he is distressed by the length of time that God's purpose will take to unfold. His experience here is like that of Daniel who was in anguish after receiving one of his visions (Dan. 10 v. 16).

Let us now sum up the first part of this interlude in the series of the seven trumpets. The context is the pattern of events that God will bring about at times when he needs to intervene in history in order to keep his purpose on track. As the world in general will not recognise God's hand in such events, it is also unlikely to acknowledge his influence in more specific historical events. So the "rainbow" angel's messages come mainly as asides, or background, to the cycle of the seven trumpets because they specifically commission John to go on to prophesy about nations and kings. Such prophecies may be noted by believers but will be largely ignored by the world. The full import of these new messages is to be amplified in a separate context, in the Revelation chapters 12 to 22, because the current context serves to establish generic patterns rather than specific events in history.

11. THE TWO WITNESSES
(Rev. Ch. 11 v. 1-13)

11.1 Jewish Aspects of the Witnesses

In the second vision of the interlude between the sixth and the seventh trumpets we see characters introduced as "my (i.e. God's) two witnesses". In setting the context for the witnesses (Rev. 11 v. 1-2) John is told to measure parts of the temple of God, but only those parts *not* given over to Gentiles, i.e. the Jewish part. The outer court of the temple and the Holy City are to be given over to gentile domination for a fixed period. For the same period the two witnesses are to prophesy. This gives us a very strong hint that the witnesses are not part of the gentile powers that will occupy Jerusalem and oppress the Jews; and so, if not gentile, they must be Jewish.

The witnesses are to prophesy in sackcloth (v. 3), which has been a sign of mourning and distress as far back as Jacob mourning for the presumed death of Joseph (Gen. 37 v. 34). We have assumed that the Revelation is a message for gentile times (see sections 1.5 and 1.6). If that were the case, then for most of the period the Jews would be dispersed throughout many foreign countries, with their land and holy places in gentile hands. This would give them ample grounds for mourning.

The two witnesses are further identified (in Rev. 11 v. 4) as being two olive trees and two lamp-stands, that is, stands bearing lamps burning olive oil (see **Lamp-stand** in the symbol glossary). This image is very similar to one found in the book of Zechariah, one of the key prophets who encouraged the Jews who returned from exile in Babylon to rebuild Jerusalem and the temple there. Zechariah sees a vision of two olive trees providing oil directly to the lamps on a single, seven-branched lamp-stand (Zech. 4 v. 2-3, 6, 11-14). The seven-branched lamp-stand was a major symbol of the enlightening power of God's word, and was used at the heart of Jewish worship in the Tabernacle and then the Temple. So it is an apt symbol for the temple that the Jews were attempting to rebuild.

As for the two olive trees, these are identified as "the two consecrated with oil, who attend the Lord of all the earth" (Zech. 4 v. 14). According to ancient Jewish law and practice, the two leadership roles initiated by anointing with oil were those of king and high priest. In Zechariah's time the monarchy had ceased, but the equivalent role of secular leadership had been given to Zerubbabel, the governor of the returned exiles. He was accompanied by Joshua, the high priest. These two, the secular and the religious leaders of the people, were guides who enlightened the people about the importance of re-establishing a place of witness and worship to God in Jerusalem. The purpose of Zechariah's vision was to encourage these two leaders to act in God's strength as a witness to the people that it was God's purpose to rebuild the temple, so their representation as sources of fuel for the light is very fitting. Thus when very similar imagery, based on olive trees and lamp stands, is used about the "witnesses" in John's vision, it adds support to the view that the symbolism has very strong Jewish connotations. We will go on to consider the full meaning of the image in its context in the Revelation shortly.

The actions performed by the two witnesses in the Revelation vision have further Jewish associations. Their ability to emit fire from mouths (Rev. 11 v. 5) is very like Elijah calling down fire on those opposing him (2 Kings 1 v. 10), and their ability to cause drought (v. 6) is also reminiscent of Elijah (1 Kings Ch. 17). The turning of water to blood (v. 6) was one of the plagues that Moses brought down on Egypt (Ex. Ch. 7), and the promise of vengeance on those who try to harm them (v. 5) carries echoes of the song that Moses recited to the people towards the end of his life (Deut. 32 v. 40-43).

11.2 A Period of Witness

The purpose of the two witnesses is described as being to bear testimony (Rev. 11 v. 7). The duration of their activities and other parallel events is given as a couple of specific time periods. It is said that they will prophesy for 1260 days (Rev. 11 v. 3), which is a period of 42 months of 30 days each. Similarly the period of down-treading by the Gentiles is 42 months (Rev. 11 v. 2). Christ also talks about a period of gentile domination over Jerusalem in his prophecy on the Mount of Olives (Luke 21 v. 24), but he indicates that this period of oppression lasts from the Roman dispersion of the Jews to a time close to his future return to the earth in glory – a period of millennia not months. This means that the period of 42 months mentioned in the vision is most unlikely to be literal, and so we need to look for some symbolic significance.

Another representation of 1260 days or 42 months is as a period of 3½ years. When we think about it in this way, two other occurrences come to mind. First when Elijah called a drought as a sign or witness against the people's idolatry it lasted 3½ years (James 5 v. 17). For most of that time Elijah was in hiding, but the sign he had invoked was there for the thoughtful to understand, and at the end of the period there was a much more dramatic and public climax in the fire from heaven that consumed Elijah's sacrifice on Mount Carmel. Then in New Testament times Christ's public ministry of witness to his people lasted for 3½ years. Again this went largely unrecognised or unaccepted by most of the people, particularly those in authority, but for those who heeded it brought the hope of salvation. This witness period also ended with an earth-shaking climax in the crucifixion and resurrection of Christ. Thus 3½ years can be seen as representing a divinely appointed period of witness about the reality of God's purpose to a largely unbelieving world, with the period ending in a dramatic and public intervention from God himself.

God speaks of the Jews as witnesses to him and his purpose through the prophet Isaiah (Is. 43 v. 9-10; and Is. 44 v. 7-8). The use of the word "witness" in the Old Testament does not always refer to spoken evidence but includes the passive evidence that some things provide just by their existence, such as the pillar or cairn that Jacob and Laban raised as a token of the pact between them (Gen. 31 v. 44-48). So in one sense the Jews were witnesses because they saw, or witnessed, all the works that God did amongst them. In another sense they have been a form of passive witness to the rest of the world, because all that God has said about them has been fulfilled in the course of their history. God's words have included both warnings of punishments for the Jews' lack of faith and promises that he will preserve them, for example "I shall make an end of all the nations among whom I have dispersed you, but I shall not make an end of you" (Jer. 30 v. 11). Thus in their continuing existence as a people, as represented in Zechariah by Zerubbabel their secular leader, and in the continuation of their religion, as represented by their high-priest Joshua, they have played the role of the two witnesses.

For most of the Christian era the Jews have been without a homeland and yet, despite much persecution and many attempts to destroy them in the various lands where they have been dispersed, they have not been destroyed as a people. The significance of their survival, as being a fulfilment of God's promises, has largely gone unrecognised, and so their passive witness has followed the pattern of the 3½-year "witnessing" of Elijah and Jesus. In the case of the Jews their role has lasted far longer than a literal 3½ years, but in a book of symbols the nature and purpose of such a period is likely to be more significant than the actual duration. So, taken symbolically, this time period represents a divinely appointed time of quiet or background witness that will end in a much more dramatic climax. The on-going witness of the Jewish people and their history forms a backdrop to the event of the Trumpets, hence its inclusion in this "trumpet interlude". The climax is described in the next few verses of this part of John's vision.

11.3 The Climax of the Trumpet Interlude

When the period of their testimony is complete, a final oppression of the two witnesses brings about their short-lived destruction (Rev. 11 v. 7-10). The location for this event is identified as being the city "where also their Lord was crucified" (v. 8) which is obviously Jerusalem. Identifying this as the location ties in with the witnesses representing the Jews, and with the final attack by their enemies occurring close to the return of Christ, after the Jews have been re-established in the land of Israel. The "death" of the witnesses is followed by a miraculous return to life (v. 11), in other words modern Israel appears to have been destroyed, but in fact manages to survive and recover. On seeing this, the enemies of the witnesses are terrified and appear to suffer some form of destruction themselves, with the survivors paying fearful homage to God (v.

13). The power behind these events seems most likely to be a divine intervention to save Israel by repulsing and destroying the enemies who are fighting against them, as God has done before for his people, for example in saving Jerusalem from the Assyrians at the time of king Hezekiah (Is. ch. 36-37). A series of events like this is prophesied by Zechariah (Zech. 14 v. 1-11), who tells of nations warring against Jerusalem, but being defeated when God fights for it. The prophet then goes on to speak of God establishing his worldwide Kingdom with Jerusalem as its capital. A number of other prophecies reinforce this message but we will not examine them until section 19 where we attempt a synthesis of "last days" prophecies from the Revelation with related prophecies from the rest of the Bible.

In the vision in Revelation the enemy of the witnesses is spoken of as the "beast" (Rev. 11 v. 7). This beast makes further, more significant appearances in later chapters, with the event most relevant to the current context being the great battle described in Revelation chapter 19. Rather than starting to deal with the beast symbol somewhat out of context here, the main interpretation has been left until section 14 for the introduction to the beast symbol and to section 18 for the great battle.

After the witnesses are revived they are elevated to heaven (v. 12). As explained in section 4.2 and under **Heaven** in the symbol glossary, "heaven" refers to an elevated condition or status, particularly where this is connected with God's power and purpose. So this elevation could signify the Jews' re-acceptance by God as being part of his people. From the earlier analysis it would not seem to support a meaning of their being transported to some kind of realm beyond the skies. Indeed, as these events are happening, "heaven" comes to earth, because the Kingdom of God comes, as revealed under the seventh Trumpet (v. 15-19), and the returned Christ sets up his capital in Jerusalem. So the background events of the "trumpet interlude" (Rev. 10 v. 1 to Rev. 11 v. 13) move forward into the same climax as the main cycle of the seven trumpets. Indeed all three of the main cycles of seven in this first half of the Revelation, namely the letters, the seals, and the trumpets, come to their climax in the return of Christ to the earth.

12. HALF-WAY REVIEW

12.1 Summary of Revelation Chapters 1-11

At this half-way point in the Revelation it is helpful to look back at the ground that has been covered and to draw out the main messages. Right at the beginning we saw how John was called to recognise the gentile future of the Christian church. This sets the context of the book as being about "gentile times" lasting from the birth of the new church up to the return of Christ and the setting up of his Kingdom on earth. This first half of the book has set out three major patterns explaining God's dealings with men in that time. The patterns have turned out to be generic templates showing how certain types of events will repeat at different times and on different scales of magnitude throughout this period. The three cycles are each based on the number seven which, as the root of many of the periods in the biblical calendar, has powerful connotations of repeating patterns. While the imagery of these visions can sometimes be seen to correspond to specific events in the experiences of the early church, and in later history, understanding them as patterns or cycles reveals powerful messages of value to believers of every generation throughout the Christian era. The three cycles of seven were the letters to the churches, the seals, and the trumpets.

The seven letters were addressed to the predominantly gentile churches of Asia Minor. We saw how the range of different levels of praise and rebuke in the letters gives an insight into how faith could wax and wane over time. The letters thus represent a cycle of faith that can be applied to spiritual growth and possible decline at the level of individuals, churches, or whole religious movements. So, the seven letters form a pattern for the relationship between God and the Christian believers.

The seven seals relate to the outcome of opening up the message of the Christian gospel. The sealed scroll indicates how the "mystery" of the gospel, which was hidden in symbols, types and allusions in the Old Testament, was revealed, or "unsealed" in Christ. The opening of the sealed scroll reveals the cycle of the effects of Christian preaching, showing how the preaching would meet with some success but that this would only be limited; in fact it would also rouse opposition and bring martyrdom, with large numbers ignoring its message altogether and being caught up in the harvest of death. The cyclic nature of the seven seals indicates that repeated waves of preaching would occur throughout the Christian era, in different places and at different times, but each would have the same pattern of success and failure.

As an interlude or aside to the cycle of the seals we were shown that underlying the preaching activity was a steady process of the saints being "sealed" or receiving the imprint of God in their minds and lives. The cumulative effect of gathering this relatively small number repeatedly out of each generation will be that they are ultimately revealed as a great multitude sharing in Christ's glory. The seven seals thus form a pattern of how God will reach out to the unbelieving world through the preaching work of the Christian believers.

The seven trumpets reveal the cycle of God's control of the world through his intervention in history. They convey the message that the Babylonian emperor Nebuchadnezzar had to learn from Daniel, that "the Most High is sovereign in the kingdom of men; he gives the kingdom to whom he wills, and may appoint over it the lowliest of men" (Dan. 4 v. 17). The actions revealed by the trumpets show that God will depose any forces that threaten to quench the light of his Word, whether the forces arise from governments or peoples and operate in the spheres of secular or religious influence. The cyclic nature of the seven trumpets means that God will need to intervene in these ways repeatedly in different parts of the world at different times.

As an aside to the cycle of the trumpets we are shown that in the background to the history of the "Christian" world, the Jews will still play a role as God's witnesses. They will play no part as a major world power and their mainly passive witness will be largely unrecognised until the dramatic events of the end of gentile times and the return of Christ. In a further aside the "rainbow" angel commissions John to witness further about nations and kings, which gives us some clue as to the content of Revelation chapters 12 to 22.

The division of the messages of chapters 1 to 11 in the way described above is shown pictorially in the structure chart below.

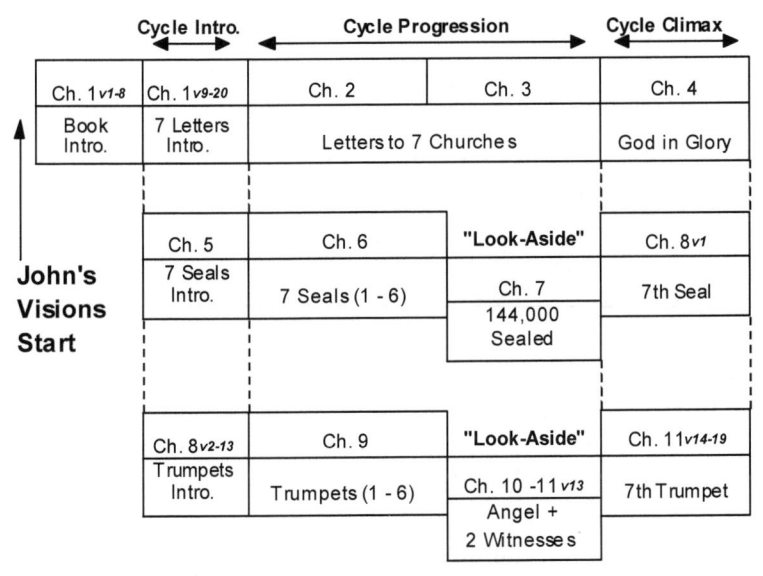

	Cycle Intro.		Cycle Progression		Cycle Climax	
	Ch. 1 v1-8	Ch. 1 v9-20	Ch. 2	Ch. 3	Ch. 4	
John's Visions Start	Book Intro.	7 Letters Intro.	Letters to 7 Churches		God in Glory	
		Ch. 5	Ch. 6	"Look-Aside"	Ch. 8 v1	
		7 Seals Intro.	7 Seals (1 - 6)	Ch. 7 144,000 Sealed	7th Seal	
		Ch. 8 v2-13	Ch. 9	"Look-Aside"	Ch. 11 v14-19	
		Trumpets Intro.	Trumpets (1 - 6)	Ch. 10 -11 v13 Angel + 2 Witnesses	7th Trumpet	

Figure 5: Schematic of Revelation 1 to 11

One feature of the structure worth noting is that the first cycle of seven, the letters, has a couple of differences from the other two cycles. Firstly, the second and third cycles, the seals and the trumpets, both have an aside or interlude between their sixth and seventh events. These two cycles both deal with the largely unbelieving world. The seals deal with preaching to it and the trumpets deal with controlling its worst excesses. Despite what this world sees as relevant and important, God has a purpose that he is progressing unstoppably. He is gathering people to be his own and is steering history, including that of his special people the Jews, towards the establishment of his kingdom on earth. The progress of this purpose is not noticed by most of the world, so under the seal and trumpet cycles, which dealt with the world at large, it is handled as a background interlude or aside. In contrast, the first cycle of the letters deals with those who believe and who earnestly desire to be a part of God's purpose. The whole of the cycle deals with their grasp of that reality, so there is no need to put in any aside about it.

Secondly, the seal and trumpet cycles are both brought to an end in a climax triggered in their seventh phase. For both cycles this grand climax is the coming of Christ and his setting up of God's kingdom on earth. Once that happens and the world enters the new millennial age, then situations of the type described in the two cycles no longer occur in the same way as before. Preaching about an unseen Christ, as under the seals, will not be necessary because he will be on earth again in person. God's unseen hand controlling history, as under the trumpets, will also not be needed in the same way because Christ and his saints will wield supreme authority in the earth. So in reaching their climax, the main activities of both of these cycles cease. However the realities of the believers' relationship with God through Christ, that are dealt with under the seven letters, do not stop when the kingdom comes but rather become more powerful and wonderful. So each of the letters contains its own promise of future blessing and the cycle of the letters does not come to an end but rather makes a transition into a more glorious reality. This is shown by the progression from the letters into the vision of the throne of glory in chapter 4.

So, the apparent anomalies in the symmetry of the three cycles of seven turn out to reflect real differences in the realities underlying their messages, namely that the things that relate to God's purpose are lasting, while the things that relate to the present state of the world are transient; as Paul says "our eyes are fixed, not on the things that are seen, but on the things that are unseen; for what is seen is transient, what is unseen is eternal" (2 Cor. 4 v. 18)

12.2 A Peep at Revelation Chapters 12-22

When we move on to Revelation chapters 12 to 22 we find visions that involve dragons, beasts, horns, kings, the city of Babylon, etc. This is very like the imagery in Daniel's prophecy, and as his visions often have accompanying explanations we know that they refer to specific nations and rulers from the ancient world. This would seem to reinforce the idea we gained from the message of the "rainbow" angel to John, that he is to go on to prophesy more specifically about "nations and kings". Thus while chapters 1 to 11 establish general patterns of events, we can expect chapters 12 to 22 to show the outworking of those patterns in history by detailing for us some of the major scenes and "milestones" in the story of the Christian era. However, as we saw in section 1.4, we should still not expect the sequence of visions to map on to a continuous narrative account of the course of history. We shall find that the text often gives us an overview first, followed by one or more visions highlighting particular details. Sometimes multiple views of the same events are given from different viewpoints. For example Revelation chapter 20 covers the start to the end of the kingdom millennium, with Rev. 20 v. 4 showing the saints taking their thrones to rule with Christ, while Rev. 20 v. 12-15 covers the end of the millennium with the second judgement and the final destruction of death itself. Then chapter 21 revisits the same period with a vision of the saints as the Bride of Christ and with some insights into life in the Kingdom, while chapter 22 adds further details of the kingdom age before ending with an epilogue.

Before proceeding with chapter 12 we would do well to repeat the warning in section 1, that the Revelation contains much strange and exciting imagery that can be very stimulating to the imagination. On one hand this can quickly lead us into realms of speculation. On the other hand, in an attempt to rein in that imaginative impulse, we can be tempted to follow an over-dogmatic adherence to a preconceived plan of interpretation. To help us to find a safe middle way between these pitfalls our primary guide and interpretative key should be the rest of the scriptures. This requires us to recall and reflect upon so much else of God's word as we try to understand the Revelation that it is surely part of the blessing in Revelation 1 v. 3 – "happy are those who listen if they take to heart what is here written".

13. THE "FIRST FRUIT" (Rev. Ch. 12)

13.1 Introduction

After the very structured format of chapters 1 to 11, where many shorter passages were arranged in three groups of sevens, the Revelation now moves on to a more narrative style. We get more of a sense of a story unfolding, but the cast of characters involved seems so unusual that it is hard at first to make out what is going on. Nonetheless, despite the narrative style, the visions are still making powerful use of symbols and as before we will look for earlier scriptural precedents to help in finding meanings for those symbols. Having understood the symbols we will then try to make better sense of the messages they are intended to convey in the context of the Revelation. As the narrative unfolds we will see that chapters 12 to 14 follow the pattern of an agricultural season from the firstfruit, through the vicissitudes of the main growing season, and into the harvest. However we are not looking here at literal crops, but at the successes and failures of spiritual growth as conveyed by the parable of the sower and the outworking of the pattern we met when looking at the seven seals.

13.2 The Woman (Rev. 12 v. 1-2)

The first character encountered in Revelation chapter 12 is a woman, and this is often used as a symbol in scripture (see ***Woman*** in the symbol glossary). The typical usage is to represent a group of people capable of receiving seed from God; that is accepting his word or spirit, and bearing offspring or fruit for him. When such people obey their Lord they are referred to as his faithful wife (see ***Wife*** in the symbol glossary), but if they become unfaithful, for example by making liaisons with the world and turning away from God, then they are referred to as an adulteress or a harlot (see ***Harlot*** in the symbol glossary). Initially it is not clear what sort of woman this is in chapter 12 and we have to look at some of the details to find out.

The woman is described in verse 1 as being adorned by the sun, moon, and twelve stars. This imagery is used in a vision given to Joseph in one of his dreams (Gen. 37 v. 9-10) and we understand from Joseph's talk with his father and the reaction of his brothers that the sun represents Jacob, the moon represents his wives, and the other 11 sons are represented as stars. This would suggest very strongly that the woman in Revelation chapter 12 is a person, or persons, very strongly linked to God's purpose with Israel.

The woman is also pregnant (v. 2) which fits with the general woman symbol, but in the absence of any other details we need to know more about the child before we can fully identify the mother.

13.3 The Man-Child and his Relatives

The male child that is to be born is obviously an offspring or seed of the woman. This idea takes us back to the very first promise of a hope of salvation from death in Genesis 3 v. 15 where Eve is promised that one of her offspring will overcome the power of sin and death. This idea is presented in the image of the woman's offspring crushing the head of the serpent. The idea of this "seed of promise" to carry out God's plan is repeated in special revelations to the Old Testament patriarchs, e.g. to Abraham in Gen. 12 v. 7; Gen. 13 v. 15; etc.

The man-child in Revelation chapter 12 is further described, in verse 5, as "destined to rule all nations with a rod of iron". This phrase originates in a prophecy of Christ's future rule over the earth in Ps. 2 v. 6-9. The relevance of the phrase to the role of Christ is reinforced by its being applied again in Revelation to the victor of the last great battle against the powers of the world (Rev. 19 v. 15). As we shall see when we reach that chapter, the other titles and descriptions applied to that victor clearly identify him as Christ. So evidence is mounting that the events of chapter 12 are briefly describing the birth and mission of Christ, and the opposition he experienced from the ruling powers of his day.

Further on in the narrative we see that the child is caught up to God and to his throne (Rev. 12 v. 5). This is a clear reference to the resurrection and ascension of Christ, and fits in well with other references to his being raised to sit at God's right hand (e.g. Heb. 1 v. 3, 13 and Heb. 12 v. 2). Thus the language used and the scriptures directly or indirectly invoked all point to the man-child in Revelation chapter 12 being Christ. Getting this identification clear helps to further identify other actors in the drama, such as the mother of the man-child.

A first reaction might be to say that if the child is Christ then the woman who bears him must be Mary. However, as referred to in the previous section and in the symbol glossary, the symbol of a woman is often used for a group of people. Also the events that happen to the woman in chapter 12 after the birth do not fit with the interpretation of the woman being Mary.

When Isaiah used symbols to convey ideas about the human side of the origin of Christ he used the picture of a "branch" that would "grow from the stock of Jesse (King David's father)" (Is. 11 v. 1). The image of a stock or stump conveys the idea that the prominent and powerful house of David would, together with all the other tribes of Israel, be cut down to leave only a weak remnant by the time of Christ. We find corresponding prophecies of punishment and reduction to a remnant in Isaiah's previous chapter (Is. 10 v. 21, 22). In view of this "stump" and "branch" symbolism, and the Jewish symbols accompanying the woman at the start of Revelation chapter 12, it seems most appropriate to see the woman as representing the faithful remnant of Israel that was waiting for their messiah at the time of Christ. In terms of the symbolic use of "woman" this remnant was a "good" woman, and it was as a member of this group of faithful Jews that Mary arose to give birth to Jesus.

One other set of characters occurring later in the chapter is the group described as the "rest of her (the woman's) offspring" (Rev. 12 v. 17). If these people are children of the woman then they are in some way the siblings of the man-child, that is brothers and sisters of Christ. In the letter to the Hebrews (2 v. 11) it says of the believers that Christ "does not shrink from calling men his brothers". More specifically they are described at the end of the chapter as "those who keep God's commandments and maintain their witness to Jesus" (Rev. 12 v. 17). So this group seems to represent Christian faithful, not descended literally from the faithful Jewish remnant but adopted into the same family through a common faith. As Paul says, "If you belong to Christ, you are the 'issue' of Abraham and heirs by virtue of the promise" (Gal. 3 v. 29).

Figure 6: The Woman and the Dragon (Rev. Ch.6:1-6)

13.4 The Dragon / Serpent Symbol

Opposing the woman (i.e. the faithful remnant of Israel) and her offspring (i.e. Jesus and the Christian faithful) is the power of the dragon. The image of a "dragon" is used in the Bible to represent the spirit or intent of major powers that contend with God. Such powers aspire to world domination and have a philosophy that raises up man into God's place, often going so far as to deify and worship their human rulers (see **Dragon** in the symbol glossary). It is interesting to note that in Revelation chapter 12 the dragon power is related to the "ancient serpent" (Rev. 12 v. 9), which is a common biblical symbol of individual sin (see **Serpent** in the symbol glossary). Thus while the symbol of the serpent represents sin, which puts individuals into conflict with the will of God, the dragon symbol seems to move this conflict up to a larger scale, raising it up from a personal level to a national level to represent a pervasive spirit of man replacing, or contending with, God.

13.5 Representing Empires in Daniel and Revelation

To understand some of the finer details of the dragon symbol it is very helpful to compare it with the images used in Daniel's prophecies to represent human empires. Here, as in prophetic biblical usage elsewhere, beasts are used as symbols for significant governing powers in the world, such as major nations or empires. Sometimes the additional detail of a horn is used as a symbol for a king ruling such a nation (see **Horn** in the symbol glossary). For example, in Daniel 8 v. 8 we are shown a he-goat representing ancient Greece. At first this has one great horn representing Alexander the Great, but this is broken and replaced by four prominent horns representing the four generals that followed Alexander and divided up his empire between them.

In another prophecy (in Dan. Ch. 7), Daniel is shown visions of four different beasts to represent the major empires that would rule over Israel and influence the Mediterranean and Middle-Eastern areas from his day onwards. The first three beasts in the sequence are depicted, reasonably naturally, as a lion, representing Babylon, a bear, representing Medo-Persia, and a leopard, representing Greece. Then the fourth beast is described as "fearsome" and "different from all the beasts that went before", and it seems to be more mythical than natural as it has ten horns. This fourth beast is generally accepted as representing the Roman Empire. No other animal images in prophecy are shown as having ten horns apart from the dragon in Revelation (Ch. 12 v. 3) and the closely related sea beast (Ch. 13 v. 1). This linking detail, of having ten horns, suggests that Daniel's fourth beast and the dragon in Revelation both represent some aspect of the Roman Empire. Further, if Revelation chapter 12 is dealing with events around the birth, death, and resurrection of Christ, then the dominant pagan power operating in the region is Rome, so making the link between the dragon symbol and the Roman Empire more likely.

One difference between Daniel's fourth beast and the dragon is that the dragon in Revelation is described as having seven heads, while this feature is not mentioned in Daniel. We can get a clue to the meaning of this in a different vision in Daniel. In the interpretation of Nebuchadnezzar's dream (Dan. ch. 2) a different symbol is used to describe the same sequence of four empires. The symbol used is that of a huge statue of a human figure, like a giant pagan idol. Although there is only one statue, the sequence of empires is denoted by the use of different metals for its different levels, namely a golden head for Babylon, silver chest and arms for Medo-Persia, bronze belly and thighs for Greece, and iron legs for Rome. Thus, whereas the use of four separate beasts in chapter 7 emphasizes the different geographical origins and different periods of rule of the four empires, the use of a single image in the form of a man in chapter 2 emphasizes their shared spirit of human opposition to God. Also the fact that idol statues of this kind were frequently used as objects of worship highlights the common inclination of such empires to put man and his creations into the place that God should occupy.

As a quick aside we can point to further reinforcement of this inference in the following chapter (Dan. ch. 3) where Nebuchadnezzar actually builds a huge idol of a human figure and commands all his subjects to worship it. This time he commands that the idol is to be made all of gold, the representative metal for Babylon, which is surely the emperor's way of saying that he does not want his empire to be succeeded by others, but to last for ever. Truly this is a real act of pride and rebellion against God's word.

This spirit of opposition to God is the one we have already recognized as being characterized by the dragon symbol. So while the dragon of Revelation chapter 12 is like Daniel's fourth beast, in having ten horns and representing Rome, it also shows, like the idol in Nebuchadnezzar's dream, that Rome is only one of several powers that would embody the spirit of human antagonism to God. Thus the depiction of the dragon as having seven heads is a means of portraying the recurrence of major powers in the world that share this common spirit or culture. The number of heads, seven, may be literal or symbolic but is typically used for events or periods that repeat (see *Seven* in the symbol glossary). So the dragon symbol in Scripture represents not just one power but a sequence of major powers which all share a spirit of antagonism to God. Just as with the levels of the image in Nebuchadnezzar's vision, where only one level at a time was active in history, so only one of the seven heads of the dragon is active at any one time. In Revelation 12, the active head represents the pagan Roman Empire.

The fact that the heads are individually crowned (Rev. 12 v. 3) suggests that the different powers represented by the heads could each have their own form of ruling power or dynastic succession. The amount of power wielded by these rulers appears to be large, since the dragon seems to be able to depose lesser secular or religious powers, as signified by its ability to cast down stars (Rev. 12 v. 4) – see *Stars* in the symbol glossary.

Summing up our findings about the dragon in Revelation chapter 12, we see that it represents one phase of a many-headed dragon power. The phase, or active dragon's head, that was in power in John's day represents the pagan Roman Empire, which actually opposed Christ and his followers. However the whole creature also epitomizes the "dragon spirit" that would be shared by other empires and so is shown to have seven heads in all. This seems to emphasize the universality of Christ's struggle and victory, as if to say that if he had come in the reign of any other "dragon power", he would have experienced the same opposition.

13.6 The Action Takes Place in Heaven

The woman is described as appearing "in heaven" (Rev. 12 v. 1) which is also where the dragon appears (v. 3) and makes war (v. 7). As already discussed (see *Heaven* in the symbol glossary), heaven refers to the realm of God, not in any physical sense of "up there" but in a more abstract sense of the dimension or domain of the spirit in which mankind can participate in the unfolding of God's purpose. Thus the woman, representing faithful Israel, is "in heaven" in the same sense in which for the Christian believers God has "raised us up in union with Christ Jesus and enthroned us with him in the heavenly realms" (Eph. 2 v. 6).

Thus when the pagan Roman Empire deems Christ to be an enemy of the state and persecutes the Christians to reinforce the pre-eminence of pagan culture, it is in fact trying to exert spiritual dominance and is contending for spiritual authority against God himself. In the shorthand of biblical imagery, this is "war in heaven". As Paul says (NKJV Eph. 6 v. 12), "we do not wrestle against flesh and blood", i.e. against literal, physical opponents, "but against principalities, against powers, against the rulers of the darkness of this age, against the spiritual hosts of wickedness in the heavenly places", i.e. against those powers and authorities that seek to adversely influence our spiritual outlook and obscure the light of the gospel.

13.7 The "Firstfruits" of God's Harvest

Having now identified the main participants in this vision, we can go on to get a better understanding of the events in which they are involved. In the first six verses of chapter 12 we see the faithful remnant of Israel, represented by the woman, taking her appointed place in the timetable of God's unfolding purpose (v. 1). She provides the environment into which Christ is to be born, as the man-child (v. 2). Right from the start he is opposed by a major, pagan power, represented by the dragon (v. 3-4). At that point in history the dragon "head" holding power is the pagan Roman Empire that seeks to destroy Jesus both at his birth, by the actions of the Roman puppet-king Herod, and at his death which is ordered by the Roman governor Pilate. However God's purpose cannot be thwarted by these human agencies. Instead of death being a defeat, Christ triumphs through the resurrection and ascends to heaven, as represented by the man-child being caught up to God's throne (v. 5).

Being the first to rise from the dead to immortality, Christ is referred to as "the firstfruits of the harvest of the dead" (1 Cor. 15 v. 20). Although that term is not used explicitly here in Revelation, it fits in with the structure of this part of the book, which reaches a climax in the grain and grape harvests depicted in Revelation chapter 14.

After Christ's ascension, the woman flees to the wilderness (v. 6). In other words she has to leave her home and go to live in a more hostile environment, which represents the Jewish dispersion throughout the Roman Empire in the second half of the first century. The verses that follow give more details of the effects of this struggle between the pagan world and the purpose of God.

13.8 The Struggle Continues

In the next six verses of the chapter (Rev. 12 v. 7-12) we see the pagan "dragon" power depicted as engaging in a war in heaven (v. 7). We have seen earlier that "heaven" represents the realm of spiritual influence (see **Heaven** in the symbol glossary). So placing the war there indicates that it is not a literal war but a struggle for dominance as the pre-eminent spiritual authority (see also **Warfare** in the symbol glossary). The two sides in the war are both shown as having leaders and followers. Since this is essentially a spiritual conflict for the hearts and minds of men, these leaders are not actual kings or generals so much as personifications of conflicting ideologies. This is borne out by the followers or soldiers on each side being called "angels" which means "messengers"; that is they are advocates and teachers of the two ways of thinking.

The leader of the forces of good is named as "Michael", a name which means "Who is like God?" and which is also given to an angel referred to elsewhere in the Bible as "the prince of my people". This seems to be a symbol of divine power being exercised through or for God's people when no divinely appointed king is physically present (see **_Michael_** in the symbol glossary). The followers on this side are Michael's angels, or messengers; that is the faithful Christians who spread the gospel through their witness, in other words, the growing body of the early church.

The leader of the evil forces is the dragon, which we have already identified as the spirit of human opposition to God that seeks to put man in God's place (see **_Dragon_** in the symbol glossary). As discussed in Section 13.5 above, the actual worldly power that is characterized by this spirit at this point in history is the pagan Roman Empire. The dragon's angels are therefore those who espouse and support its way of thinking.

In the vision the dragon, paganism, loses the struggle because it is too weak (v. 8). The resulting victory of the forces of good is explained in two ways. Firstly (v. 9), there is the image of the "ancient serpent" being thrown down (see **_Satan_** and **_Serpent_** in the symbol glossary). This is a symbol for Christ winning his victory over the serpent-power of sin. Being free of sin, Christ cannot be held by death and in rising from the grave he becomes the "firstfruit" of God's harvest. This spiritual victory won by Christ is expressed in a second way by its being referred to in the words "by the sacrifice of the Lamb ... they have conquered" (v. 11). The "they" who have conquered are Michael's angels, representing the Christian faithful with their apostles and preachers. They share symbolically in Christ's death and resurrection in the waters of baptism. This makes them able to share in Christ's victory, but they also have their own part to play as referred to in the words "and by the witness they bore, they have conquered" (v. 11). Thus the early church is shown actively spreading the gospel and winning the kind of victories represented by the "white horse" phase of the seven seals cycle (see section 7.2). These successes are gained through faithful preaching and service, often at considerable personal cost due to the opposition of the servants of the dragon power, that is the Roman authorities with their allies and colonies. So as the victories in the spiritual battle are won by the believers, the dragon power, Rome, loses its attempt at spiritual pre-eminence but it still keeps its secular power, shown as it being thrown out of heaven but still exercising power on earth (v. 12).

In the last few verses of the chapter (Rev. 12 v. 13-17) we see further details of the ensuing secular results of this spiritual conflict. Verse 13 shows the dragon power, Rome, persecuting the woman, Israel, as happened in the major Roman military repressions in AD 70 and AD 100. As already indicated in verse 6, such repression did not result in complete annihilation because the Jews fled, or were transported, into exile. Just as their entry into the Promised Land under Moses and Joshua was the end of a literal wilderness wandering, so their expulsion from the land is represented figuratively by a return to the wilderness (v. 14). It is noteworthy that the time allotted to this new wilderness existence is expressed as 1260 days in verse 6, which, as 42 months of 30 days each, is the same as the three and a half year period in verse 14. This expression of the same time period in different ways is strongly reminiscent of the description in chapter 11 of the period that the two witnesses were to testify (see section 11.2). This correspondence seems to strengthen the interpretation that the symbols of the two witnesses and the woman both represent the role of the Jewish people as "God's witnesses" (see section 11.1).

13.9 Eagle's Wings and the Dragon's River

Within the last few verses there are a couple of details where it is difficult to identify enough biblical precedents to provide a really secure interpretation, but we can suggest some reasonably plausible ideas. The first detail is that the means or agency by which the woman is enabled to flee is expressed as "the wings of a mighty eagle" (verse 14). Because the Roman army used the image of an eagle on its battle standards, some interpreters have taken the eagle as a symbol for Rome and its empire, and have taken this phrase to relate to the outer edges of the empire where the dispersed Jews could find relative safety. Although this is a useful historical observation, the reasoning behind the interpretation draws on secular rather than biblical correspondences.

In earlier biblical uses "eagle" is used in prophecies about nations, but never about Rome. One key use of the eagle as a symbol derives from the bird's visual acuity that gives it so much more accurate vision than human beings. This leads to it being used as an image of the Holy Spirit or spiritual insight, as in the eagle-face of the cherubim (see **Cherubim** in the symbol glossary). In this sense we have a very relevant passage in Exodus where God is indicating how he has been using his power or spirit to support the Israelites in their journey through the wilderness towards the Promised Land. It describes how God "carried you on eagles' wings and brought you here to me" (Ex. 19 v. 4). So surely the eagles' wings that carry them back out of their land into the "wilderness" of exile, and give them safety from the Roman persecutions, is the same divine power.

The second detail is that the dragon tries to undermine or destroy the dispersed Jews (the woman) with a flood of water out of its mouth (verse 15). Now James likens a mouth that utters both blessings and curses to a fountain that issues both fresh and brackish water (Jas. 3 v. 10-11). Also, in a number of places, good words are likened to fresh, sweet, life-giving water, particularly words that relate to the purpose or teachings of God (for example in Jesus' talk with the woman at the well at Sychar, John 4 v. 14). So it is reasonable to see the image of life-threatening water issuing from the mouth of an opponent of God (the dragon) as representing evil words in the form of propaganda or false teaching. In this case it could be propaganda aimed at inciting the common people to continue the authorities' persecution of the Jews. Indeed incidents of misinformed anti-Semitism have been a common experience of the Jews in exile from the time of the Caesars onwards.

In this case the desired destructive effect is not fully achieved, as the water is soaked up by the earth (verse 16). Since "earth" is often used as a symbol for the people that live on it (see **Earth** in the symbol glossary), then here it could represent the peoples of the Roman Empire, the territory of the current "dragon" power. Thus the image seems to indicate that despite official propaganda inciting persecution of the exiled Jews, the people at large do not act on it, allowing the Jews a continuing existence in their witnessing role.

Thwarted in its intention of eliminating the woman, the dragon persecutes the other offspring of the woman (verse 17). As already identified at the end of section 13.3, these "other offspring" are in fact the brethren of Christ, that is the Christian church, which did suffer persecution at the hands of the Roman empire and yet was still able to "keep God's commandments and maintain their witness to Jesus" (end of verse 17). So the revelation of Jesus as the "firstfruit" led to a growing harvest of faithful believers. The gathering in of that harvest will be covered in Revelation chapter 14, but first the main characteristics of the intervening epoch are outlined in chapter 13.

14. THE TWO BEASTS (Rev. Ch. 13)

14.1 Introduction – Reminder of Earth & Sea Symbols

Before starting the interpretation of Revelation chapter 13 it will be helpful to set the context by reminding ourselves of the meaning of "earth" and "sea" when used as biblical symbols. We encountered these and related symbols earlier as targets for the judgements under the seven trumpets (see sections 9.3 and 9.4). We took "earth" (see *Earth* in the symbol glossary) to represent the populations of well-organized, civilized nations. Such people, with their superior education and communications, have the best chance of accessing the word of God, though they do not necessarily choose to accept it more readily than others. Mountains, which are raised up areas of the earth, then become symbols for nations which raise themselves up over others and exert widespread influence as empires (see *Mountains* in the symbol glossary).

The "sea" is also used as a symbol for peoples, but given its fluid and always-changing nature it is natural to use it to represent less-developed nations made up of relatively loose tribal or nomadic groupings of peoples, often with little or no access to the word of God (see *Sea* in the symbol glossary). In chapter 13, notable beasts arise from each of these environments, and we will look at each of these in turn.

14.2 Beast of the Sea – Background

In our analysis of Revelation chapter 12 we looked at the similarities between the dragon described there and the "fourth beast" depicted in Daniel chapter 7 (see section 13.5). We will now go on to study the "sea beast" at the start of Revelation chapter 13, and as we do so we can see a number of further resemblances to the dragon. Both sets of "family resemblances" are laid out in Table 6 below.

We have already seen that when a beast is depicted as having multiple heads it seems to be used as a symbol of the division of a

Table 6: "Beast" Resemblances

Dan. 7 The 4th Beast	Rev. 12 The Dragon	Rev. 13 The Sea Beast
1 Head	7 Heads	7 Heads
10 Horns	10 Horns	10 Horns
No Crowns	Heads Crowned	Horns Crowned
Blasphemes (at the end) - via little horn	No blasphemy Mentioned	Blasphemes - via its mouth

single "beast" power into subdivisions or phases that have a relatively independent existence from each other while still being part of one recognizable power or culture. An additional example is found in Daniel 7 v. 6 where the leopard, that is being used to represent Greece, develops four heads to represent the four dynasties founded by the generals who succeeded Alexander. While these heads represent geographical separation of powers, we saw that the seven heads of the dragon in chapter 12 represent a separation in time of the different powers that embody the "dragon spirit" of human opposition to God.

In chapter 13 we see that the "sea beast" also has seven heads like the dragon as well as having ten horns like both the dragon and Daniel's fourth beast. Given the identification of the two earlier beasts with the Roman Empire, the further unique similarities between them and this new sea beast would lead us to expect that it is also closely related to some form or phase of the Roman Empire. We will see if this is borne out as we look in more detail at the relationship between the dragon and the sea beast.

14.3 Transition from Dragon to Sea Beast

As the new beast emerges from the sea (in verse 1) it receives power and authority from the dragon (verse 2) which also yields up its throne to this sea beast. This looks like a direct transfer of power rather than conquest and overthrow. If we look to history we see that during the third century AD the Roman Empire suffered many crises due to plague, invasion and civil strife. Attempts were made, as under the emperor Diocletian at the end of the third century, to simplify the management of the empire by dividing it into two administrative areas. By the end of the fourth century, this division had become permanent and the united Roman Empire had split into two independent parts, the Western and the Eastern Empires. The existing capital city, Rome, became the residence, or "throne", of the western emperor, while the eastern emperor was based in Constantinople, which was founded earlier that century by the emperor Constantine. Thus the details given in the vision, and the biblical clues we have to help us to understand them, seem to suggest that the sea beast is a symbol for the Western Roman Empire.

Also, in terms of its origin, this new beast rises out of the sea, and as we reminded ourselves in section 14.1 the sea is a prophetic symbol for relatively unstructured, tribal peoples. Looking at the scope of the previously united Roman Empire we see that its eastern wing was centred on Greece, Asia Minor and the Middle East which had been home to several relatively advanced, empire-building civilizations for thousands of years. The other, western wing was home to much more primitive societies with the groupings of Britons, Belgians, Gauls, Germans, and Spaniards rarely having any national cohesion but consisting rather of much smaller and more fluid tribal groupings. Thus the peoples of Western Europe fit closely the pattern represented by the symbol of the sea, which seems to confirm the identification of the sea beast as the Western Roman Empire.

As we have already noted, both the dragon and the sea beast have seven heads. In the case of the dragon we have taken this to represent multiple phases of a power standing in opposition to God, with the relevant phase in Revelation chapter 12 being the pagan Roman Empire. As the sea beast is part of what followed that pagan Roman phase, it may itself be considered to be part of the next head of the dragon (but for more details on "dragon's heads" see section 17.3). What then of the sea beast's own set of seven heads? Following the pattern, they should represent multiple phases of the Western Roman Empire. This would make them occupy a smaller time scale than the phases or "heads" of the dragon. This change of scale possibly lies behind the change of level at which crowns are placed on the dragon and the sea beast. While the dragon is shown (Rev. 12 v. 3) with crowns on its heads (indicating the rulership of separate, major imperial powers), the sea beast is shown (Rev. 13 v. 1) with crowns on its horns (to represent different royal families or dynasties within the same, western empire).

We are given some detail of one of the sea beast's heads that is shown as receiving a death blow. This might be thought to endanger the life of the whole beast, but the wound is healed and the beast stays alive (Rev. 13 v. 3), to the wonder of the rest of the world. This detail is borne out in history as, not long after the division of the empire, the barbarians overran the Western Roman Empire and Rome fell. However the conquerors quickly took over so many of the existing Roman traditions and institutions that they, and their successors, are sometimes called "sub-Roman" societies. Thus although the new power did not have a Roman emperor it was effectively a new phase of the Western Roman Empire, with many of the same territories and the same capital, Rome. This new phase, or "head", of the sea beast was the Ostrogothic Empire and over the centuries other powers such as the Visigothic, Frankish, Holy Roman, and Austro-Hungarian Empires became dominant in many of the parts of Western Europe where Rome had ruled. These then could be some of the powers represented as "heads" of the sea beast and, as with the heads of the dragon, only one of them is active at any particular point in history.

14.4 Sea Beast in Action

Under Constantine, at the beginning of the fourth century, the official religion of the Roman Empire was changed from being pagan to being, at least nominally, Christian. However, pagan worship was tolerated for some time and had an insidious influence on "official" Christianity. For example many pagan festivals and deities were "Christianised" to make the new religion more familiar and acceptable to former pagans. Also, as the church became more organised and wealthy, hierarchies of bishops were established in power structures and districts very similar to those in the Roman civil administration. Thus the state, or "beast" power as it is represented in symbol, gradually came to uphold a form of Christianity that was corrupted and significantly distanced from its first century origins. As the state church consolidated its control of religious power, it became more aggressive against those who stood up for the original gospel teachings, branding them "heretics" and persecuting them or sending them into exile. These actions are described symbolically in several ways (Rev. 13 v. 5-10). For example the beast is said to utter blasphemies and to revile the name of God, in other words it speaks falsely about God's nature and purpose. It also reviles God's dwelling, which is explained as being those who dwell in heaven, that is faithful people not a building. This calls to mind words about true believers sitting with Christ in heavenly places (Eph. 2 v. 6) and being God's true temple (1 Pet. 2 v. 5). The beast also uses its considerable power to wage war on God's people, which leads to a call for them to show endurance and faithfulness. This is very like the call to the martyrs, as represented by the symbol of the "souls under the altar", under the fifth of the cycle of seals that revealed the effects of the preaching of the true gospel (see section 7.8).

The fact that the sea beast's words are described as blasphemous reinforces the link already made between it and Daniel's fourth beast (Dan. Ch. 7). We have recognized that both are prophecies about the Roman Empire. In Daniel the fourth beast changes appearance and develops a new, small horn that has a mouth uttering blasphemies. So in Daniel the change from pagan Rome to a Rome supporting a corrupt form of Christianity is shown by the fourth beast developing its "little horn", while the same change is shown in Revelation by the transition of power from the dragon of chapter 12 to the sea and earth beasts of chapter 13. Thus, in Revelation, when men follow or worship the sea beast (Rev. 13 v. 4), they are still in fact worshipping the dragon, because the sea beast is still putting man's ways and ideas in the place of those revealed by God. So despite the change in name from dragon to sea beast, there is little significant change in the nature of the ruling power. This is probably why the descriptions indicate that the sea beast has such a close family resemblance to the dragon; so close that it may well be the next phase or "head" of the dragon. The fact that the dragon is not described as uttering blasphemies in chapter 12 may be accounted for by it representing a pagan power which didn't know or recognize God, and so could not use his name and teachings falsely.

14.5 Beast of the Earth – Rev. 13 v 11-15

Following the description of the sea beast, a new beast appears which rises out of the earth (Rev. 13 v. 11). As we reminded ourselves in section 14.1, the earth is used as a scriptural symbol for organized, civilized peoples. In terms of the geography of the Roman Empire, such powers had preceded Rome in its eastern territories, and on that side the empire had absorbed the remnants of several earlier empires such as those of the Persians and the Greeks.

Another important detail about this earth beast is that it has the authority of the sea beast and exercises that authority in the presence of the sea beast (Rev. 13 v. 12). So whereas the sequences of beasts in both Daniel chapter 7 and chapter 8 represent a succession of powers, the earth beast in Revelation chapter 13 does not supersede the sea beast but co-exists with it, described as acting "in its presence".

Putting the above information together, we are looking for a power which follows the unified, pagan Roman Empire, which arises from the territory of earlier civilized powers, and which coexists with the sea beast power which we have already identified as the Western Roman Empire. This can only lead to the identification of the earth beast as the Eastern Roman Empire.

As we saw above, the unified, pagan Roman Empire was represented as one phase, or "head", of the dragon. This is now followed by a new phase in which authority is divided between two co-existing powers. The whole of this divided Roman Empire becomes one new "head" on the dragon, but the histories of the two halves are sufficiently different to require the details to be represented by two further symbols, the Sea and the Earth beasts. This aspect of the two powers being "similar but different" was also highlighted in Nebuchadnezzar's vision of the statue (Dan. Ch. 2), in which Rome is portrayed as being divided, as shown by the two legs, but having much in common, with both legs being made of iron and belonging to the same statue.

In John's vision the new beast from the earth has two horns like a lamb (Rev. 13 v. 11), which is reminiscent of the Old Testament vision in which Daniel sees a two-horned ram (Dan. 8 v. 3-8) that is explained to him as representing the eastern empire of Medo-Persia (Dan. 8 v. 20). The two horns in that case represented the twin power base of that empire, in the form of the earlier power of the Medes that ruled the emerging Persian power until they grew too strong and eventually took over as the dominant power. This two-sided nature was also characteristic of the Eastern Roman Empire. Unlike the western empire, which changed its scope and ruling dynasties several times, the eastern empire was more stable, and in its first phase as the Byzantine Empire it ruled for about a thousand years. However, over this period its influence gradually shrank and its territories were slowly taken over by the Ottoman Empire. Thus over many centuries the dominant influence in the eastern empire gradually shifted from the Christian, Byzantine power to the Islamic, Ottoman power. This two-sided division of power accounts for the "two-horned" appearance of the eastern, earth beast power. We will look again at the transition from being a Christian power to being an Islamic power when we reach Revelation chapter 19.

14.6 Earth Beast in Action

The earth beast is shown as making an image of the previously revealed sea beast (Rev. 13 v. 14-15). In terms of the powers we have identified, this indicates that in some way the eastern empire creates a replica or likeness of the western empire. In fact Eastern Rome (Byzantium) set up very similar state institutions to the west with an identical state religion, at least at first. After some time, doctrinal differences caused a split in the state church, and the church in the east became the Eastern Orthodox faith in the 11th century. Thus, with its secular and religious institutions modelled on those in the west, the eastern empire was very much "an image" of the west.

Although the church in Constantinople had its own spiritual leader, or patriarch, it nevertheless, for a considerable period, recognized the supremacy of the church leader in the west, i.e. the Bishop of Rome, or Pope. Over time the powers claimed for the papacy gained wider acceptance within, and beyond, the church. In fact, due to periods of weakness and turmoil in the secular leadership in the west, the Pope also gained political power, both by having direct rule over the Papal States and by having powerful influence over kings and emperors in both west and east. Thus, in terms of biblical imagery, the Pope, and the institutions he ruled or influenced, became part of the power represented by the sea beast. The language of Revelation chapter 13 presents this power as continuing in the spirit of the dragon in opposing the true teachings and people of God. It also indicates (Rev. 13 v. 12, 14-15) that the earth beast is similarly deluding the inhabitants of its territories (the "earth", or eastern empire countries) and effectively causing them to worship the sea beast rather than God. This is because the earth beast, in its long first phase as Byzantium, follows the same form of religious worship as the west and acknowledges its spiritual authority. Given the very close links between the secular powers and the church leadership at this time, these regrettable trends look like a natural outworking of the old adage that "power corrupts". However the failings of the church leaders do not automatically consign all members of these churches to the way of error; rather they emphasize the warnings, given under the cycle of the seven seals, that the preaching of the true gospel will often suffer opposition and achieve only limited success.

As an additional detail, the earth beast is shown as being able to call down fire from heaven (Rev. 13 v. 13). This is surprising as such a power is often the sign of a prophet, for example Elijah who calls down fire to consume his sacrifice on Mount Carmel (1 Kings 18), and also to destroy soldiers sent to capture him (2 Kings 1). However, in this case, it is a false sign because the earth beast, although it has some resemblance to a lamb, which is one of the symbols for Christ, does in fact speak like a dragon (Rev. 13 v. 11), the symbol for human opposition to God. Thus this earth beast deludes the people and executes those who do not follow its ways (Rev. 13 v. 15).

14.7 Mark and Number of the Beast – Rev. 13 v. 16-18

The idea of there being pressure to conform to the state system, as alluded to above, is reinforced by using the image of the earth beast making its people or followers receive a mark or imprint from the beast's seal (Rev. 13 v. 16-17). The mark is received in the right hand, a symbol for personal actions (for example not letting the left hand know what the right hand does – Matt. 6 v. 3), or in the forehead, a symbol for the seat of the will (see for example Ezek. 3 v. 8-9). Thus the earth beast seeks to impose conformity of action and thinking amongst its peoples. This contrasts with an earlier symbol of much more desirable conformity when the true believers, under the symbol of the 144,000 (Rev. 7 v. 2-3), are sealed in the forehead with the seal of the living God (see section 8.2). The pull between these two pressures to conform is referred to by the apostle Paul when he writes, "conform no longer to the pattern of this present world, but be transformed by the renewal of your minds; then you will be able to discern the will of God" (Rom. 12 v. 2). In other words, our minds can be moulded, like softened wax under a seal, and it is far better to seek the influence of God's word and his holy spirit than to succumb to the pressures of the world around us.

It is further predicted that those without the mark of the beast will not be able to buy or sell goods (Rev. 13 v. 17). In other words the conformity sought by the powers of the eastern empire would be so rigid that people who did not follow its approved ways would be unable to engage in trade. In fact history bears out that the Byzantine Empire had a very extensive civil service through which it administered a rigid guild system with associated state controlled and taxed markets. Without state-approved guild membership there was no access to these markets and the only other opportunity was to sell one's skills as a contracted labourer to an employer who would then own the goods produced. This state control was so effective that it was very difficult to amass private wealth, and for a long time there was virtually no middle-class of wealthy tradesmen and merchants in Byzantium.

One last detail in chapter 13 has been the root of much speculation down the ages. That is that the earth beast is given a number, 666, the number of the beast. Many interpreters have tried to "decode" this number by allocating a set of number values to the letters in the alphabet and using this equivalence to show that the total number value of some historic individual's name or title computes to 666. Many languages and numbering schemes have been tried, with very varied outcomes. However there is no scriptural precedent for doing this kind of number-for-letter calculation. Rather there is a good scriptural precedent for a significant use of the number 666 itself. In 1 Kings 10 v. 14 the figure 666 is given as the number of talents of gold that came into king Solomon's treasury in the course of a year. This is significant because it is a large amount and because its acquisition by Solomon is in direct contravention of a divine command. The law through Moses states that kings over God's people should not amass large quantities of gold (Deut. 17 v. 17); rather, a faithful king was to make and study his own copy of the law, and learn from it to fear God and keep his commandments (v. 18-20). This implies that believers trust in God to support them in difficulties, while those who turn away from him trust in wealth. Seeking wealth was a common trait of both the Eastern and Western Roman Empires, but Eastern Rome (Byzantium) was particularly successful as a trading nation and was famous for its wealth, which was mainly acquired for, and by, the state. So the number of the beast, 666, is not a secret code hiding the identity of a particularly "beastly" individual, but rather a symbol for the materialism of the earth beast power that we have already identified as the Eastern Roman Empire.

15. THE SEVEN ANGELS & THE HARVEST (Rev. Ch. 14)

15.1 The 144,000 – Rev. 14 v. 1-5

So far in this second half of the Revelation we have seen, in chapter 12, the victory that Christ won over the powers of sin and the world, with his resurrection making him the firstfruit from the dead and launching the spread of the gospel in the early church. Then, in chapter 13, we saw the predictions that the growth and establishment of the church would involve compromise with the secular ruling powers and corruption of the truths of the gospel, to the extent that true followers of God's way would be oppressed and persecuted. These events all fulfil the pattern, revealed under the cycle of the seven seals, of gospel preaching having some limited success, but stirring up opposition and yielding only a scant harvest of true believers.

This gloomy outlook at the end of chapter 13, where the peoples of the earth beast take his mark in their hand or forehead, is now sharply contrasted at the start of chapter 14 by the picture of the 144,000 who have the name of the Lamb and the Father written on their foreheads. The vision is actually revisiting the imagery of the "sealing" of the 144,000 that was first introduced in the "interlude" passage between the sixth and seventh seals. We saw there (in sections 8.2 and 8.3) that 144,000 was not a literal number but a symbolic figure representing those who are God's elect through faith, most likely representing the living saints at any one point in time. The repeating factors of 10 and 12 that make up 144,000 may well indicate that the repeated process of election goes on in every generation as those who respond to God's call come out from the teeming masses of humanity. This process of sealing goes on alongside the preaching cycle of the seven seals as its desired and intended outcome. However it is less visible to the observer than the other effects of the cycle, hence its introduction as an "interlude" within the seals cycle. The image is revisited at the start of chapter 14 to remind us that the process of choosing out a people for God will still continue, even when conditions in the world seem very dark from a spiritual viewpoint.

This new description of the 144,000 (Rev. 14 v. 1-5) makes it clear that they belong to God and stand with Christ as his redeemed. Indeed, they are described as "the firstfruits of mankind for God and the Lamb" (Rev. 14 v. 4), which has echoes of the words of James who says "he brought us to birth, by the word of truth to be a kind of firstfruits of his creation" (Jas. 1 v. 18). This is using symbols like the parable of the sower, in which Christ sows the "seed" of the word which, when received into the "good ground" of believing hearts, bears fruit for God. Thus the image of having the names of the Lamb and of God written in the forehead is a metaphor for having one's mind, with all its thoughts and resultant actions, profoundly influenced by the word of God. Christ of course was the perfect example of this, being the word made flesh (John 1 v. 14). Because of this total obedience to God's will, Jesus remained sinless and so the grave could not hold him. Through his resurrection he became "the firstfruits of the harvest of the dead" (1 Cor. 15 v. 20). This use of the term "firstfruits" as a metaphor to describe Jesus is quite obvious. However, applying the same term to generations of believers living right up to Christ's second coming raises an issue. In the Jewish calendar the feast of firstfruits marked the start of the harvest, and the later feast of ingathering celebrated its completion. So far the text has only used the symbol of firstfruits, so when will the rest of the harvest be gathered? The most obvious inference is that that the process of the harvest will continue beyond the second coming into the kingdom age, and the harvest will not be complete until there are no more mortals who can accept God's offer of salvation. We will look at this when we get to Revelation chapter 20.

As remarked above, the first account of the sealing of the 144,000 in Revelation chapter 7 occurs between the sixth seal, representing the judgements of a day of the Lord, and the seventh seal, representing the second coming of Christ. It is presented like an aside, out of the main stream of history, indicating that the preparation of God's people will progress quietly and relatively unnoticed by the observers of the "great" affairs of the world. So too, here at the start of chapter 14, it comes as something of an aside between the main historic milestones of the beasts of chapters 12 and 13, and the final harvest images in the rest of Revelation chapter 14.

15.2 The Seven Angels – Rev. 14 v. 6-20

The remainder of chapter 14 contains a series of announcements and actions by a sequence of seven heavenly beings or angels. As we come to understand the implications of what the angels do, and see how the visions of the following chapters relate to this, we will see that the angels are providing an outline or framework for the events of the end-times leading up to the return of Christ. While the number seven can be representative of a repeating cycle, like the seven seals or trumpets, it can alternatively carry implications of finality and completion (see *Seven* in the symbol glossary). The "seven" of these seven angels conveys this latter sense, that of bringing an era of history to a close.

The first angel (v. 6-7) has a message for the whole world. It draws attention to the importance of the eternal gospel so that, in the context of the previous verses, others can accept its influence and join the body of believers represented by the 144,000. It is a last warning because the time for God's judgements on the world is very close. Following closely, and so presumably coming as part of those divine judgements, the second angel announces (v. 8) the fall of Babylon. No further details of this are given at this point, but we will find that the whole of Revelation chapters 17 and 18 deals with the judgements on Babylon and we will leave further comment until then.

The third angel's message complements those of the first two angels. First (v. 9-11) it warns of the condemnation that will befall those who receive the Beast's mark, rather than accepting God's name like the 144,000. This has echoes of the harvest of death under the fourth seal. Next (v. 12) the message turns to a call for endurance by God's people. In this there is an implicit warning that these final judgements may be very terrible, but a reassurance that they will be shortly followed by the return of Christ, which the faithful so earnestly desire. This understanding is reinforced by the answering voice from heaven (v. 13) which promises rest for the faithful and seems to imply that their death at this point, with its hope of imminent resurrection at Christ's very near return, might be preferable to living through these final times of judgement on the earth. These words echo the call for endurance and promise of rest made to the faithful under the fifth seal.

The first angel is described as "flying in mid-heaven", and as the second and third angels are said to follow it, we may assume that they fly there too. We met the phrase "flying in mid-heaven" earlier when an eagle flew there in Rev. 8 v. 13, and we took the meaning there to be a divine or spirit-inspired warning. We have already identified heaven as relating to the spiritual realm and the nature or existence of God. The phrase mid-heaven, or "the midst of heaven" (AV), does not refer to a middle layer but rather to a central or middle zone, i.e. the very heart of heaven. Any message originating from here would therefore seem to have great significance, as coming from the core of God's power and purpose. This proves to be the case here as the messages deal with issues of eternal life and death, calling the world to pay heed to the life-saving message of God's word before it is too late.

The last four angels in this group of seven appear as two pairs. In each pair the first carries a sickle and the second gives the order to start reaping. The first pair, of the fourth and fifth angels, initiates the harvest of the wheat crop (v. 14-16), which we look at in more detail in section 15.3. The second pair, of the sixth and seventh angels, commences the grape harvest (v. 17-20), which is covered in section 15.4.

15.3 The Wheat Harvest – Rev. 14 v. 14-16

Christ in his parables often uses grain, and wheat in particular, as a symbol for the word of God. For example in talking about the growth of the influence of God's kingdom in men's hearts he talks about the ear of corn filling with grain, but then, when the whole crop is ripe, the farmer, God, starts reaping, or, in the KJV, "putteth in the sickle" (Mk. 4 v. 26-29). This follows on from the parable of the sower (Mk. 4 v. 3-20), which likens the effects of preaching the gospel to the results of sowing grain into four kinds of ground. We have already seen how similar consequences were predicted under the first four of the seven seals (see sections 7.2 to 7.7). The parable of the wheat and the tares (Matt. 13 v. 24-30; 36-43) uses similar imagery to show how the believers (the wheat) and the unbelievers (the tares) will be left to grow together until a final divine intervention (the harvest) when they will be separated to meet their different fates. The vision of the wheat harvest in Revelation chapter 14 builds on this symbolism.

Figure 7: The Wheat Harvest (Rev. Ch.14:14-16)

We can also see parallels between this vision and Christ's own prophecy about his return, which he gave on the Mount of Olives. In the same way that the first angel stresses the need to hear the gospel (Rev.14 v 6-7), so Christ explains that "this gospel... will be proclaimed as a testimony to all nations; and then the end will come" (Matt. 24 v. 14). The start of the wheat harvest is signalled when the fourth angel appears in heaven (Rev. 14 v. 14), though this being is not explicitly called an angel, but is described as being like a man wearing a gold crown. This is perhaps because it represents the returning Christ coming in glory, which is announced in the Olivet prophecy in Matt. 24 v. 30. The fifth angel (Rev. 14 v. 15-16) acts as a herald or assistant to the harvest process, and in the Olivet prophecy Christ says "with a trumpet blast he (the Son of Man) will send out his angels, and they will gather his chosen from the four winds" (Matt. 24 v. 31).

The fifth angel, and later the sixth, are described as coming out of the temple (Rev. 14 v. 15) or the heavenly sanctuary (Rev. 14 v. 17), in other words, from the presence or dwelling place of God. If these events are at the time of the second coming, then the angels will be accompanying Christ, who "has entered heaven itself.... and will appear a second time.... to bring salvation to those who eagerly await him" (Heb. 9 v. 24, 28). Thus this image of coming from the temple appears to signify a divine intervention in the affairs of the world, and this fits with a view that the vision of the wheat harvest represents the return of Christ to the earth and the gathering to him of the faithful believers.

15.4 The Grape Harvest – Rev. 14 v. 17-20

After the depiction of the wheat harvest, the vision moves on to the grape harvest. This is trodden in "the winepress of God's wrath" (v. 19) and out of it flows blood (v. 20) rather than juice or wine. In an age when warfare was conducted in hand-to-hand struggles using cutting and piercing weapons, a major victory often left the battlefield heaped with corpses and literally awash with blood. So the use of the image of treading a winepress to portray the utter defeat of opposing forces is not surprising. Indeed, Isaiah uses the image in his prophecy when he speaks of Christ's victory over all the nations that will resist him when he appears in power to save his people (Is. 63 v. 1-6). The context for this prophecy is a time when Israel, having rebelled against God's wishes and suffered for it, finally turns back to him and finds him ready to forgive and support them (Is. 64 & 65). This message, being in the Old Testament, is addressed to the Jews, but like much of Isaiah it contains very powerful Messianic overtones and links strongly to the events of the second coming. A shorter prophecy about the same events, which also uses the winepress image, can be found in Joel 3 v. 9-16.

Figure 8: The Grape Harvest (Rev. Ch.14:17-20)

In Revelation chapter 14, the initiation of the grape harvest is the work of sixth and seventh angels. The seventh angel is described as coming out from the altar and having power over fire (Rev. 14 v. 18). Fire is often used as part of an image of cleansing or refining, as for example in the prophecy of the second coming, quoted in Handel's Messiah, where Christ is described as being "like a refiner's fire" (Mal. 3 v. 2) whose purpose is to purify and purge away impurity like a refiner of silver burning away the dross. The idea of this power of fire coming out of the altar identifies it as having divine origin and carries echoes of the events preparing for the start of the cycle of the seven trumpet judgements. Then (Rev. 8 v. 3-5) the prayers of the saints were mixed with fire from the altar in heaven and cast on to the earth, as a symbol of the destructive power of the judgements to come (see section 8.2).

Already in the vision of the wheat harvest we noted parallels with Christ's parable of the wheat and the tares. That parable ends with the gathering of the wheat into the farmer's barn, representing the gathering of the faithful into the Kingdom, while the tares are gathered in bundles to be burnt, indicating the destruction of those who reject and oppose Christ. Now these two actions are reflected in the two harvest visions. The wheat harvest depicts the gathering of the faithful, while the grape harvest and the treading of the winepress represents Christ's judgements on the nations who oppose him in the great day of the Lord. We will meet the same winepress image again when we reach the more detailed account of the setting up of Christ's kingdom (e.g. Rev. 19 v. 15).

15.5 Summary of Rev. Chs 12-14: Firstfruits to Harvest

In these first three chapters of part 2 of the Revelation we have found an overview of the Christian era. It has taken us from Christ's first coming as the "man child", who became the firstfruit from the dead and ascended to God, to his second coming as the saviour of his faithful believers and the judge of the nations. It has set the selection of a chosen people, his firstfruits, against the historical context of the major world power of pagan Rome. This was shown as one phase, or "head", of the dragon power which characterises human opposition to God. That phase of the dragon was then superseded by two coexistent powers shown as beasts, namely the sea beast of Western Rome and the earth beast of Eastern Rome. This division of power lasts, in various guises or phases, until the time of the end. This is very like the later stages of Nebuchadnezzar's image vision (Dan. 2 v. 31-35) where the Roman period is shown as the two iron legs that become more fragmented in the feet and toes of iron mixed with clay. Then, just as Nebuchadnezzar's image was shattered by a divinely created stone which grew to fill the earth, so the divided empire of the "beasts" is overturned by the returning Christ who holds his two harvests, one of ingathering and one of judgement and cleansing.

With this overview of the Christian era brought to an end, the remaining chapters of the Revelation deal in much more detail with the events of the return of Christ and the establishment of his kingdom. It is rather like a film scene using a wide-angle shot to establish the context before zooming in to pick up the action in close-up.

16. THE SEVEN LAST PLAGUES (Rev. Chs 15 & 16)

16.1 A Vision of Heaven (Rev. Ch. 15)

The seven angels in chapter 14 came, or spoke, from heaven, but their actions were directed towards the earth. Now in Revelation chapter 15 John's attention is directed back toward heaven by a partial recapitulation of the vision of the throne of glory from chapter 4 (see sections 5.1 & 5.2). In this new version of the vision (Rev. 15 v. 2) the actual throne where God is seated in glory is not specifically included, but the crystal sea before the throne (as in Rev. 4 v. 6) is shown. Now it is surrounded by the multitude of victorious believers (Rev. 15 v. 3) who are described as singing Moses' song. This song is almost certainly the one that Moses and the Israelites sang to God in celebration of their deliverance from the Egyptians during the exodus from Egypt when they crossed the Red Sea to begin their journey to the Promised Land (Ex. 15 v. 1-18). The use of this song is most apt at this point in the Revelation as the believers are celebrating their deliverance from an evil world, as already represented by the vision of the wheat harvest. In their rejoicing over this and the imminent establishment by Christ of their long promised kingdom they go on to predict (Rev. 15 v. 4) the dawning of a wider recognition of God by all the nations. This will no doubt be inescapable for most of the previously unbelieving peoples as they witness the overwhelming power that Christ displays on his return, as already predicted in the vision of the grape harvest.

The other inhabitants of this new vision of heaven are seven more angels who are preparing seven bowls containing the seven last plagues to be inflicted on the earth (Rev. 15 v. 1, 7). This is another image related to the same theme as the grape harvest. Just as the grapes were described as being trodden in the winepress of God's wrath (Rev. 14 v. 19), so the seven bowls are said to contain the wrath of God, and the seven plagues are described as bringing God's wrath to an end. Thus, like the grape harvest, these seven plagues are to be the final judgements of godless nations before Christ's kingdom is fully established.

At this point the temple in heaven, the symbol for God's presence among his people, is described as being filled with the smoke of God's glory that prevents anyone from entering it until the plagues are over (Rev. 15 v. 8). This is very like the events at the dedication of Solomon's temple when the musicians sounded out praise to God and then the temple was filled with the glory of God which stopped the priests ministering there for a while (2 Chron. 5 v. 13-14). So in this new vision, the faithful celebrate a new phase of their relationship and service to God as they are being granted new roles as immortal kings and priests in Christ's new kingdom. Then the smoke stops access to heaven for a while.

The exact meaning of this temporary bar to access is difficult to determine, as there is no clear scriptural precedent other than the one just quoted, and a very similar incident during the consecration of the tabernacle (Ex. 40 v. 34-35). However we could venture a hypothesis. As already noted in the interpretation of the imagery of the wheat harvest, the believers at this point in the sequence of visions are being, or have been, gathered to Christ to be granted immortality and given their new roles in his kingdom. Thus, until the kingdom organisation is established, there is no active preaching and much of the world is in turmoil or active rebellion against Christ. He and his now immortalised followers are not at first recognised for the divine power they truly are, but are only seen as threats to the established world order and the current holders of power. Thus it is very likely that during this time of upheaval and conflict, access to God, via understanding, repentance and baptism, might be barred until the last judgements are complete, i.e. when the grape harvest is completed.

16.2 Number Seven: Cycle and Completion

The events of chapter 14 were heralded by a sequence of seven heavenly beings or angels, and the seven plagues of chapter 15 are being prepared by another seven angels. With earlier significant sets of "sevens" we took the number seven to signify a cycle or repeating pattern. So, in the interests of consistency, it is natural to wonder whether these two sets of seven angels might be considered in the same way. In researching the meaning of the number (see *Seven* in the symbol glossary) we found good precedents to demonstrate that it could refer to a cycle, and in Revelation part 1 (chapters 1 to 11) the main "sevens" of the letter, seals and trumpets were seen to represent cycles. However, we found that it can also carry connotations of divine completion or bringing to a close, as in Genesis 2 v. 2, where "... on the seventh day, having finished all his work, God blessed the day." We have seen how the seven angels of chapter 14 lead up to the events at the return of Christ and the close of the Christian era, and the seven angels with bowls are preparing the seven *last* plagues. Thus it seems that in these cases the "seven" of the angel sequences is one of completion. Indeed these are the final events that bring the earlier cycles of seven to their conclusion.

So, in Revelation part 2 (chapters 12 to 22) a pattern seems to be emerging that the main "sevens" seem to be singular rather than cyclic. They point forward to God's purpose with the earth coming to its climax. Thus the seven heads of the dragon and sea beast each represent singular phases of earthly powers, with each head occurring once. Also the seven angels' warnings prepare for the actions of the final wheat and grape harvests, which are concluding events rather than a repeating pattern. Also the seven bowls contain the seven final plagues to come on the earth before the kingdom era starts.

There is a possible link between Revelation parts 1 and 2 in the form of an earlier "seven" that was not fully explained when we first encountered it (see section 10.1). This is the voice of seven thunders that spoke to John and whose words he wanted to include in his writings (Rev. 10 v. 3-4). However he was stopped by a heavenly voice that told him to seal up the words. As we are given no further information we cannot be sure what these thunders said or represented, but a speculation springs to mind. John heard the seven thunders between the sounding of the sixth and seventh trumpets, in other words they occurred towards the end of one of the visions presenting cyclic patterns of events. Indeed, as we have seen, all the significant "sevens" in the first half of the Revelation represent cyclic patterns. So perhaps it was not appropriate to explain the thunders in that context because they represented a group of singular events, not another cyclic pattern? If so, they may have been mentioned as a possible pointer or forward reference to the second half of the Revelation that we are considering now, and in which the significant "sevens" represent groups of singular, non-repeating, and concluding events heralding the return of Christ and the start of the kingdom age.

16.3 The First Bowl (Rev. 16 v. 1, 2)

We will now start to consider the details of the seven last plagues as they are poured out of the seven bowls. For each of them we will try to understand their target area, their nature or effect, and the scope of the damage they cause. In each case we will find some correspondence with the earlier trumpet judgement that carried the same number.

The target of the first plague is the earth, which was also the target affected by the punishments under the first trumpet in Rev. 8 v. 7. We have taken the earth to represent structured, civilized nations (see section 9.3, and also **Earth** in the symbol glossary). The effect of the trumpet was that one third of the earth was burnt up, while this final plague brings evil sores or boils on everyone who accepts the influence of the beast. There is actually a scriptural link between these two plagues. The effect of burning, as under the first trumpet, is to produce ashes, and at the time of the exodus Moses initiated the sixth plague on Egypt by throwing ashes into the air. That plague too brought boils or sores on the unbelieving Egyptians (Ex. 9 v. 8-11). Though the link is a little tenuous, it can be seen to suggest that when men do not respond to repeated incidents of a partial "burning" or exposure to a "refining fire", as under the first trumpet judgement, they should in the end suffer personally and visibly, as under the first bowl. To explain the imagery a little more explicitly, it appears to represent men reaping in full the results of their failure to heed God's earlier (trumpet) judgements, by finally having their mortality and moral corruption become as obvious as visible sores would be. These visible sores could be either literal, as physical illnesses, or symbolic, as the increasingly visible adverse effects of a materialistic and ungodly way of life. This warning about "reaping what you sow" is supported elsewhere in the scriptures, such as in Gal. 6 v. 7-8 and Rom. 1 v. 24-32.

16.4 The Second Bowl (Rev. 16 v. 3)

The target of the second plague is the sea, which was also the target of the second trumpet judgement in Rev. 8 v. 8-9. We have understood the sea to be a symbol for the relatively unstructured, undeveloped nations (see section 9.4, and also *Sea* in the symbol glossary). It is quite a natural sequence to have this as the second target following on from the first "plague" aimed against the developed world, since major problems or failures in the world's prosperous regions often have further consequences in the poorer nations; such as the way that drug taking in the consumer nations often brings violence and instability to the supplying countries.

Under the second trumpet one third of the sea turned to blood, but now under the second of these last plagues all of the sea is turned to blood, "like a dead man's". In other words this last plague is a completion, in a full, 100% measure, of the earlier trumpet judgement of God. The understanding of this plague is similar to the first, with men reaping in full the consequences of their lack of response to God's earlier judgements as everything becomes contaminated with the corruption of mortality and death. This stagnant and lifeless condition may refer to literal problems arising from conflict and disease, but it also carries connotations of there being no remaining spiritual life or development.

16.5 The Third Bowl (Rev. 16 v. 4-7)

The third plague falls on sources of fresh water, which were also affected by the third trumpet judgement in Rev. 8 v. 10-11. In interpreting that passage (see section 9.5) fresh water was taken to represent the sphere of religion and the influence of the Spirit (see *Water* in the symbol glossary). Under the third trumpet judgement one third of the fresh water became wormwood, which we understood as signifying that in some areas true religion became corrupted by false teaching. Now under the plague from the third bowl, all of the waters become blood, and this is described as being a just judgement on those who have persecuted the true faith (Rev. 16 v. 6). Thus the meaning behind this plague is that many of the forms of "religion" that the world recognizes will prove to be sources of death, not life, because the saving power of the true gospel will become obscured by the reworking and replacement of key elements of the message. This process will often lead to the suppression of those who wish to keep and preach the true faith. There are many sources from which such corruption can arise, but some of the most common are the use of religion to reinforce political power and the use of positions of church leadership to enhance personal power, wealth or status. The New Testament contains several warnings about this, such as Matt. 7 v. 15, Acts 20 v. 29-30, Gal. 1 v. 6-9, Tit. 1 v. 10-11.

16.6 The Fourth Bowl (Rev. 16 v. 8, 9)

The target of the fourth plague is the sun, which was also, together with other heavenly bodies, the target of the fourth trumpet judgement in Rev. 8 v. 12. The sun is typically a symbol for political power in kingdoms or empires (see **Heavenly Bodies** in the symbol glossary). The effect of the fourth trumpet judgement was that one third of the heavenly bodies were darkened, which we took to represent part of the world's governing powers being overthrown (see section 9.6). The reverse of this seems to be happening under the plague from the fourth bowl, as it shows the sun becoming too hot and scorching the people. With a little reflection we can understand this extension of the symbol to mean that ruling world powers, in their death throes before being finally extinguished by the reign of Christ, exercise excessive, repressive powers over their subjects, i.e. they will cease to be beneficially "warming" and will become destructively "scorching" to their peoples. We will find more details of this later when we look at the actions of the Beast in Revelation chapter 17.

16.7 The Fifth Bowl (Rev. 16 v. 10, 11)

The fifth plague falls upon "the throne of the Beast", a symbol very similar to one encountered earlier in Revelation chapter 13. There we met two beasts, one from the sea and one from the earth, and it was to the sea beast that the "dragon" gave his power and his throne (Rev. 13 v. 2). In Revelation chapter 16 and later passages there are references to "the beast", unqualified by any mention of "sea" or "earth". However, the earlier reference to the handing on of the dragon's throne is explicitly linked to the sea beast, and no mention of a throne is made in connection with the earth beast. So we can take this unqualified reference to "the throne of the beast", and other references to just "the beast", as relating to a latter day equivalent of the sea beast. Earlier we took the sea beast to represent the Western Roman Empire (see sections 14.2 to 14.4). The natural equivalents to this power in modern times are the developed nations of the West, predominantly Western Europe and the Western nations historically influenced by Europe, such as the USA. These are nominally Christian nations, but they have let their pursuit of wealth and power undermine their Christianity to the point where they are largely apostate; for example, surveys indicate that across these countries, the percentage of the population that regularly attends a Christian place of worship varies from around 20% to under 10%. This failure to stay true to the real spirit of Christ is a key characteristic of Western, "sea beast" powers. Despite some superficial adherence to the outward forms of Christianity, and a few prominent members of governments who publicly declare their faith, these powers actually take after the "dragon" in the way they put the thinking and ways of men above the teachings of God.

The fact that this plague falls on the beast's throne would indicate that its primary effect is to damage the seat(s) of government of the advanced Western nations. This is borne out by the description of the plague's result, which is that the kingdom of the beast falls into darkness. The darkness is an image of the lack of guidance and direction brought about by the damage to the centres of government power and control. This is where the parallel with the fifth trumpet judgement arises. That judgement was depicted as a swarm of locusts, which we understood as being a destructive wave of decadence and immorality (see section 9.8). One significant detail was that the locusts came out of the smoke from the bottomless pit and that the smoke caused the sun to be darkened (Rev. 9 v. 2-3). We saw this as representing a weakening or flouting of government power, which is just what is happening under the fifth plague as it falls on the Beast's throne and plunges its kingdom into darkness.

Thus we can understand this image of the plague to indicate that in the rich and largely apostate "Christian" countries of the West, the governments suffer a major loss of authority, possibly as an unforeseen effect of encouraging their citizens to adopt goals and attitudes leading to self-seeking and decadence. This loss of central control leads to great uncertainty and anguish in which men "gnaw their tongues in agony" (Rev. 16 v. 10), which calls to mind Christ's words about the latter days when "people will faint with terror" (Lk. 21 v. 26). The anguish of this fifth plague seems to be worse because of the ongoing effects of an earlier plague, as men "curse the God of heaven for their pain and sores" (Rev. 16 v. 11), and we remember that the first bowl brought a plague of sores or boils over the inhabitants of the organized, civilized countries, depicted as "the earth". Thus although the seven "bowl" plagues are being described in sequence, they may well overlap and interact in their timing and effects.

It might at first seem strange that this fifth plague bringing loss of government power follows the fourth plague under which that same power became "scorchingly" oppressive. However this is not necessarily a contradiction. Recent history in the UK and the US contains a number of examples of large scale protests over issues such as war or taxation that have turned into violent confrontations with law enforcement forces. It is not too difficult to envision circumstances under which a similar conflict could turn into a vicious circle in which increasing governmental oppression might arouse increasing civil disobedience and unrest, to the point of rioting, looting and the introduction of martial law.

16.8 The Sixth Bowl (Rev. 16 v. 12-16)

The area of influence of the sixth plague is the river Euphrates, which was also the location mentioned at the beginning of the sixth trumpet judgement in Rev. 9 v. 13-15. Under the sixth trumpet four angels of destruction were released at the river Euphrates and the nature of the destruction unleashed was characterised by hosts of military horsemen, representing a major outbreak of war. As some kind of preparatory action at the start of the sixth plague, the river Euphrates is depicted as being dried up. As already mentioned in section 9.9, this is a reference to an actual historical event that led up to the fall of the city of Babylon at the time of Daniel. The fall of Babylon is now about to be used as an important symbol at the end of Revelation chapter 16 and throughout chapters 17 and 18. The interpretation of this will be covered in the next section (Section 17), so we will defer the explanation of the drying up of the river until we have dealt more fully with the use of Babylon as a symbol. Then, having established the context for the event, we will refer back to the drying up of the Euphrates in section 17.5.

After the drying up of the river, three frog-like spirits appear. Under the Mosaic Law the frog was unclean as it is a water-dwelling animal that does not have fins and scales (Lev. 11 v. 10). We have little in the way of scriptural precedents for interpreting the frog as a symbol, since it is only mentioned in the account of the plague of frogs on Egypt (Ex. Ch. 8), and then here in the Revelation. However we can get some pointers by considering the basic elements of the frog's life cycle. It starts life, as eggs and tadpoles, in fresh water, which we have seen to be a symbol for the spiritual realm (see ***Water (fresh)*** in the symbol glossary). Then when mature it becomes an amphibian and lives both in water and on land, with the land or earth being a symbol for the human, mortal nature and the worldly realm (see ***Earth*** in the symbol glossary). Finally, the word "spirit" conveys the idea of some kind of power or vital essence. This can be divine power, as in "the Holy Spirit", or the inner character of a man, as in "who knows what a human being is but the human spirit within him?" (1 Cor. 2 v. 11).

Putting the above ideas together, we can start to see that a frog spirit represents some kind of abstract power that has its origins in God's truth (the fresh water), but becomes unclean by the corruption of the world and human nature (the earth). When such an abstract power has the ability to influence men's actions, as in this case, it is likely to take the form of a shared mind-set or commonly accepted set of principles, such as an ideology. We will see more clearly how this fits the interpretation of this passage as we examine the sources of these three spirits.

16.9 Nature of the Frog Spirits

The three frog spirits are described as emerging from the mouths of three different creatures, that is from the dragon, the beast and the false prophet. In Revelation chapters 12 and 13 we also met a group of three creatures representing worldly powers that existed at the start of the Christian era. Those earlier powers were the dragon, the sea beast and the earth beast. By the end of Revelation chapter 16, time has moved forward to the end of the Christian era, close to the return of Christ, and it seems that a similar group of three powers can still be identified. A comparison of the two groups shows that two of the powers have clear equivalences. Obviously the dragon is common to both groups, but the creature just described as "the beast" in the latter group could match either the sea beast or the earth beast in the earlier set. However the beast is also referred to in this unqualified way in subsequent chapters where (for example in Rev. 17 v. 3 etc.) it is portrayed as having seven heads and ten horns, and is said to be blaspheming. That matches the description of the earlier sea beast (Rev. 13 v. 1), which was also depicted with seven heads, ten horns, and blasphemous names. Thus the beast in the later group is clearly the latter-day equivalent of the earlier sea beast.

Having matched two members of each trio, we are left with just one remaining creature in each of the two groups. So is there some correspondence between the false prophet and the earlier earth beast? Earlier we identified the earth beast as the Eastern Roman Empire (see section 14.5), which initially had a form of Christianity that was to become the Eastern Orthodox faith. The sea beast, representing the Western Roman Empire (see sections 14.2 and 14.3), was also "Christian" and has retained that ideology, at least nominally, into its later phase as "the beast". However in most of the lands comprising the eastern, "earth beast" power, the dominant ideology has changed over the centuries from that of eastern orthodox Christianity to the newer religion of Islam. While having no desire at all to insult Islamic believers or question their sincerity or morality, it cannot be denied that, by rejecting the position of

Christ as the Son of God, and treating Mohammed as a greater prophet, the teachings of Islam contradict those of Bible-based Christianity. Thus from a position that accepts Bible-based Christianity as true, some of the key tenets of Islam must be seen as false. Therefore, for someone holding this stance, it is logical to represent the latter-day equivalent of the Eastern Roman Empire as the lands of the "false prophet".

One detail of the imagery that indicates a two-phased nature for the eastern power is that the earth beast was shown as having two horns (Rev. 13 v. 11). This is very like the way the Medo-Persian power is shown as a ram with two horns in Daniel chapter 8. There the culture of the Medes was most influential at first but later the Persians came to dominate. In a similar way the two horns of the earth beast may represent the Eastern Orthodox and Islamic phases of the same power bloc in the eastern Mediterranean region.

Having identified the sources of the three frog spirits we can now suggest the ideologies that they represent. We have previously seen how the dragon represents an attitude that tries to put man in the place of God (see **Dragon** in the symbol glossary). So the dragon spirit is one that rejoices in what people can achieve when they share common aspirations, and in fact shares the biblical teaching that all men are equal, but corrupts the Bible message by denying the existence of God. Such ideas are found in the ideology of humanism. The second force, that is the sea beast or beast, takes on the name and rituals of Christianity but allows the gospel truths to be corrupted with man's thinking and the desire for wealth and power. This is characteristic of the ideology of institutionalised Christianity. The third frog spirit is that which has arisen in the lands of the Middle East characterized as the "false prophet". There the dominant ideology is that of Islam, which accepts Abraham and some of the Old Testament writings, but can be seen as opposing the Bible's teachings by denying that Christ is the son of God.

The effect of the three frog spirits is to "muster all the kings of the world for the battle on the great day of God the sovereign Lord... at the place called in Hebrew Armageddon" (Rev. 16 v. 14, 16). Thus the effect of the three ideologies, of humanism, apostate Christianity, and Islam, will be to blind the nations to the true nature of the returned Christ. Because of their preconceived ideas, they will not recognize Christ as God's appointed world ruler, and they will try to keep hold of their own power and status in the world. This will result in them actually going to war against the returned Christ, as portrayed in Ps. 2. More details of this conflict will be given later when we consider Revelation chapter 19.

16.10 The Seventh Bowl (Rev. 16 v. 17-21)

With the pouring out of the seventh bowl a loud voice from the temple in heaven declares, "It is over" (Rev. 16 v. 17). This is a clear indication that the judgements represented by the seven bowls are now over. Since these were stated at the outset to be the seven last plagues by which God's wrath would be completed, their cessation must mean that the world must now be at peace with God, and that can only happen when Christ has established his kingdom on the earth.

The heavenly declaration is accompanied by a great earthquake, but once again, as this is a book of signs, we should look primarily for the symbolic meaning of the earthquake. There is in fact a very relevant prophecy of a final shaking to be found in Haggai chapter 2. This predicts that God will "shake the heavens and the earth" (v. 6 & 21) but it then goes on to clarify that what this really means is that God will "shake all the nations" (v. 7) and will "overthrow the thrones of kings, break the power of heathen realms, overturn chariots and their riders" (v. 22). Thus the earthquake is a symbol for the overturning of the structures by which men govern their kingdoms. This is consistent with the use of the earth as a symbol for the structured, civilized nations of the world (see **Earth** in the symbol glossary). This view of the symbolic meaning of an earthquake is confirmed by a New Testament passage in Hebrews chapter 12, which quotes and clarifies the prophecy by Haggai. The phrase about shaking the heavens and the earth is quoted first, in Heb. 12 v. 26. This is then amplified by saying that it indicates "the removal of all created things", i.e. those things that are being shaken, "so that what cannot be shaken may remain" (Heb. 12 v.

27). Further clarification is given by saying that "the kingdom we are given is unshakeable" (Heb. 12 v. 28), and it is therefore this new kingdom, Christ's kingdom on earth, which must remain after the shaking. Thus the great earthquake represents the removal of the shaken kingdoms of men, so that the unshakeable kingdom of Christ may remain.

After this shaking no islands or mountains remain (Rev. 16 v.20), and a key feature of islands and mountains is that they are elevated above the normal level of the sea or the earth. We have seen earlier that sea and earth represent types of nations in the world, so islands and mountains, the eminent places in the sea and earth, represent eminent nations who rise above their neighbours as overlords and empire builders (see **Islands** and **Mountains** in the symbol glossary for further examples of these images used in scripture). These powers will be done away with because, once his kingdom is established, the only eminent power in the world will be Christ. This levelling of human powers was foretold by Isaiah using very similar language where he says, "Let every valley be raised, every mountain and hill be brought low" (Is. 40 v. 4).

This overthrow of world powers is accompanied by thunder and great hailstones (Rev. 16 v. 21). In the Bible such powerful phenomena are usually taken to be great demonstrations of God's power, and the overthrow of major political and military powers in the world will definitely require a major exercise of divine power. What is not clear here is whether these storms will happen literally or whether they are to be seen as symbols of God's power. Certainly the Bible records some instances of God using the power of the elements when He fought for his people in the past, as happened in the plagues on Egypt (Ex. ch. 9) or the defeat of the Amorite kings (Josh. 10 v. 11). What is clear is that God will use his great power to subdue all the nations that oppose Christ when he returns.

Amongst all the nations that are subdued, particular mention is made of the fall of Babylon (Rev. 16 v. 19). However this brief reference is greatly amplified in the next two chapters, so we will leave the interpretation to the next main section where it can be covered in much more detail.

16.11 Summary Chart – Bowls (Vials) in Context

We have seen earlier how the three main sets of "seven" in part 1 of the Revelation point to cycles of events taking place during the Christian era, i.e. the seven letters, seals and trumpets relating to the cycles of faith, preaching, and God's judgements, respectively. This was summarized in the halfway review (see section 12.1). In part 2 of the Revelation we met the seven last plagues released from the seven bowls. As we looked at each of these we noted similarities to the earlier trumpet judgements. In the table below we compare the first six of these two groups of seven. The rows show firstly the number of the event, secondly the target of the judgement, thirdly the scope of the damage inflicted, and fourthly the result of the judgement.

Table 7: Comparison of Trumpet and Bowl Judgements

(a) TRUMPETS

1	2	3	4	5	6 a	6 b
Earth	Sea	Water	Sun	Sun	Euphrates	Mankind
1/3 Burnt	1/3 Blood	1/3 Bitter	1/3 Dark	Hidden by Smoke – Locusts released	4 Angels Released	1/3 Killed by Horsemen
Ashes	Death	Death	No Power	No Power	Initiate War	War

(b) BOWLS (VIALS)

1	2	3	4	5	6 a	6 b
Earth	Sea	Water	Sun	Beast's Throne	Euphrates Dried Up	Armageddon
All Boils	All Blood	All Blood	Burns People	Darkened	Babylon Falls	Final War
Death	Death	Death	Suffering	No Power	Ruined	Defeat

The sixth event in each group has been presented as two columns, 6 a) and 6 b), to show how the text prefaces the main event with some kind of preparatory action. For both the trumpets and the bowls, the seventh in the series marks the cessation of action because the climax of the series has been reached.

A comparison of the two sections of the table shows the complementary nature of the two series that represent God's judgements on those who reject or oppose his purpose. The trumpet judgements are cyclic, occurring repeatedly throughout the Christian era. They typically affect only a third of their target, and so leave two thirds to regenerate while awaiting a possible recurrence of the cycle. On the other hand, the final plagues in the bowl sequence fall on similar areas but have their impact on the whole of the target, leaving nothing unaffected. This is because they are singular events that bring about the world-shaking upheaval by which "sovereignty over the world has passed to our Lord and his Christ, and he shall reign for ever" (Rev. 11 v. 15).

So far in part 2 of the Revelation chapters 12 to 14 have provided an overview of the Christian era, ending in the wheat and grape harvests. Then chapters 15 and 16 have "zoomed in" to give more details about the punishments of the grape harvest, in the form of the seven last plagues. As part of the events of the sixth of these plagues we were told that Babylon had to drink of the cup of God's wrath (Rev. 16 v. 19). Now in chapters 17 and 18 the visions "zoom in" even closer to give details of the fall of Babylon.

17. THE FALL OF BABYLON
(Rev. Chs 17 to 19 v. 10)

17.1 The Two Symbols for Babylon

At the beginning of Revelation chapter 17 an angel invites John to look at the fate of a woman described as a prostitute, but when the woman's name is revealed it is not a personal name, but the name of a famous historical city, Babylon. So, to get the full import of these next two chapters we need to understand how the scriptures present both prostitutes and ancient Babylon. We will start with the use of a prostitute or harlot as a biblical symbol.

17.2 Babylon the Harlot

In scriptural usage the symbol of a harlot is used as the evil side of the more general "woman" symbol (see ***Woman*** in the symbol glossary). We met the other side of the symbol earlier in the form of the good woman who bore the man-child in Revelation chapter 12 (see section 13.2). This idea of the good woman is used in the Bible to personify the whole body of faithful believers. The closeness of the relationship that these believers have with God is sometimes indicated by referring to the good woman as the bride of God, or of Christ. Some commentators use the term "multitudinous bride" to convey the idea of a single relationship shared by many. Initially in the Old Testament the believers are of Jewish origin and are portrayed as God's "wife" (see ***Wife*** in the symbol glossary). Later, with the inclusion of the Gentiles into the gospel hope, the believers from all nations are represented as the bride of Christ.

The scriptural use of the harlot as a symbol tends to focus not so much on the idea of a commercial prostitute but more on the unfaithful wife who has left her husband to commit multiple adulteries (see ***Harlot*** in the symbol glossary). This idea of the "good woman gone bad" is used to represent people with knowledge of God's purpose, and opportunities to be joined to him as "brides", but who turn away from God to the material and sensual attractions of the world. These ideas lie behind the way the harlot is presented in Rev. 17 v. 2. Often some gifts or financial inducements provide additional temptations for the former wife to leave her husband and commit her adulteries. So it is in this case where the harlot's relationship with the world has made her wealthy (Rev. 17 v. 4). Also the fall from the previous faithful state usually leads to a rejection of former beliefs and companions, and, if opportunity arises, may progress to active persecution of the true "bride", which again is the case here (Rev. 17 v. 6). Such persecutions are also a trait of the dragon (see Rev. 12 v. 17).

The location of the harlot provides another interesting detail. In order to see her, John had to be carried "in spirit into the wilderness" (Rev. 17 v. 3). Now the wilderness was last mentioned when the good woman went there to escape her persecution by the dragon (Rev. 12 v. 14). We understood that to represent the faithful Jews being dispersed into a godless world (see section 13.7). If all had then gone well, subsequent generations of the good woman's spiritual offspring should have continued as faithful Christian people, in lands which would then have become spiritually fruitful. However what actually happened during the Christian era was that most of her spiritual offspring, in the form of Gentiles who had chance to hear the gospel, largely lost the conviction of their faith. Although still nominally "Christian", such peoples and nations were driven more by worldly concerns and ambitions than by the hope of the gospel. As a result the lands they occupy have remained a spiritual wilderness, that is places of drought and death, lacking the fresh, life giving "water" of salvation. People in this situation are aptly represented by the symbol of the harlot in the wilderness.

The harlot is not alone in the wilderness. She is shown in a close relationship with the beast, and as we have seen before, beasts are used in scriptural prophecies as symbols of secular governing powers (e.g. Dan. ch. 7). Now in the ancient world women rarely had power in their own right, but derived power and status indirectly from their husbands or lovers. As this was the real-world context for the biblical writings, it is highly likely that the same conditions apply to the use of a woman as a symbol. So we can expect the harlot to represent some or all of the populace who have abandoned a primary allegiance to God, and transferred it to their worldly rulers and governments in the hope of improved status and greater affluence.

Initially the harlot is mounted on the beast as its rider (Rev. 17 v. 3, 7). Since the rider of an animal is usually not just being passively carried but is normally steering it in some way, this would seem to convey that the harlot has some ability to control or collaborate with the beast. This co-operation may be the means by which the harlot has gained her power and dominion (Rev. 17 v. 18). However the co-operative relationship does not last as she is rejected and hurt by the beast (Rev. 17 v. 16). These interactions between the harlot and the beast deserve closer examination, but they will be better understood after the nature and identity of the beast have been more clearly established.

17.3 The Beast

The new creature simply referred to here as "the beast" has a very close resemblance to two powers that occurred earlier in Revelation chapters 12 and 13, namely the dragon and the sea beast (see sections 13.4, 14.2 & 14.3). Notably this new beast has seven heads and ten horns, features that are only otherwise seen in the dragon and the sea beast. However it also has the same red colour that was a particular attribute of the dragon (Rev. 12 v. 3), and additionally displays a blasphemous nature (Rev. 17 v. 3), which is only otherwise attributed to the sea beast (Rev. 13 v. 1). With this combination of identifying characteristics, we can see that this beast is in some way a latter day equivalent of both the dragon and the sea beast. The similarity to the sea beast, which we understood as representing the Western Roman Empire, indicates a territorial base in the West and an outlook that is nominally Christian but practically apostate. The family likeness to the dragon indicates that the new beast is likely to share the "dragon spirit" and be motivated to ignore, or actively oppose, the purpose of God.

Before completing the identification of the Beast, we need to understand the symbolism of the multiple heads on these strange creatures, which is not easy. The text itself says, "this calls for a mind with insight" (Rev. 17 v. 9). However with the understanding of symbols that we have already gained, we can attempt a solution. The heads are described as "hills" (v. 9), which can equally well be translated as "mountains", and the heads are also identified as "kings" (v. 10). Now we have already seen that elevated areas, like mountains, are used to represent world powers or empires (see **Mountains** in the symbol glossary), and the additional reference to kings reinforces this concept of ruling powers. Further information is given that of these seven heads, five have fallen, one still exists at the time of the vision in John's day, and one head is still to come (Rev. 17 v. 10). This confirms the earlier suggestion that creatures with multiple heads are symbols for a sequence of ruling powers, with only one power, or "head", being active at any one time (see section 13.5). So this new, seven-headed beast can be seen to represent a sequence of world powers or empires spread out through the course of history. The heads all being attached to the same creature, such as the dragon, shows that they share the same characteristics and attitude, i.e. promoting the thinking and ways of men over the teachings of God, and opposing the spread of God's word.

The dragon phase, or "head" that was active in John's day was the unified, pagan Roman Empire, and the Western Roman Empire, represented by the sea beast, was still in the future. So, the information that some of the beast's heads had already fallen must mean that the set of heads being described are those of the dragon, which can be identified as a symbol for nations opposing God back in the Old Testament. If the number of this set of seven dragon powers or empires is literal rather than symbolic, then one set of candidates could possibly be: Egypt, Assyria, Babylon, Persia, and Greece (five empires that had fallen before the time of Christ), plus the unified, pagan Roman Empire (the current major power at the time of the Revelation), plus the divided, "Christian" Roman Empire as the seventh power that was still to come after John's day.

This seventh "dragon's head" power, which is also represented as a divided power by the two separate symbols of the sea and earth beasts (see Sections 14.2 and 14.5), is said to remain only a little while (Rev. 17 v. 10). This could possibly be a reference to the "fatal" wound inflicted on the sea beast (Rev. 13 v. 3), which we took as the fall of the western empire to the barbarians. However the sea beast also had seven heads, so the demise of the first head was to be followed by subsequent phases of similar empires in the lands of Western Europe (see Section 14.3).

The new beast in chapter 17 is described as being "an eighth" power, but still "one of the seven" (Rev. 17 v. 11). We can perhaps take these phrases to mean that this beast has some significantly unique characteristics that mark it out as a new, eighth power, separate from the other seven "dragon's head" empires in some way, but at the same time being like, or "one of", the other seven in sharing similar, dragon-like characteristics. One of the special characteristics of this beast is that it "was once alive, and is alive no longer, but has yet to ascend out of the abyss" (Rev. 17 v. 8). So apparently it was not in existence in John's day, but had an earlier counterpart and would take on a new phase of existence in the latter days. When it appears again, it ascends from the abyss, or "the bottomless pit" (A.V.), just like the cloud of locusts that appeared as part of the fifth trumpet judgement (Rev. 9 v. 3). We took that imagery as a picture of widespread decadence, arising from a common, worldly mindset of the people, rooted in the realm of mortality and death, and having no ruler other than "the destroyer". Since the imagery shows the new beast arising from a similar dark abyss, could that indicate a similarity of worldly mind set and of direction being shaped by the common will of the people? If so, that might point to one of the special characteristics of the beast being that of having a form of government somewhat similar to modern democracies. That would certainly distinguish this beast from previous scriptural images of ruling powers, since they typically represent instances of authoritarian rulers governing subject peoples.

As noted above, the other special characteristic of this future eighth power is that it had a counterpart earlier in history. The feature making the two occurrences similar may well be their distinctive style of government. If the new "eighth" power is to be in some way "democratic", then to find a counterpart we should look for earlier examples of other non-autocratic powers. We can find just one early Old Testament case that could possibly represent the "was once alive" phase of the beast. When we read about the original city of Babel (Gen.11 v. 1-9) we find that there is no indication of it having a ruler. We also find that there was a spirit of rebellion against God, and that men worked together in a common cause, as indicated by the words "They said to one another, 'Come, let us make bricks and... let us build ourselves a city and a tower'". These actions and attitudes fit those of a dragon-like power arising from a common will of the people, without an autocratic ruler.

If the inferences made in this section are correct, then the beast is some sort of coalition of democratic powers that makes an eighth dragon-like power, additional to the first seven autocratic "dragon's head" powers. It will also have similar territorial origins and apostate Christian attitudes to those of the sea beast power of the Western Roman Empire, and its horns will be the governments or leaders of the individual nations making up the coalition. Looking at what the beast does will help to confirm whether or not this interpretation makes sense in the context of this part of the Revelation.

17.4 Harlot / Beast Interaction

Initially, as we remarked in section 17.2, the harlot and the beast co-operate. While the harlot is shown as being carried by the beast (Rev. 17 v. 7), she is also described as having dominion over kings of the earth (Rev. 17 v. 18). This seems to be an apt image of the roles of the governments (the beast) and the peoples (the harlot) in advanced western democracies that have built up power and wealth by dominating and exploiting less developed nations.

As for the beast's ten horns, these are the constituent sovereign powers or governments making up the power bloc represented by the whole beast (see *horns* in the symbol glossary). These powers come together to take concerted action, shown by them throwing in their lot with the beast (Rev. 17 v. 12, 13). They act together in turning on their peoples (the harlot) in a wave of repression (v 16, 17). This fits in with the images of the fourth and fifth of the final judgements represented by the seven bowls (see Sections 16.6, 16.7) which we understood as representing fiercely oppressive government powers and unruly, disaffected peoples. Despite the sufferings of the people, the governments represented by the beast retain some power, most likely in the form of armies and similar forces, because the beast goes on to participate in the final conflict with the Lamb and saints, and only then is it destroyed.

The duration of the events of these final power struggles is very short, and is described in symbolic terms as being just "one hour" (Rev. 17 v.12). Another telling use of this phrase occurs in the account of the events in Gethsemane, just before the arrest of Jesus, when he rebukes the sleepy disciples for not being able to stay awake "for one hour" (Matt. 26 v. 40, 41). There may be an implied warning to believers here, stressing the importance of staying spiritually alert in the dark and difficult days of the last times, so as not to be caught unawares by the rapid unfolding of events.

The interaction of the harlot and the beast has revealed something of the events in the last days, but has shed little light on how or why these events occur. We are given more information about this in the use of the alternate imagery for the harlot, when she is shown as the city of Babylon. We will look at that symbolism, and the events of the fall of the city, in the next section.

17.5 The City of Babylon and the Euphrates

Although Babylon is being used as a symbol, the ideas behind the symbol are firmly rooted in the history of the city-state of Babylon, which was the capital of the ancient Babylonian Empire. It was there that the Jews were taken into captivity at the time of Daniel and Jeremiah. However the Babylonians faced divine retribution because they thought that their own power had given them the victory over Israel, and they refused to recognize the hand of God. Their fate was prophesied in several places (e.g. Is. 13 & 14), and the fall of the city is recorded in Daniel (Dan. Ch. 5). This history makes Babylon a symbol for forces in the world that rejoice in human power and success, while ignoring God and oppressing his people.

The historic city was situated on the river Euphrates that was an artery for her trade. The river was also a major contributor to her defences, particularly when under siege, as it flowed through the city and provided fresh water for drinking and for irrigating market gardens within the city walls to provide the citizens with food. Eventually, Babylon fell to Medes when the upstream waters were diverted through a canal, and the section of the river through the city was dried up enough to allow the attackers to get under the defensive water gate by night and penetrate the heart of the city.

As we have already seen, the symbol of Babylon is equated with the harlot (Rev. 17 v. 5), who we took to represent the affluent peoples of the western, apostate Christian, nations. These are predominantly the people of Europe and the USA who, by their long possession of the word of God, have had the best opportunities to become part of the bride of Christ, but who have largely rejected that role, and have committed their hopes and aspirations to the achievement of materialistic rather than spiritual goals.

If Babylon, like the harlot, is a symbol for the peoples of the advanced western nations, what is the counterpart of the symbolic river Euphrates? For ancient Babylon, the real river was fundamental to her strength, being an artery of her trade and a major contributor to her defences. What, in modern times, performs a similar role as it flows through all the countries of the west? No physical feature or structure is sufficiently dominant to match the symbol, but there is a set of inter-linked facilities that act as the heart and lifeblood of these countries and their governments. That is the banking and exchange mechanisms which channel the stream of wealth through their government treasuries, corporate accounts, and individual wallets.

When we looked (in section 16.8) at the penultimate plague in the set of the seven last "bowl" judgements, we saw a picture of the Euphrates being dried up (Rev. 16 v. 12). We left the interpretation of that vision partly unresolved, as we were waiting to identify the modern counterpart to the symbol of the city of Babylon. Now that we have identified the modern Babylon as the peoples of the West, and the counterpart of the river Euphrates as their banking and exchange mechanisms, we can see how the drying up of the symbolic Euphrates, in terms of the collapse of the financial systems in the West, would be a huge blow that would cause massive turmoil and chaos in the countries affected. In the global financial crisis, or "credit crunch", of 2008 / 9 we have seen some banks fail, causing people and businesses to lose all their money. Governments have used enormous sums of money to support their countries' financial systems, and it is still not clear whether a wider set of failures has been averted. Should this, or some future crisis result in massive failure of financial institutions then the impact in the largely urbanized West would be disastrous. Ordinary people would quickly run out of money, as many banks and cash points would not be open. Without the means to legally purchase daily necessities they would have to resort to looting to get even basic foodstuffs. To avoid total anarchy, governments would have to impose martial law.

With this understanding of the events occurring under the later "bowl" judgements of Revelation chapter 16, we can start to see how chapters 17 and 18 provide a greater level of detail for the same events. This is laid out schematically in Table 8 below, which outlines the nature and outcome of each "bowl" judgement and then aligns these with the key events of chapters 17 and 18.

Table 8: "Bowls" summary aligned with later detail

Later Bowls (Vials) – Rev. 16 v. 8-20:				
4th Bowl	**5th Bowl**	**6th Bowl (a)**	**6th Bowl (b)**	**7th Bowl**
Sun Burns	Beast's Kingdom Dark	Euphrates Dried Up	Armageddon	Done ! Babylon Drains Dregs
Government Oppression	Civil Disorder	Financial Collapse	Major war	Worldly Forces Defeated
Alignment with events from Revelation Chs.17 & 18:				
Introduction to Harlot / Babylon and the Beast – then Beast & horns strip and burn the Harlot (Babylon) Rev. Ch. 17			Beast fights the Lamb & Saints Rev. 17 v. 14	Babylon is a smoking ruin Rev. Ch. 18

The fall of the modern "Babylon" has now been covered in our consideration of Revelation chapter 17, and we progress to chapter 18 to see a "close up" of the "smoking ruins".

17.6 Babylon Fallen (Rev. Ch. 18)

Chapter 18 follows on from the events of chapter 17, and gives a detailed picture of the fallen city and the effects of that fall. One striking feature is the stress that is put on the wealth and trade of the city that is destroyed by the fall. In all, this chapter of just 24 verses uses 10 of those verses to describe the wealth of the modern "Babylon" and the sudden loss of that wealth. For example, the account relates that the merchants of the world had grown rich on her wealth (Rev. 18 v. 3), and that her own traders were the "merchant princes of the world" (Rev. 18 v. 23). The passage also describes many aspects of her trade and the distress that her sudden fall creates in the wider world of trade and cargo transport (Rev. 18 v. 11-19).

The other main emphasis in the chapter is the use of images of harlotry as a vivid portrayal of sensual worldliness and the persecution of true believers that so often accompanies apostasy. So, the passage describes the harlot's wealth and luxury (Rev. 18 v. 3, 7, 9, 16, & 19), and records how the kings of the earth have committed fornication with her (Rev. 18 v. 3 & 9). It also explains that the judgements now falling on her are in retribution for her mistreatment of the saints and apostles (Rev. 18 v. 20 & 24).

The language used in this chapter carries many echoes of Old Testament prophecies pronouncing sudden and catastrophic judgements over two particular historic cities. Firstly the description of the collapse of trade is very like that in the prophecy of the fall of Tyre (Is. Ch. 23), but the closest similarity is with a prophecy against Babylon. In particular the harlot's boast of being a queen and never being widowed (Rev. 18 v. 7) is strikingly similar to the words attributed by Isaiah to the "virgin daughter of Babylon" (Is. 47 v. 1 & 7, 8), and there are similar references to the speed of the fall, being "in a single hour" in Revelation (Ch. 18 v. 19), and "in a single day" in Isaiah (Ch. 47 v. 9). These similarities are so close that it looks as though we are being specifically directed to the earlier passage as forming a pattern that will be followed again in the events of the last days. In fact the prophecy in Isaiah is quite extended, covering chapter 45 which predicts that the

Persian Cyrus will be instrumental in carrying through the overthrow of the Babylonian Empire, chapters 46 and 47 which describe the fall, and chapters 48 and 49 which describe the restoration of Israel and their rise to eminence and widespread recognition as God's favoured people. In the replication of this pattern in the last days, we see the returned Christ acting as judge and redeemer (like Cyrus), the rich, apostate peoples of the West suffering a punishing fall (like Babylon), and the resurrected saints being seen as God's people in the new kingdom age (like the Jews returning from exile).

17.7 Lessons for Believers

Although the events of chapter 17 and the after-effects described in chapter 18 were still in the distant future in John's day, and are still in the future today, most of the descriptions in chapter 18 are in the past tense, for example "fallen is Babylon the great" (Rev. 18 v. 2). This may be a form of emphasis to stress that this judgement is certain and unavoidable. However some of the words are addressed to faithful believers, and these use the present tense, for example the warning "come out of her" (Rev. 18 v. 4). This shows that the words apply to all those who have the faith and spiritual perception to recognize the harlot power for what she is, before she is judged, so that they can resist its influence in their own lives and, with Christ's help, avoid the fall into compromise and apostasy. Since the believers must, in some sense, be in or amongst her in order to then come out of her, the need for this warning reinforces the understanding of the harlot image as one of apostasy.

The exultation of the saints over the downfall of the harlot (Rev. 18 v. 20) is not intended to be vindictive, but rather to be an expression of relief and joy that a major hindrance to the spread of the gospel has been removed. Indeed, this punishment of a spiritual oppressor is the vindication promised to the martyred saints when they asked God "how long... before you will vindicate us?" in the vision of the fifth seal (Rev. 6 v. 10).

17.8 The Lamb's Wedding and Bride (Rev. 19 v. 1-8)

This exultation of the saints is continued as a kind of commentary by the redeemed on the events that have just happened (Rev. 19 v. 1-10). This section seems to be a natural conclusion to chapter 18, and of course the chapter divisions in our Bibles are not part of the original text, but later additions to aid reference and quotation. In this section there is rejoicing over the fall of the harlot (Rev.19 v. 1-3) as being a justified judgement, because of her corrupting influence and the way she has persecuted the true believers. This "vast throng" (Rev. 19 v. 1) direct their heartfelt praise to God (Rev. 19 v. 1-3, 6-8), with their repeated "Hallelujah", which is actually Hebrew for "praise be to God". The phrase "vast throng" is the same as that used in the vision of the whole multitude of the redeemed (Rev. 7 v. 9-17) that came between the opening of the sixth and seventh seals (see section 7.4). Also, in the current passage, the people in this throng are encouraged in their praise by a heavenly voice (Rev. 19 v. 5) that addresses them as "all you his servants, you that fear him, both small and great". This very inclusive salutation, together with the use of the description as a "vast throng", linking to the earlier description of the redeemed, provide a strong indication that the faithful of all ages have now been assembled, implying that Christ has finally returned and the resurrection has now occurred.

This interpretation also fits with the way the earlier vision of the wheat harvest, at which the faithful are gathered in to their master, preceded the vision of the grape harvest with its wine press of God's wrath. As mentioned at the outset, sequentially related visions need not be fulfilled as sequential events, and there may actually be a considerable degree of overlap, but by the time the judgements of the grape harvest are over it is very likely that the gathering in of the saints will also be complete.

This implication, that Christ returns and gathers the saints from wherever they may be amongst the chaos of the fall of the modern Babylon, gets further support from the way the throng and the events around them are described in the next few verses (Rev. 19 v. 6-8). Firstly the phrase "the Lord... has entered on his reign" (v. 6) indicates that the kingdom era has begun. This is reinforced by the statements that "the wedding day of the Lamb has come" and "his bride as made herself ready" (v. 7), which carry strong echoes of the parable of the wise and foolish virgins (Matt. 25 v. 1-13), where it is the wise virgins, the true faithful, who meet the bridegroom and go into the wedding feast. In this passage the Lamb's bride is described as being clothed in "fine linen, shining and clean (v. 8), which is a symbol for the righteousness made complete in resurrection splendour. So we are presented here with a picture of the good woman, as the Bride, now united with her husband, the Lamb. This is in stark contrast to the fate of the evil woman, the harlot, whose fall has been so graphically portrayed in the two previous chapters.

17.9 A Footnote to the Wedding Feast (Rev. 19 v 9-10)

After the vision of the Lamb's wedding feast, an angel confirms to John the blessedness of those who are invited to the feast. The phrase "happy (or blessed) are those who... " is the opening phrase of each of the beatitudes in the sermon on the mount (e.g. Matt. 5 v. 3-12), so the angel's use of the same phrase points to the invitation to the wedding feast being the completion or summation of those earlier blessings. The importance of this benediction is underlined by the additional words: "these are the very words of God" (Rev. 19 v. 9).

In awe at the power and importance of these words, John attempts to worship the angel, but he is restrained by the angel insisting that worship should only be addressed to God. In fact the angel likens his role, as the messenger from Christ to John, with the role of John and other preachers who bear witness to Jesus out in the world. This is not to minimize the importance of the angel's revelation but to stress the importance, in God's sight, of the believers' work in spreading the gospel, which of course was the theme of the vision of the opening of the seven seals.

The angel's concluding words, as translated in all of the more literal English versions, declare that "the testimony of Jesus is the spirit of prophecy". It is worth analyzing this statement in a little more detail. The phrase "the testimony of Jesus" is used right at the beginning of the Revelation to describe what John was recording in writing down his visions (Rev. 1 v. 2); in other words, the Revelation itself is Jesus' testimony. The word "spirit" in both English and biblical usage carries the connotation of "essential essence" or "distillation" of something, in this case the essence of prophecy. Thus this statement is emphasizing the consistency of the Revelation with the rest of scripture by saying that it conveys the very essence of the messages of God's earlier prophets. This reinforces the importance of basing any interpretation of the book in harmony with those prophecies and the precedents they set for the use of prophetic symbols.

17.10 Chart of Chs. 17 & 18 in Wider Context

We have now covered enough of the second part of the Revelation to begin to see the underlying structure of that part of the book. The figure below shows how the parts fit together.

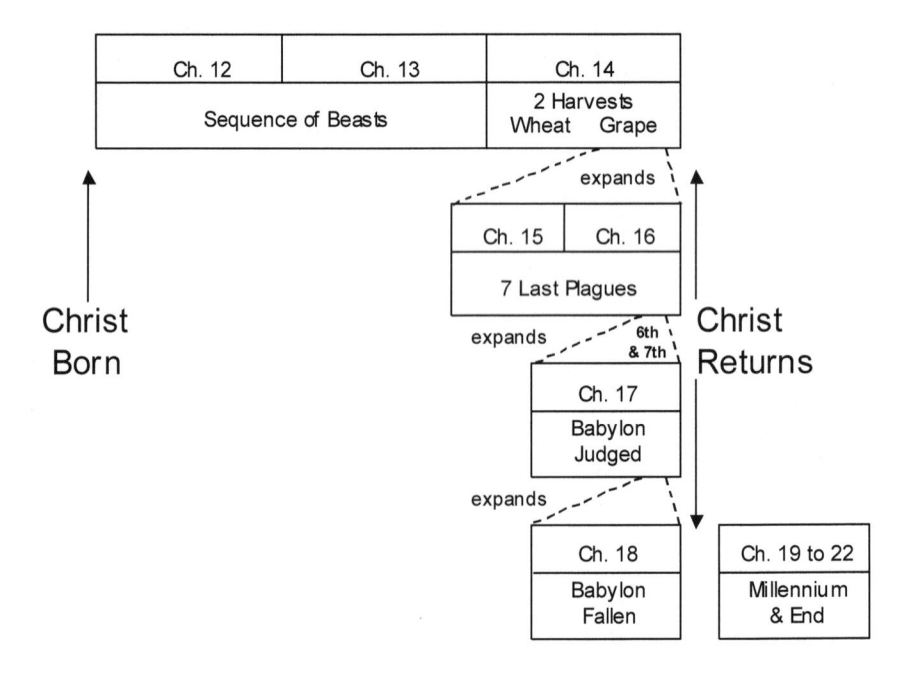

Figure 9: Schematic of Revelation 12 to 22

Part 2 of the Revelation started in chapters 12 and 13 with the birth of the "man child", Jesus, and the sequence of "beast" powers that struggled against him and his "offspring", the faithful believers. The implications are that this kind of struggle will continue throughout the Christian era, coming to a climax in the times at the end of that era. Chapter 14 depicts those end times as a harvest season, with the wheat harvest representing the gathering of the faithful, and the grape harvest representing the punishments arising from the treading of the wine press of the wrath of God. The lord of those harvests is Jesus, so by the time they are over he has returned to the earth and started to establish his kingdom.

The next chapters, 15 and 16, describe the seven bowls with the seven last plagues to fall on the earth before the end of the age. Effectively these are an expansion of the vision of the grape harvest, giving more details of how the final judgements will unfold. In the events of the sixth bowl the river Euphrates is dried up, which historically was a precursor to the fall of the city-state of Babylon, and under the seventh bowl the judgements are ended and Babylon has fallen. So since chapter 17 describes the fall of the symbolic Babylon, it must be a further expansion of the events of the sixth and seventh bowl judgements. Then chapter 18 describes the after-effects of the fall of Babylon, so it forms yet another expansion, this time of the end of chapter 17.

The beginning of chapter 19 changes focus from the fallen harlot to the bride of the Lamb, and forms a bridge into the concluding chapters of the Revelation which describe the kingdom era.

18. THE KINGDOM AND THE END (Rev. 19 v. 11 to Rev. 22)

18.1 The Last Battle (Rev. 19 v. 11-21)

As already indicated by the vision of the two harvests, the role of the returned Christ is twofold. Firstly he comes as Lord of the wheat harvest to gather his saints to the wedding feast of the Lamb, and secondly he comes as the one treading the grapes of wrath, to judge and overthrow the apostate "harlot" peoples. The first ten verses of Revelation chapter 19 relate to the former role, but from verse 11 the narrative swaps over to carry on the account of his actions in the role of warrior and judge. This passage starts with John seeing heaven wide open. Given our understanding of heaven as being the realm in which God's ways and purpose hold sway (see *heaven* in the symbol glossary), then this opening of the heavenly realm shows that God's purpose with the earth is now being made obvious to all.

The being that appears as the agent of God's purpose is shown as the rider of a white horse who is to judge and make war. This is obviously the returned Christ, and the way he is described includes many back references to earlier passages that described him and the role he is to have when he returns. So he is depicted as having:

- eyes like fire (v. 12) – as he had in the introductory vision in Rev. 1 v. 14
- a secret name (v. 12) – as was also promised to the faithful in Rev. 2 v. 17
- a blood stained robe (v. 13) – a consequence of the wine press in the Grape Harvest running with blood, as in Rev. 14 v. 20, and in fulfilment of Is. 63 v. 1-3
- a sword coming from his mouth (v.15) – again as in the introduction in Rev. 1 v. 16
- the ability to rule nations with an iron rod (v. 15) – the destiny of the "man child" as predicted in Rev. 12 v. 5, and in fulfilment of Ps. 2 v. 7-9
- the titles of king of kings, lord of lords (v. 16) – which were also given to the Lamb in Rev. 17 v. 14.

On top of all these back references, the rider is also named as "Faithful and True" (v. 11), and called "the Word of God" (v. 13), recalling John's words in his gospel that "the Word became flesh; he made his home among us, and we saw his glory, such glory as befits the Father's only son, full of grace and truth" (John 1 v. 14).

Figure 10: The Armies of Heaven (Rev. Ch.19:11-16)

155

So this can be none other than Christ, now revealed in power as the Word of God in action.

Now, at his return, Christ is not alone but is accompanied by the armies of heaven (Rev. 19 v. 14). These are clothed in white linen, which identifies them with the Lamb's bride (Rev. 19 v. 8) and with the fulfilment of the promise made to the faithful in the letter to the church at Sardis (Rev. 3 v. 5). So although this army may include angels, the language used points to it being composed primarily of the now justified and immortal believers clothed in divinely provided righteousness. This army, like their lord and leader (Rev. 19 v. 11), are mounted on white horses, which also echoes their earlier role in winning smaller victories for Christ by spreading the gospel of salvation, as depicted by the white horse in the vision of the first of the seven seals (Rev. 6 v. 2). Now they are not gaining only limited successes, but are joining their master in the final battle in which they will be totally victorious.

18.2 Overthrow of the Enemy

Having identified the rider and his armies of heaven as the returned Christ and his saints, we now need to clarify the nature of the enemy who opposes them. This power is described as "the beast and the kings of the earth, with their armies mustered to do battle against the rider and his army" (Rev. 19 v 19). As the only named power at this point, it would seem that the beast is the leader of the forces of opposition against Christ. We have already met this beast in Revelation chapter 17 and identified it as representing the government powers of the affluent, apostate "harlot" peoples of the West (see Section 17.3), probably a grouping of Western European and North American countries, something like the NATO alliance. Thus even though western peoples (the harlot) and much of their infrastructure and institutions (the city of Babylon) have fallen into chaos in the punishments described in chapters 17 and 18, the government powers and their armies still have enough resources left to lead the attack on Christ. Being joined by "the kings of the earth" would seem to indicate that the beast power calls on a wider network of allies to support this war effort. This could be done, for example, through a United Nations initiative.

It might at first seem surprising that "Christian" nations should actually lead an attack on the returned and glorified Christ. However we have already been told that "three foul spirits like frogs... muster all the kings of the world for the battle on the great day of God" (Rev. 16 v. 13-16). In considering that passage earlier, we understood the spirits to be the three dominant ideologies of humanism, apostate Christianity, and Islam, which will so condition men's thinking as to blind them to the true nature of the returned Christ (see sections 16.8 and 16.9). Thus humanism and Islam deny that Jesus is the Son of God and will not expect him to return to the earth with divine power, while many Christian churches teach that the kingdom of heaven is in some realm beyond the skies and is not on earth. Because of these preconceived ideas, many world governments will not recognize Christ as God's appointed world ruler. As a result they will try to keep hold of their own power and will defend it by going to war against the returned Christ.

The fate of the defeated beast power is to be captured and thrown into a lake of fire. This symbol of the lake of fire is probably based on the historic rubbish pit outside the walls of ancient Jerusalem in the valley of the sons of Hinnom, or "Gehenna", where all the rubbish that was thrown over the city wall was consumed to ashes in the continual fires that burned there. For example, Jeremiah foretold that during the siege in king Zedekiah's reign, so many would die that there would be no burial places left and the bodies would have to be burned there (Jer. 7 v. 32-33). This is an apt symbol for complete destruction, leaving no trace or memorial, indicating that once the beast power is destroyed it will never emerge again. In this fate the beast is joined by the False Prophet. As we identified earlier (see Section 16.9), this "false prophet" seems to be a symbol for a coalition of nations situated in the territories of the former Eastern Roman Empire that at first were "Christian" but in the end-times have become Islamic nations. This group is not named among those directly opposing Christ. So their role in the final battle is not made clear here, but in the final part of this exposition (Section 19), we will attempt to show their part in the wider sweep of events that occur at the return of Christ. However, despite the lack of detail here, it is clear that this power has also showed major resistance to Christ, because, like the beast, it is to be totally destroyed.

A further image of destroyed armies is shown as a vision of heaps of corpses providing a feast for flocks of carrion birds (Rev. 19 v. 17-18, 21). This would have been a common sight after battles between massed armies using cutting and stabbing weapons. In the context of modern warfare it is likely that the primary significance of the imagery is to convey the completeness and finality of the military defeat inflicted, rather than to paint a literal picture of the outcome of the battle.

One noteworthy feature of the language used here is its striking similarity to words in Ezekiel that also describe a great day of the Lord in which nations are defeated and God's people are vindicated (Ez. 39 v. 4,17-20). The similarity is so strong as to give us a powerful hint that these two prophecies relate to the same event. Rather than make a digression here, we will address this in a postscript in section 19. Aside from these tantalizing hints arising from the details, the main message of the passage is clear, showing that the enemies that oppose Christ are destroyed (Rev. 19 v. 20-21), and this includes the government powers and armed forces of the East (the false prophet) and the West (the beast). This leads on to a vision of the reward of the victors in the battle.

18.3 The Saints in Glory (Rev. 20 v. 4-6)

Before looking at the further constraints imposed by Christ on the powers of evil, we will skip forward a few verses into chapter 20 to look at the reward given to the faithful. John sees a vision of thrones being set up, to be occupied by those who are to exercise powers of judgement in Christ's new kingdom (Rev. 20 v. 4). This is a reward that was promised in the letters to the seven churches to those who would be victorious (i.e. in Rev. 2 v. 26-27 and 3 v. 21). It also represents a fulfilment of promises elsewhere that the faithful believers will be made kings and priests (e.g. 1 Pet. 2 v. 5, 9). Here in Revelation this reward is given to those who have endured the temptations and the opposition of the world without being corrupted (Rev. 20 v. 4).

These faithful ones are further described as being martyrs, like those who were encouraged to wait patiently for their reward in the vision of the fifth seal (Rev. 6 v. 9-11), or who have not received the mark of the beast (as in Rev. 13 v. 15, 16) but rather, by implication, have received the imprint of God's seal (as in Rev. 14 v. 1, 4-5). As part of their reward these believers will have participated in the resurrection at Christ's return and will have been granted eternal life. It is for that reason that they cannot be harmed by the second death (Rev. 20 v. 6), which we will consider in more detail in section 18.5.

These roles that the immortal saints will take in assisting Christ in the administration of his world-wide kingdom are to last for 1000 years (Rev. 20 v. 4-5). This could be a literal figure, but since we have seen repeatedly that the whole book conveys its message in symbols, it is more likely to be a symbolic figure. Looking for possible keys to this symbol, it is interesting to note that it is very close to the longest human life span recorded in the Bible, that of Methuselah who lived for 969 years (Gen. 5 v. 27). Thus 1000 years represents a period of time longer than any man has lived, and by the end of such a period all the mortal inhabitants of the kingdom will be second-, third-, or later generation kingdom citizens, with no mortals left alive who were original, first-hand witnesses to the earth-shaking events of Christ's return. We will look at the implications of this in the next section.

In summary then, Christ's victory in the great battle at the end of the age ushers in a new kingdom age. The citizens in that kingdom will be the human population from all the earth's peoples who have survived the judgements and conflicts of the last days, while their governors, priests, and teachers will be the faithful who have gained immortality in the first resurrection at Christ's return. King over all will be the returned Jesus, and no other power or government will be left to oppose him.

18.4 The Dragon Bound and Freed (Rev. 20 v. 1-3, 7-10)

The section above, based on Rev. 20 v. 4-6, gives us an understanding of the supremacy of Christ and his saints in the new kingdom age. This helps us to interpret the surrounding verses about the role of the dragon. In the description of the final battle in chapter 19, the dragon is not recorded as one of the enemies directly opposing Christ; but the beast is named and is destroyed (Rev. 19 v. 20), as the implied leader of the opposing forces. Now when we considered the nature of the beast earlier (see Section 17.3) we saw that it was a new and different type of head on the dragon, being "an eighth – and yet he is one of the seven" (Rev. 17 v. 11). Thus the death of the beast marks the end of this particular dragon head, but it does not mean the end of the whole dragon force. Indeed, at the end of the battle the dragon is described as being bound, not killed (Rev. 20 v.1-3).

When considering the identity of the dragon (see Section 13.4) we found it to be a representation of the spirit of man in rebellion against God. It is this spirit that continues into the kingdom age amongst the human kingdom citizens. Thus the place of confinement for the dragon is described as being in the "bottomless pit", or "abyss" (Rev. 20 v. 1, 3), which, as we have remarked before, is the realm of mortality and death (e.g. Rev. 9 v. 1-2, 11; also see section 8.8). However in the new kingdom age the influence of this power is greatly restricted, or "bound" (v. 2), by the authority and abilities displayed by Christ and his saints, since they rule with divine power. Thus in any conflict against this kingdom government, ordinary mortals will be at a considerable disadvantage, no matter how strong a spirit they share.

A further element of the restraining power may also lie in the memories and experiences of the human subjects of the kingdom, many of whom will remember the conditions and events that preceded the return of Christ. The experience of the peace and blessings of the kingdom age, compared to the problems and conflicts of the end-times that preceded it, may convince many of the value of accepting and obeying the new kingdom government. Indeed there are some hints in scripture that human life expectancy may increase in the kingdom age (e.g. Is. 65 v. 20), and if so many eyewitnesses to the return of Christ and the events that preceded it would live on well into the new era.

Although the spirit of human rebellion is restrained for a long time during the kingdom age, it does eventually resurface. This is conveyed by the image of the dragon being released from its bondage at the end of a 1000-year period (Rev. 20 v. 7-10). A possible factor contributing to this may be that after this length of time all the people, who were eyewitnesses of the return of Christ, and the period of upheaval immediately before it, will have died. Also, even the longest extended life spans will have been ending and death will have become more common. Thus the human kingdom citizens will become increasingly aware that they are mortal and do not exercise any real authority, while Christ and the saints are immortal and have all the real power. It is understandable that this realization should breed a sense of unfairness and discontent, especially when the memory of the mess that human rule created in the earth has faded. Eventually this discontent leads to active rebellion and conflict. The language used, particularly the mention of Gog and Magog, carries strong echoes of Ezekiel chapters 38 and 39 which we saw earlier as prophetic of the nations fighting against the returned Christ and the saints (see the end of section 18.2). This new and final attack is defeated and the dragon is now destroyed in the same way as the beast and the false prophet were destroyed at the end of the earlier great battle. The overthrow of this final rebellion of men against God is followed by a great judgement and calling to account.

18.5 The Second Death (Rev. 20 v. 11-15)

The end of chapter 20 describes a great judgement of the dead. Those whose names are not recorded in the book of life are destroyed by being thrown into the lake of fire; the same fate that befell the beast and the false prophet who had opposed Christ at the start of his reign (see section 18.2). In order for these unfaithful dead to be judged and destroyed in this way, there is a necessary implication that they would first have to be raised back to life. Since there was a resurrection earlier, at the return of Christ, to allow Christ's followers from earlier ages to be judged and rewarded, this resurrection at the end of the kingdom age is a second resurrection. Also for those who are brought back to life but have to face death again because they are judged unfaithful, the lake of fire is a second death. This is exactly what it is called in Rev. 20 v. 14.

The first resurrection was a fulfilment of the parable of the ten virgins, with the five wise virgins representing those who were truly faithful to their master and who enter the marriage supper (as in Rev. 19 v. 6-8). These are the saints who have reigned with Christ as kings and priests during the kingdom age, and who were granted immortality to allow them to take up these roles. They therefore cannot die again, and indeed one of the promises in the letters to the seven churches was that those who are victorious could not be harmed by the second death (Rev. 2 v. 11). So who are the dead who are judged in the second resurrection? They must be all the mortal citizens of the kingdom age, both those still alive at the end of that age and those who have lived and died during the millennial period time. All of these mortal citizens will have witnessed Christ in glory in his kingdom, and been taught about God's ways by the saints who act as priests and teachers for them. The mortal populace therefore will all be responsible for how they have responded to this knowledge during their lives, and will face the great judge at this final judgement. As we have already seen, those who are found to have been unfaithful have to die in the second death (Rev 20 v. 14-15), while those whose names are found in the book of life stay alive, to be made immortal and join the company of the saints.

When this last judgement has finished death itself is destroyed (Rev. 20 v.14). That means that no one else can die after this, because all those who were mortal have now been judged, and have either been destroyed in the second death or granted immortality. Thus all those who remain with Christ after this time will be the immortalized saints, and death will be no more (see also Is. 25 v. 8, and 1 Cor. 15 v. 26, 54-57).

18.6 The End (Rev. 21 v. 1-8)

With the end of death, a new era in God's relationship with his creation is going to start. This is shown in the vision at the beginning of Revelation chapter 21 where John sees a new heaven and a new earth (Rev. 21 v. 1). This represents a new form of government or leadership and a new type of people (see *heaven* and *earth* in the symbol glossary) which replace the previous forms of social structures that were needed when at least some of the people were mortal. Those earlier forms are no longer needed now that mortality and death have ceased. This new state represents a final and perfected fulfilment of such prophecies as Is. 65 v. 17-19 and 2 Pet. 3 v. 13. One of the details of this vision seems very strange if taken literally, that is the absence of any sea (Rev. 21 v. 1). However once we remember the use of seas as a symbol for unenlightened and primitive peoples existing in spiritual darkness (see *sea* in the symbol glossary, and also section 9.4), we see how accurately this characterizes an era inhabited only by immortal saints.

The community that is to live in this new spiritual era is further pictured as the holy city, New Jerusalem (Rev. 21 v. 2). The city is described in more detail later in the chapter (and this is covered in the next section, 19.7), but some features are mentioned immediately. Firstly, in being described as the new earth, replacing what went before, it is apparent that this new community is to fill the whole earth, like the divinely prepared stone in Daniel's interpretation of Nebuchadnezzar's vision of the great image (Dan. 2 v. 35, 44). Also, because all forms of sin and evil have been removed or excluded from this era (as restated in Rev. 21 v. 8), it is now finally possible for God to make his dwelling with mankind (Rev. 21 v. 3) in their new state as purified and immortalized saints (Rev. 21 v. 4). This is the final phase of God's purpose when he is to be "all in all" as described by the apostle Paul (1 Cor. 15 v. 24-28).

The fact that this is the final stage of God's plan is revealed by the words "it is done" and the use of the title "Alpha and Omega" (Rev. 21 v. 6). Alpha, as the first letter of the Greek alphabet, makes God the beginning of everything and the creator of all, as in Genesis chapter 1, while Omega, as the last letter, puts God as the purpose and end of all things, which we now see being worked out in the way that God becomes all in all. This final state of harmonious coexistence of God and his people marks a return to the blessings and perfection of the newly created earth when everything was "very good" in God's sight. The way in which this final state represents a kind of Eden restored, was highlighted by one of the promises in the letters to the seven churches, which said "to those who are victorious I will give the right to eat from the tree of life that stands in the garden of God" (Rev. 2 v. 7). One of the other promises prepared us for the use of the New Jerusalem as a symbol for this final age, by saying "I shall write on them the name of my God, and the name of the city of my God, the new Jerusalem" (Rev. 3 v. 12). Having looked at the final perfection of this holy city, the following verses of chapter 21 describe the emergence of the city as it rises to prominence. Here the image of the bride is used in parallel with the symbol of the city.

18.7 Vision of the Bride (Rev. 21 v. 9 to 22 v. 5)

We have already met the use of the parallel symbols of a woman and a city to represent the same thing. In Revelation chapters 17 and 18 we saw how the apostate "Christian" nations of the West were represented as both the harlot and the city of Babylon. We now turn from the evil and worldly version of these images to the good and spiritual version in the form of the bride and the city of New Jerusalem. The contrast seems to be deliberate, as the language in which the two women are introduced to John is almost identical (for the bride in Rev. 21 v. 9, and for the harlot in Rev. 17 v. 1).

Although John is shown a vision of the bride, the description proceeds with metaphors relating to the city. However when we look at the meaning of the symbolic language used, we see that it relates to the process of spiritual salvation and the end purpose of sharing the glory of the returned Christ. So the city shines with the glory of God, having radiance like jasper and clarity like crystal (Rev. 21 v. 11). These are the terms used in John's early vision of heaven to describe the radiance of God's glory (Rev. 4 v. 2, 3) and the purity of everything in the heavenly realm (as in the sea of glass, Rev. 4 v. 6). Thus, what is being described is not a literal city but a symbol for the community of the perfected, immortal saints, the bride, now united with their (her) Lord. This understanding is reinforced when we look at some of the symbols used to describe the city.

The numbers used to measure or quantify the features of the city are predominantly multiples of twelve: twelve gates (v. 12 & 21), twelve foundation stones (v. 14), sides 12,000 furlongs long (v. 16), and walls 144 (=12 x 12) cubits high (v. 17). As we discussed when looking at the vision of the sealing of the 144,000 (see section 8.2), twelve is the number of divine election. So with this proliferation of "twelves", we see that the city is a representation of the full assembly of God's elect.

The materials described as used in the city are pearls and gold (Rev. 21 v. 21), and various precious stones (Rev. 21 v. 19, 20). Pearls are formed by the gradual clothing of sharp, irritating grit with white, shining beauty. This is a beautiful image of the process by which mortality is clothed with God's gift of righteousness (e.g. 2 Cor. 5 v. 2-4; and Rev. 19 v. 7-8), and the pearls here form the gates, so that the only way to enter the city is by going through this spiritual transformation. As for the use of gold, this is a frequent biblical symbol for a tried faith (e.g. 1 Pet. 1 v. 7), and this is another key characteristic of those who will please God and be included in his elect.

Precious stones are also used symbolically in connection with God's people. Their high value makes them a natural metaphor for anything that is especially treasured, so in speaking of the people who are named in God's record of "those who feared him and had respect for his name", the prophet Malachi (Mal. 3 v. 16-17) says that they will be God's "own possession" (AV "jewels"; RV "peculiar treasure"). Also, the gems named as forming the twelve foundation stones of the city link closely to the twelve jewels set into the breastplate in the Jewish high priest's sacred vestments (Ex. 28 v. 17-20). Although it is not always easy to match the Hebrew and the Greek names for particular types of gems, at least eight, and perhaps all, of those jewels listed as city foundation stones also were used in the high priest's breastplate. Each of the stones in the breastplate was engraved with the name of one of the twelve patriarchs who founded the twelve tribes of Israel, and these tribes were God's people in the Old Testament period. Thus their high priest carried their names close to his heart when he ministered before God. In the New Testament period, Christ is the high priest for the Christian believers (e.g. Heb. 9 v. 11-12), and as their mediator he carries their name and prayers to God. So the jewels are a symbol of those who are close to Jesus' heart and who are precious to God. Hence the symbol of the jewels as foundation stones for the holy city. In a further parallel with the breastplate, these foundation stones bear the names of the twelve apostles (Rev. 21 v. 14), the founders of the body of believers, the bride.

The city is said to have no need for a temple (Rev. 21 v. 22). That is because a temple is a sacred place where worshippers can find some reminder or symbol of their God, a God they can only see with the eye of faith. But now the bride has been united with her bridegroom; and Christ, in his full glory and divine splendour, is present for all to see. Thus it is no longer necessary to have a temple as a representation and reminder of his presence. The symbol for the presence of Christ is the throne of the Lamb and of God shown as being within the city (Rev. 22 v. 3-5). The visible presence of Christ not only delights the faithful who have waited for this so long, but it also gives light to the rest of the world (Rev. 21 v. 24). The saints, as Christ's kings and priests also share this role of bringing light to the world (Rev. 22 v. 4-5), in fulfilment of many earlier prophecies (e.g. Is. 2 v. 2-3; Is. 60 v. 1-3).

18.8 The City as a Temple

In Revelation chapters 19 v. 9 to 21 v. 8, we are taken from the founding of the millennial era to its end in the final rebellion, the last judgement, and the progression to the new age when God is all in all. This new age is represented by the symbol of the holy city, but the key elements of that new order are already present during the millennial age, since Christ was united with a great multitude of immortalized believers at the start of his kingdom on earth. However more believers will emerge from the mortal citizens of the kingdom during the millennium and they will be joined to the saints at the final judgement, thereby making the holy city complete. So, in chapters 21 v. 9 to 22 v. 5, we are given a picture of the emerging holy city during the kingdom age but before the final "all-in-all" stage is reached. During this period the city, representing immortal saints, brings light to nations, made up of mortal citizens, and they offer tribute in response (Rev. 21 v. 24). The fact that there is need for a source of healing for the nations (Rev. 22 v. 2) confirms that not all of the kingdom's inhabitants have become immortal.

We have already seen (in section 18.3) that the role of the immortalized believers in the kingdom age is that of kings and priests in support of the reign of Christ. The symbol of the holy city is another representation of that same body of believers, and indeed we read that the inhabitants of the city bear God's name in their foreheads (Rev. 22 v. 4), which is in marked contrast to the inhabitants of "Babylon" who had the beast's mark in their foreheads. So during the kingdom period the community of the saints forms a living church or temple (see 1 Pet. 2 v. 5-6) to which the mortal populace can come for instruction about the ways of God. If they respond positively to that instruction they too will have the opportunity of becoming part of the community themselves.

This spreading of the knowledge of God's plan of salvation is pictured as a river of life flowing out of the holy city (Rev. 22 v. 1-2). The imagery used here is very reminiscent of that used in Ezekiel's vision of a future temple, which has an ever-deepening river of water flowing from a spring under its threshold (Ez. 47 v. 1-12). In Ezekiel's vision the water flows into the Dead Sea to make it become fresh and produce abundant fish (Ez. 47 v. 9), in other words it brings life where previously there was death. Given that fresh water is a symbol of the spiritual realm (see *water* in the symbol glossary, and also see Section 9.5), we can see how the underlying symbolism of Ezekiel's vision anticipates the role of the spiritual community of the holy city.

The parallel between this part of Revelation and Ezekiel's temple vision is even closer. The power of the community of the holy city to bring spiritual growth and healing to the world is pictured as the stream of water promoting a growth of trees that miraculously gives monthly fruit, and whose leaves can heal the nations (Rev. 22 v. 2). This is almost identical to Ezekiel's vision where the water from the temple also promotes a growth of monthly fruit and healing leaves (Ez. 47 v. 12). In the Revelation vision, the trees are each described as being "a tree of life". The original tree of life grew in the Garden of Eden but access to it was barred after Adam's fall (Gen. 3 v 22-24). The use of this name for the trees of the holy city indicates that the healing process being promoted is bringing about a return to the perfection of the newly created Eden.

So the holy city is a symbol for the community of the immortal saints, starting as the bride supporting Christ in his cleansing and healing work in the millennium, and then being joined by the new believers from that age to go forward into the even closer union with God when God becomes all-in-all. It is quite fitting that the sequence of John's visions of the holy city started with a view of the completed city (Rev. 21 v. 1-8, covered in section 18.6), before going back to see the emerging city and its role in the millennial age (Rev. 21 v. 9 to 22 v. 5). By doing this, the last main vision before the epilogue echoes some of the main positive themes encountered earlier in the book, such as the presence in the world of a community of believers, their role in spreading the light of the gospel, and the promises "to those who overcome" that they will ultimately be united with their master and share in his glory. This is surely a great exhortation to all those who now struggle to live faithful lives in a world dominated by the thinking of the beast and the ways of the harlot.

18.9 The Two Women – a Summary

In much of the second part of the Revelation from chapter 12 to 22, we have encountered two women used as symbols: the good woman or the bride, and the bad woman or the harlot. It is helpful to illustrate the depth of these symbols by summarizing what we have discovered about them in a table, and that is shown below.

These symbols of the two women highlight the key differences between those who try to follow the ways of God and those who conform to the ways of the world. A similar extended allegory can be found in the book of Proverbs where the first nine chapters contrast the call of Wisdom, pictured as the good woman, with the allure of the world, as represented by the harlot.

Table 9: The Two Women Compared

Aspect	Good Woman	Bad Woman
Known as:	The Bride	The Harlot
Is Consort of:	The Lamb	The Beast (or kings of the earth)
Made up from:	Those sealed with God's seal	Those with the mark & number of the Beast
Shown as a City:	New Jerusalem	Babylon
City is on a River:	Water of life	Euphrates
River water action:	Flow & increase – to cleanse and heal	Dry up – causing city to fall
City foundations:	12 Apostles	7 World Empires (mountains)
City history:	Hidden, humble beginnings; finally revealed in glory	Always sought power; finally has total collapse

Having reached the stage where the good woman has finally been revealed as united with her master in glory, the Revelation concludes with a short epilogue.

18.10 Epilogue (Rev. 22 v. 6-21)

The epilogue starts in a similar way to the initial introduction to the Revelation, with an angel who has been sent to John to tell him what must soon take place (compare Rev. 22 v. 6 with Rev.1 v. 1). John's response is one of awe and he starts to worship the angel (Rev. 22 v. 8). This has happened before (see Rev. 19 v. 10), and the response in both instances is the same. John is restrained and told to worship only God (Rev. 22 v. 9). This is because an angel is just a messenger of God (the Greek word for "angel", *angelos*, means "messenger"), and so only has powers derived from God, and has no inherent power or authority that would make him an object of worship. Now the Bible indicates that men rank lower than angels, since even Christ in his mortal state "was made subordinate to the angels" (Heb. 2 v. 9), but in his risen and glorified state it its God's intention to "put everything in subjection beneath his feet" (Heb. 2 v. 8). So, at present, we are also lower than the angels, but the promise to the faithful is that they will be like Christ (1 John 3 v. 2), and we can see representations of this in the symbols of the bride and the holy city. The faithful, in that future role of aiding Christ in bringing light to the world, will also be bearing messages from the heavenly realm and so be at least equal to angels. Therefore those who seek God must not be tempted to worship angels, though despite this warning the Gnostics did later introduce this as part of their false teachings.

One of the key messages in this epilogue is that "the time of fulfilment is near" (Rev. 22 v. 10), and this again is an echo of the words in the introduction to the book (see Rev. 1 v. 3). At first this can seem puzzling as nearly two millennia have passed since John saw these visions and not all of them have been fulfilled yet. However when we look back and see the content of the visions with their cyclic patterns of events (in Rev. Chs. 2-11) and the initial historic pictures of the struggles of the early church (Chs. 12 & 13), we see that many significant elements of the visions were already starting to happen, even though they were to carry on for a very long time.

This emphasis on the immediacy of the visions is reinforced by the words "I am coming soon" that appear to come directly from Christ (Rev. 22 v. 12). This saying is probably better rendered as "I come quickly", as it is given in the KJV, since this fits in with other uses of the same Greek word in the New Testament. The saying then refers to the suddenness of Christ's coming rather than its closeness to John's day. This fits in with the warning (in Rev. 22 v. 11) that we should not turn from righteousness or become deeply engrossed in evil, because the suddenness of Christ's return will not leave time for warnings or special preparations, and once he is here it will be too late to change.

The epilogue continues (Rev. 22 v. 13-16) with many reminders and recapitulations of what has gone before. Thus Christ claims the titles of "the Alpha and the Omega" (v. 13) that we met in the introduction (Rev. 1 v 8, & 17). Also the faithful are described as those who "wash their robes clean" (v. 14) like the great multitude in Rev. 7 v. 14, and they may also "eat from the tree of life" (v. 14) as promised in the first of the seven letters (Rev. 2 v. 7) and described in the vision of the holy city (Rev. 22 v. 2).

In a further echo of earlier themes, the faithful are rewarded by being able to "enter the city by the gates" (v. 14), reminding us of the use of the pearl gates as a metaphor for the clothing of mortality with immortality (Rev. 21 v. 21, as remarked in Section 18.1). Jesus also used the image of entering by the gate in his analogy of himself as the door of the sheepfold (John 10 v. 7-9), and in his parable of the wide and narrow ways (Matt. 7 v. 13-14). In the parable, only the narrow gate leads to salvation, but there are many who do not search for it and who take the easier broad way that leads to the wide gate of destruction. This idea seems to be reflected in the following words (Rev. 22 v. 15) that characterize the immorality of those who remain outside the holy city.

More reminders of the opening of the Revelation occur in verse 16, where Jesus reiterates that these visions are his testimony to the churches, which he has sent to John by his angel (cf. Rev. 1 v. 1, 4). He also likens himself to the "dawn star" which is the first visible source of heavenly illumination to be seen when the darkness of the night starts to lift. This is an excellent metaphor for the way his appearing on his return will bring light to a spiritually dark world and herald the dawn of a new era of righteousness on the earth. The same metaphor was used at the end of the fourth letter to the churches (Rev. 2 v. 28) where Jesus uses it to imply that the faithful will share in this "light-bringing" work.

Amongst all these echoes of the earlier material of the Revelation Jesus includes a significant pointer to the way he is also fulfilling the messianic prophecies and allusions in the Old Testament. He does this by identifying himself as "the offspring of David, the shoot growing from his stock" (v. 16) which is a direct reference to Is. 11 v. 1 and is obviously intended to draw attention to the promises of the blessings in the kingdom age which follow in the rest of that chapter. The reference to David also invites investigation of all the divine promises to David about the great son who was to come in his line of descent (e.g. 2 Sam. 7 v. 12-16; Ps. 72; Ps. 110; Matt. 22 v. 41-45; Acts 2 v. 34-35).

The epilogue now concludes with an exhortation, two warnings, and a blessing. The exhortation is that all those who hear the words of the Revelation should heed the appeal contained in the message, which comes in the power of the Holy Spirit (Rev. 22 v. 17). The call is also repeated by the bride, which is surely an allusion to the duty of the faithful hearers to take their own part in spreading the gospel, as portrayed in the earlier vision of the opening of the seven seals (Rev. Chs. 5 & 6). The nature of the appeal is indicated in language about thirst and life-giving water. This not only alludes to the water flowing out of the holy city (e.g. Rev. 22 v. 1) but is also very close to the words at the opening of Is. Ch. 55, where the passage goes on with an extended appeal to turn away from the materialism of the world and find real value in the ways of God.

The first warning is against altering the message that has been given to John. Since the message has been sent directly from the glorified Christ (v. 16), it carries the full force of divine authority and truth, so anyone who deliberately tries to alter it is corrupting that truth and making a lie. As has just been proclaimed (v. 15), "all who love and practice deceit" (or KJV "maketh a lie") are left "outside" the holy city, which is the community of the saints. That fate is expressed again here using terms we have encountered earlier in the book, so that those who add to the inspired message are to suffer in the final outpouring of God's wrath as in the seven last plagues poured from the seven bowls (v. 18), and those who take anything away from the message are to be barred from the tree of life (v. 19), which epitomizes the idea of Eden restored in the kingdom age and the revealing of the holy city.

The second and final warning is "I am coming soon" (Rev. 22 v. 20). This is a repeat of the same words as occurred in verse 12, which, as we commented earlier in this section, is perhaps better understood as coming quickly or suddenly. This is very like the message of Jesus' parable of the ten virgins, where all ten have fallen asleep and so the call to attend the bridegroom comes suddenly and unexpectedly. The implication is that there will be no time for last minute preparations. Only those who have fully prepared themselves beforehand, like the five wise virgins, will go in to the wedding feast with the bridegroom.

The final blessing (Rev. 22 v. 21) is "the grace of the Lord Jesus be with all (of you). Amen". Thus Christ's love and forgiveness are offered to all those who read this message. This gift is offered freely, but the choice to accept or decline the offer is a matter for each reader to decide.

18.11 Final Summary Charts

As stated in the Preface, we did not begin our study of the Revelation with any pre-existing theories about its structure or key messages. However as we progressed and saw features and patterns emerging from the text, one key structural feature struck us quite forcefully. That is that the book starts with Jesus sending his message to John and the early church in chapter 1, and builds to one of its climaxes towards the end of chapter 11 with the rejoicing that Christ has set up his kingdom on earth, with such words as "Sovereignty over the world has passed to our Lord and his Christ, and he shall reign for ever!" (Rev. 11 v. 15). Then Jesus appears again in a more historic context of Roman opposition in the vision of the birth of the man child attacked by the dragon in chapter 12, and the narrative progresses through a series of increasingly detailed visions of the build-up to the end-times, Christ's return and the millennial age. This seems to divide the book up into two main parts, i.e. chapters 1 to 11, and chapters 12 to 22. We drew up some charts in an attempt to summarise our growing understanding of the book's structure and these are shown below.

Revelation Part 1 (chapters 1-11) introduces the three main, cyclic patterns of events as shown in the chart below (see also the chart in Section 12.1). Here the three main cycles of seven deal largely with the spiritual work of Christ and his church, covering the growth, and sometimes decline, of faith amongst the believers (the seven letters), the effect of the believers going out into the world to preach the word (the seven seals), and the divine interventions in, or punishments of, the unbelieving world so as to prevent the light of the gospel being extinguished (the seven trumpets).

Table 10: Summary of Revelation 1 to 11

Scene Setting	Main Cycle	Look Aside	Completion
Ch. 1: Prologue	Chs. 2, 3: The 7 Letters	(None)	Ch. 4: A Vision of Heaven
Ch. 5: The Lamb & the Scroll	Ch. 6: The 7 Seals (1 to 6)	Ch. 7: The 144,000 & the Multitude	Ch. 8 v. 1: The 7th Seal
Ch. 8 v 2-5: Lighting the Censer	Ch. 8v7 to Ch. 9: The 7 Trumpets (1 to 6)	Ch. 10, 11: Angel & Witnesses	Ch. 11 v.15-19: 7th Trumpet

The second two cycles are interrupted between their sixth and seventh events with asides that look at what is happening in the background, largely unrecognized by the world at large. These asides cover the way the body of believers is being built up to become eventually a great multitude, and the passive witness of the Jews. All three cycles are completed with visions of some aspect of the eventual outcome, that is the kingdom of heaven being set up on earth, and God ultimately being all-in-all.

Revelation Part 2 (chapters 12-22) shows, in expanding levels of detail, some of the key events in the Christian era that form the historic backdrop to the repeating cycles. The structure of this part is shown in the next chart (see also the chart in Section 17.10).

Here the narrative starts with a summary of how the main groups of political powers will be formed in the Judaeo-Christian areas of the world. These power groups are relevant to most of the period of the Christian era, as covered by the three cycles of sevens in the first part of the Revelation. Next, the events of the end-times are summarized using the symbols of the two harvests, with the wheat harvest being the gathering of the faithful into Christ's kingdom, and the grape harvest being the expression of God's wrath against those who reject and oppose him. The events of the grape harvest are then expanded into the seven last judgements coming from the seven bowls. As a further level of expansion, a key event of the sixth bowl judgement is broadened out in the vision of the fall of Babylon, with a further "zooming in" to focus on the ruined city and the impact of the fall. After a final addition of the details of the great battle against the returned Christ, the narrative moves on to cover the millennial age and the final glory of God being all-in-all.

Table 11: Summary of Revelation 12 to 22

Christian Era	End-Times & Expansions	Millennial Age	End & Epilogue
Chs. 12, 13: Beast Sequence	Ch. 14: The two harvests		
	Chs. 15, 16: 7 last plagues		
	Ch. 17: Babylon judged		
	Ch. 18, 19 v.1-5: Babylon fallen		
	Ch. 19 v.6-21: The last battle	Ch. 20: The Kingdom	Ch. 21 v. 1-8: The final glory
		Ch. 21v9 to 22 v5: The Bride / City	Ch. 22 v. 6-21: Epilogue

19. POSTSCRIPT: THE EVENTS OF CHRIST'S RETURN

19.1 Gentile and Jewish Perspectives on the Return of Jesus

We have now progressed through the whole of the Revelation, and we have found that its message relates primarily to gentile peoples in countries where Christianity has had a strong influence. This has confirmed what we deduced quite near the beginning of the study (see sections 1.5 and 1.6). The messages and images relating to the Jews have been restricted to the passages about the two witnesses, in chapter 11 (see Section 11.1), and the woman who bore the man-child, at the start of chapter 12 (see Section 13.2). The gentile emphasis in the rest of the book means that the events of the end-time and the return of Christ are also viewed from this perspective. This stands in distinct contrast to prophecies about the return of Messiah in the rest of the Bible where the emphasis is typically on how these events affect the Jews and the land of Israel. Thus to get a global perspective on the events at Christ's return we need to fit together the prophecies in the Revelation with those in other places in the scriptures. This postscript section is an attempt to provide such a synthesis.

This section cannot be too detailed or it will stray too far from the main theme of the Apocalypse, so we will restrict our comparison to just a few of the many relevant prophecies. First we will look at two key prophecies that establish the overall historical context within which the return of Christ will occur. Then we will look at a few of the more detailed prophecies that give some details of how the Jews and the land of Israel will be affected by the events leading up to the return. Finally we will see how the events involving the gentile nations fit into the picture.

19.2 Prophecies that Set the Context

There is one key prophecy that establishes a very broad outline of the history of the struggle for power in the countries surrounding the Mediterranean basin. This region is significant in God's purpose because it is where both the Jewish and the Christian witness to God's message originated. The prophecy in question is in the form of a vision given to king Nebuchadnezzar and the interpretation of it given through Daniel, as recorded in the book of Daniel (Dan. 2 v. 28-45). In the vision the king saw a great image of a man that was struck on the feet and destroyed by a stone that then grew to fill the whole earth.

The image was made of layers of different materials, and Daniel explains that these layers, from head to feet, represent a progression of different ruling powers from the king's time onwards. So the golden head represents Babylon, and the silver chest and arms portray the Medo-Persian Empire, with the two arms showing the internal division between the factions of the Medes and the Persians. Next the belly and thighs of bronze represent the Greek empire, with the division of the thighs indicating that the empire was divided after Alexander's day. The following level of the image contains the iron legs, which stand for the Roman Empire with its division into the Eastern and Western Empires. This detail fits with the representation in the Revelation where the single pagan Roman Empire, shown as the dragon, is divided into two, in the form of the beasts from the earth and the sea. The last layer is the feet whose mixture of iron and clay indicates a mixture of strong and weak kingdoms with no single power ruling them all. The image standing on two feet portrays the ongoing division of culture and ideology between the Western and Middle-Eastern parts of the region (see Sections 14.3 to 14.6). At the time when the international situation reflects the conditions denoted by this final level of the image, the stone falls on the feet, destroying the image and growing to fill the earth. The meaning of this is that "the God of heaven will establish a kingdom which will never be destroyed" (Dan. 2 v. 44), that is the establishment of Christ's reign on earth.

On top of this broad outline we can add specific Jewish details from Christ's own prophecy, given on the Mount of Olives shortly before the crucifixion. There are records of this in the gospels of both Matthew and Luke, which show the prophecy was given in response to two questions from the disciples. They wanted to know when the temple in Jerusalem would be destroyed and what signs would indicate the start of Christ's kingdom reign (Matt. 24 v. 2-3). It seems that they expected these events to occur at about the same time, but from a few verses in Luke's account we see that Jesus indicated a gap between the fall and destruction of Jerusalem, and his later second coming. So, having described events that were to occur in the Roman siege and sack of the city, mainly around AD 70, he says "they (i.e. the Jews) will be carried captive into all countries; and Jerusalem will be trampled underfoot by Gentiles until the day of the Gentiles has run its course" (Lk. 21 v. 24). This covers nearly 2000 years during which the Jews had no control of the city, from the expulsion of the Jews by the Romans in AD 70 and AD 100 until their resettlement in the 20th century. Only then did they regain control of Jerusalem, partly in 1948 and more fully in 1967. Christ then talks about a period of distress and uncertainty that will reach a climax when "they will see the Son of Man coming in a cloud with power and great glory" (Lk. 21 v. 27).

Thus these two key prophecies, through Daniel and Jesus himself, outline a "gentile age" from the Roman period to the present, in which there would be no single power in the region of the Mediterranean basin that would have the same dominance as the Romans. In the same period Jerusalem would not be in Jewish control. That period started to close when the Jews regained Jerusalem and will end completely with the return of Christ. Many other prophecies speak of a time when the Jews will be re-gathered to the land of Israel and the city of Jerusalem. Some of these were fulfilled, in whole or in part, with the Jewish return from their earlier captivity in Babylon. However some speak of a time following a return when there will be a major conflict, involving the Jews and their capital city, in a great "day of the Lord" that will result in a divine salvation and a subsequent period of redemption and blessing. We will look at some of these prophecies next.

19.3 Prophecies of War Against Jerusalem

When we studied the vision of the two witnesses (Rev. Ch. 11 – see Sections 11.1 and 11.2), we took it to be one of the few places in the Revelation that refers to the Jews. In the vision, towards the end of their period of activity, the witnesses are killed but shortly afterwards they miraculously return to life. This terrifies their enemies who in their turn experience destruction, with their survivors paying fearful homage to God. We took this vision to indicate that in the end-times the Jews would be attacked by their enemies but would experience the power of a divine intervention to save Israel and repulse their enemies. This series of future events is spoken of in many other biblical prophecies,

One noteworthy Old Testament prophecy dealing with a latter-day war against Jerusalem is given in Zechariah chapter 12. This speaks of a siege of the city and a gathering of nations to attack it (Zech. 12 v. 2-3), but shows that God will repulse the attacking armies (v. 4, 8-9). It also indicates that the Jews will accept the Lord of Hosts as their God (v. 5), and will mourn when they see "him whom they have pierced" (v. 10-14). This implies very strongly that the leader of the divine forces that save them is Christ, and that the people now recognize that the Jesus who they asked the Romans to crucify so many centuries before has now returned as their saviour.

A similar prophecy is found in the book of Joel. This talks of a future "day of the Lord" in Zion as being a threatening day in which "countless hosts" appear (Joel 2 v. 1-2). It also presents an appeal from God for the people to turn back to him and indicates that they will heed his appeal when they repent of their earlier ways and seek his deliverance from the forces that threaten them (v. 12-17). It then shows that God will deliver his people and restore the fortunes of the remnant that survive that "great and terrible day of the Lord" (v. 18-32). The passage goes on to say that the nations will be gathered together into the valley of Jehoshaphat where God will bring his judgements on them on behalf of his people Israel (Joel 3 v. 1-3). It gives more details of this great conflict as the nations gather for war only to find that "the Lord roars from Zion and thunders from Jerusalem" as he makes himself "a defence for Israel" (v. 9-17). The language used to describe the conflict uses the image of treading the winepress, which carries strong echoes of the descriptions of God's final judgements in Revelation (e.g. Rev. 14 v. 18-20; Rev. 19 v. 11-16).

Another prophecy, this time in Ezekiel, also describes a great day of the Lord in which nations are defeated and God's people are vindicated, and it does so in language that is strikingly similar to words used in Revelation to describe the final battle of the returned Christ against the forces that oppose him (compare Ez. 39 v. 4, 17-20 with Rev. 19 v. 17-19). This passage in Ezekiel occurs in a larger section of latter-day prophecies that are relevant to our study. The relevant section starts in chapter 36 where God promises to restore Israel to their own land after it has been in the possession of their enemies. He says that he will do this for the sake of his own name, to make the nations recognize and honour him, because in their dispersion Israel have brought his name into disrepute (Ez. 36 v. 22-23). He specifically says that he is not doing this for the people's sake, so this indicates that at the time of their re-gathering the Jews are not yet properly honouring God and living in harmony with him. Nonetheless the chapter does promise that the land will be rebuilt and replanted and that eventually he will let "the Israelites pray to me for help" (Ez. 36 v. 37). The next chapter portrays the re-gathering of Israel as a heap of dry bones coming together to form a mighty company representing "the whole people of Israel" restored to their own land (Ez. 37 v. 11-12). He then promises that they will turn from their faithlessness and accept him as their God, and that then "my servant David will be king over you" (Ez. 37 v. 24), using this as a symbol for David's greater son, Jesus Christ, finally fulfilling his role of king of the Jews.

The next two chapters, 38 and 39, describe the events that bring about Israel's return to their God and the appearance of Christ as their saviour and king. The passage foretells how a host of nations will "invade a land restored from ruin, whose people are gathered from many nations on the mountains of Israel that have been so long desolate" (Ez. 38 v. 8). This attacking force gains some initial success in getting into the country, but at the very point when Israel are threatened with annihilation God shows his power and fights for them, when "on that day my wrath will boil over" and "I will show myself great and holy and make myself known to many nations" (Ez. 38 v. 18, 23). Chapter 39 adds details to this account, including the calling of the birds to feast on the flesh of the fallen which we cited above as being so similar to the account of the final conflict in Revelation (Rev. 19 v. 17-19). As a result of God's actions "All will see the judgement that I execute and the hand I lay upon them. From that day forward the Israelites will know that I am the Lord their God." (Ez. 39 v. 21-22).

19.4 Identifying Israel's Enemies

Some of the finer details of these passages in Ezekiel are worth a little extra study. A key point to notice is the list of nations who are named as making up the forces that attack Jerusalem. These include Magog, Meshech, and Tubal as the leading powers, with Persia, Cush, Put, Gomer, and Bethtogarmah as their allies, and the latter two being specifically mentioned as a northern force. In typical Bible usage countries are referred to by the names that were current at the time the writer was living. Where the message refers to the future it applies to the nations that will be living in the same geographical areas at the time the prophecy is fulfilled (e.g. in prophesying about the regathering of Israel to their land, Zechariah (ch. 10 v. 10) speaks of them coming from Assyria which ceased to be a political entity long before the return). It can be difficult to link some of these ancient names for countries or tribes to the locations they occupied when particular prophecies were written, but the combination of archaeological discoveries and the works of ancient writers such as Homer and Herodotus have helped this identification considerably. In the case of Ezekiel's prophecy there is reasonable agreement between commentators on the following equivalences:

- Magog – taken to be the Scythians in the location where they first started to have an impact on the nations of the Mediterranean and Middle East, i.e. in the lands between the Black Sea and the Caspian Sea, around where we now find Azerbaijan, Armenia, Georgia, Dagestan, and Chechnya.
- Meshech – identified with the later Moschi people in what is now north-eastern Turkey bordering the Black Sea and Western Georgia.

- Tubal – believed to be the father of the Cappadocians whose ancient capital was Mazaca which is now the modern city of Kayseri in east-central Turkey.
- Gomer – identified by Josephus as being equivalent to the Roman district of Galatia, which is now west-central Turkey, and by Homer as equivalent to the Cimmerians who were located around the north-east of Galatia, still in what is now Turkey, but possibly having their early origins on the north shores of the Black Sea around the region we now refer to as the Crimea.
- Togarmah or Bethtogarmah – a name of a son of Gomer (Gen. 10 v. 3) believed to be located near Gomer, possibly in northern Armenia.
- Persia – obviously equivalent to modern Iran, and for most of the period of its empire also including modern Iraq; possibly chosen to represent eastern powers.
- Cush – an ancient name for the region that is now Sudan and possibly also covering Ethiopia; this may have been chosen to represent southern powers.
- Put – generally taken to be the region that lies west of Egypt and is now Libya; possibly chosen to represent western powers.

So, the countries identified are the modern equivalents of peoples who were governed, or heavily influenced, by the Eastern Roman Empire that we saw in Revelation chapter 13 as being represented by the beast of the earth. In current times these countries are predominantly Islamic or have growing and influential Muslim minorities, and so fit the symbol of the "false prophet" used in the later chapters of Revelation in place of the earth beast, as discussed in Section 16.9.

While on the subject of identifying the nations that enter the final war against Israel, it is relevant to refer to a view, sometimes advanced, that one of the leading nations in the attack is Russia. This identification is based on a particular interpretation of the Hebrew word "rosh" in the prophecy in Ezekiel (38 v. 2-3, & 39 v. 1). In some versions the phrase used in these passages is "... Gog, prince of Rosh, Meshech and Tubal... ". This treats the Hebrew word as a proper name and leaves it untranslated. There is then a temptation to see a similarity between "Rosh" and "Ros" or "Rus" which was an early name for the grouping of Slavic peoples around the city of Kiev and the river Volga that formed the beginnings of what was to become the state of Russia. However there are two significant objections to this. Firstly the Bible writers generally use names that were current in their own time, and while Ezekiel dates from the 6th century BC, the name "Ros" or "Rus" was not used for the emerging Russian peoples until around the 5th or 6th century AD, over a thousand years after Ezekiel's day. If the passage was intended to refer to this name it would be the only such anachronism in the Bible. Secondly, the word "rosh" has a well accepted meaning of "chief" or "head" and is so translated more than 400 times in other scriptures. Thus the phrase in Ezekiel can be translated more consistently as "Gog... the chief ('rosh') prince of Meshech and Tubal", as it is in the King James Version. So an interpretation that points to a primary involvement of Russia in the final war against Israel rests on rather insecure foundations.

19.5 Recap of the Final Battle in Revelation

In the sections above we have seen that many biblical prophecies before the Revelation show Israel being attacked by the armies of surrounding, mainly Islamic, countries. Hugely outnumbered and faced with total destruction, the Jews turn to God as their only hope, and he responds by sending Christ back to the earth to defeat the invading armies and set up his own kingdom on the earth.

As we saw in earlier sections of this study, the sequence of events at the time of the end was predicted in the Revelation by the interpretation of the later outpourings of the seven bowls (Rev. Ch. 16), with added details given in subsequent chapters. This sequence involves an increase in government oppression (the fourth bowl), civil disorder in the kingdom of the Beast, i.e. the nations of the West (the fifth bowl), and then a financial collapse in Western states, followed by a major war (the sixth bowl). The financial collapse brings about the fall of Babylon, a symbol we saw as representing the impoverishment of the peoples and internal structures of the Western nations (Rev. Chs. 17 & 18), but enough military power is left for the West to fight a major battle, depicted as being between the Beast, accompanied by the kings of the earth, and the returned Jesus leading the armies of heaven (Rev. Ch. 19). The battle results in the defeat of worldly forces (seventh bowl) and the establishment of Christ's kingdom on earth (Rev. Ch. 20).

In the next section we will try to put the earlier, Jewish-orientated, prophecies and the apocalyptic, gentile-orientated, prophecies into a single time sequence.

19.6 Merging the Apocalyptic View with Other Bible Prophecies

The point at which the two sets of Jewish- and gentile-oriented prophecies meet is in their predictions that groups of nations will fight against the returned Christ. The possibilities are that:
a) there is one battle in which Islamic and Western nations fight together, or
b) there are two battles with the West fighting first and the Islamic nations second, or
c) still with two battles but with the Islamic nations fighting first and then the West.

The details in the prophecies help us to find the most likely of these options.

The prophecies before the Revelation all talk of an attack on the nation and land of Israel. This only becomes a battle against Jesus when the Jews are on the brink of destruction and appeal for divine help. At this point Christ returns to save Israel and repulse their enemies. In contrast, the account in Revelation describes a battle between the forces of the West (the Beast) and their allies (the kings of the earth) against the returned Christ (the "Faithful and True" and called "the word of God") with the armies of heaven (Rev. 19 v. 11-19). This account makes no mention of the Jews and suggests that this battle starts when Christ has already returned. A further point is that the vision revealed by the sixth bowl shows the kings of the earth being gathered to the final battle by three frog spirits. In the exposition in Section 16.9 these spirits were identified as being misleading, but commonly followed, ideologies.

The effect of the three frog spirits is to "muster all the kings of the world for the battle on the great day of God the sovereign Lord... at the place called in Hebrew Armageddon" (Rev. 16 v. 14, 16). The effect of the three ideologies, which we identified as humanism, apostate Christianity, and Islam, will be to blind the nations to the true nature of the returned Christ. Because of their preconceived ideas, they will not recognize Christ as God's appointed world ruler, and they will try to keep hold of their own power and status in the world. This will result in their actually going to war against the returned Christ, as portrayed in Ps. 2.

The implications of this additional detail are that the most likely scenario for the final conflict is that of alternative c) above, i.e. two battles with the Islamic nations fighting first against Israel and then the West leading a further wave of attack, unwittingly, against the returned Christ. With this clarification we can start to fit the two prophetic patterns together.

The sequence is put in context by the outline of the final chain of events given by the seven bowl prophecies. Starting out from the fourth bowl, the sequence seems to run as follows:
- Governments become oppressive. This corresponds to the fourth bowl (see Section 16.6).
    - In democratic societies this tends to be triggered by perceived or actual threats to the stability and security of the state. In recent times terrorist attacks and civil disturbances (such as the fuel tax protests in the UK) have shown how quickly governments may feel forced to take extraordinary measures and this has highlighted the possibilities of seemingly benign governments becoming oppressive.
- Civil disorder becomes a major issue in Western nations (the Beast powers). This is the interpretation of the fifth bowl (see Section 16.7).
    - History shows that in the face of increasing government oppression society will either be cowed or will react with civil disorder, or even revolution. If there is such a reaction there is a serious risk of a vicious circle in which disorder provokes more

repression, which provokes more severe disorder, and so on.
- The financial systems of the West collapse (the drying up of the river Euphrates). This corresponds to the first part of the sixth bowl (see Sections 16.8 & 17.5).
    - The possibility of such a collapse is much greater than many people realize. The speed, complexity, and interdependence of modern banking and financial trading computer systems make them very vulnerable. The collapse of various financial institutions in the US, the UK, Iceland and elsewhere during the 2008-9 financial crisis (or "credit crunch") have now highlighted this in a dramatic way. I have worked for a large part of my career in the banking industry and have seen analyses of various scenarios in which one of the possible outcomes has been a widespread collapse of financial institutions throughout the West. Once confidence in banks is seriously shaken there is a real risk that ordinary people will then only trust cash and seek to withdraw as much of it as they can from the banks. No bank in the world can sustain a prolonged "rush" against it. In the worst case they can only close their doors and turn off their cash machines. In an urban society, such as predominates in the West, the populace has no alternative food source than the shops and supermarkets. If these cease trading, or if people have no cash left to buy, the only alternative to starving is looting. If this happens against a background in which there is already considerable civil disorder (see above), then the most likely response by governments is the imposition of strict martial law.
    - The combination of the events outlined above, i.e. government oppression, civil disorder, financial collapse, and martial law, match up very well to the symbolic portrayal of the same events in Revelation chapter 17, where the Beast (the government powers in the West) turns on the harlot (the peoples of the

West) so as to "strip her naked and leave her destitute" (Rev. 17 v. 16).
- The events outlined above will leave the Western nations very weakened and probably forced to bring all their military forces home to maintain order under martial law.
  o Allies of the West, who depend on its support and ultimately on its military strength, will thus be weakened in their turn. This will particularly apply to Israel, which is so outnumbered by its potential enemies in the Middle East and depends so heavily on the might of the USA as a deterrent to prevent attacks from neighbouring states. With the USA and other Western nations seriously weakened and greatly distracted by internal affairs, that deterrent will be removed and Israel will become very vulnerable to a concerted attack by her Islamic neighbours.
  o Although the Middle-Eastern states may be affected to some extent by the financial collapse in the West, many of them will be able to fall back on a barter economy using their oil assets as a currency for continuing trade with other parts of the world. They may be thus able to avoid the internal conflicts damaging the West, and so be well positioned to take advantage of Israel's weakness. This appears to be the trigger for the prophesied attack by Islamic nations against Israel (see Section 19.3).
- As also seen in Section 19.3, the prophecies indicate that the initial success of the Islamic attack will leave Israel facing annihilation, and that in her extremity she will turn to God who will send Christ back to the earth to save them and to totally repulse their enemies.
  o Viewed from the West, the only likely means to bring about such an overwhelming victory by the heavily outnumbered Israelis is that they resort to the use of weapons of mass destruction in significant quantities. This presumed action would be unacceptable in the West, which would then be obliged to gather its remaining strength to go into

the Middle East to constrain Israel and try to restore stability.
- o However, instead of encountering just an Israeli military force, they will find themselves attacking the returned Christ and the armies of heaven. They will initially be unable to recognize him as the Son of God because of their ideological position which does not accommodate the concept of Jesus as a real and tangible force in world affairs, and so they will fight against him. This is the fulfilment of the prophecy of the frog spirits leading the nations to the battle of Armageddon (see Sections 16.9 & 18.2).
- Once the forces of the West have been defeated, or have surrendered, all opposition to Christ will cease and he will start to set up his kingdom on earth (see Sections 18.1 and 18.3).

The sequence of events outlined above is necessarily a personal hypothesis, but it seems to me to unify the prophetic visions of latter-day events in a way that is consistent with current political and social realities. If Our Lord remains away for a longer period than seems likely at present, then circumstances may change and events may work out in some other way that is hard to foresee now. However, no matter how it happens, we can be certain from the Bible prophecies that Jesus will return to earth, that he will overcome all opposition, and that he will set up his kingdom to become a place of peace and beauty, filled with the knowledge and love of God.

Even so, come Lord Jesus

APPENDIX A: SYMBOL GLOSSARY

The book of Revelation contains so many symbolic images that it would not be practical to try list them all here. The list here contains some of the more significant symbols, particularly those that occur in more than one place in the book. Entries often include additional exposition to support the choice of meaning that has been attached to the symbol, as this helps to keep the main text free of digressions and maintains a clearer narrative flow. On the other hand where a major symbol occurs only once in the book, most of the interpretation may be placed in the main text with just a simple entry in the glossary pointing to that place.

Beasts

The book of Daniel sets a powerful precedent for us to understand the use of beasts as symbols. In Daniel chapters 7 and 8, beasts of different kinds are used to represent the power and influence of major ruling forces in the world – kingdoms, empires and their rulers, governments and armies. Particular rulers or their dynasties may be represented as additional details such as horns (see ***Horns*** entry in the glossary). Beast images of note in the Revelation are:

- The dragon (see separate glossary entry for ***Dragon***)
- The beast from the sea (see Section 14.2)
- The beast from the earth (see Section 14.5)
- The creature just known as "the Beast" which in this interpretation is seen as a latter-day re-emergence of a power like the Sea beast (see Sections 16.7 and 17.3 for details).

Cherubim

Cherubim, the plural of "cherub", appear to be a manifestation of divine power and glory. Their particular role seems to be to separate the holy or eternal from the temporal. Thus their first occurrence in the Bible is to be placed to protect the tree of life from approach by fallen mankind (Gen. 3 v. 24).

Cherubim also have significant appearances as decorative figures in the furnishings of the places of worship established under the Mosaic Law. A pair of cherubim was made to flank the mercy seat as part of the lid of the Ark of the Covenant, and in the temple a larger pair was made to fill the most holy place and overshadow the whole ark. Further figures of cherubim were used to decorate the veil of the tabernacle and the inside walls of the temple. Their close relationship to the most holy place and the mercy seat seems to reinforce their role of setting, or emphasizing, a boundary between the place of men and the place of God.

Apart from the above, cherubim appear in visions, particularly in those that emphasize the glory of God. So when Ezekiel sees God on his throne of glory, he sees the throne supported by cherubim (Ez. 10 v. 1). This is like an earlier vision in which very similar beings are called "living creatures" (Ez. 1 v. 4-26). In fact Ezekiel equates the cherubim to the living creatures when he says "These were the living creatures I had seen... at the river Kebar" (Ez. 10 v. 20).

The positioning of cherubim between the temporal and the divine may symbolize the role of Christ as the mediator between man and God. Being both Son of Man, through Mary, and Son of God, through the Father, he is perfectly suited to this role. If the cherubim are a symbol for this role of Christ then their faces are also very apt. John sees four cherubim each with a different face, while Ezekiel sees them as being alike but each having four faces. The two accounts could be just different views of the same thing. For example, if the four cherubim in John's vision had kept a different face turned fully towards him, he may not have registered that they had other faces. Whether that is so or not, both prophets see the same four types of face and these are very relevant to the role of Christ. The faces, as recorded in Ez. 1 v. 10 and Rev. 4 v. 7, are those of:

- a lion
    - this represents kingship; and Christ is referred to as the Lion of the tribe of Judah (e.g. Rev. 5 v. 5) and as the future king of God's kingdom on earth.
- an ox
    - one of the main beasts of burden in biblical times, this represents service and humility; and Christ is

>> spoken of as the Suffering Servant (e.g. Is. 42 v. 1-3; Is. Ch. 53)
- a man
  - this obviously indicates humanity; and Christ is often referred to as the Son of Man
- an eagle
  - having much sharper vision than humans makes the eagle a symbol for spiritual insight and omniscience (see entry for *Eagle*); this can be seen as a metaphor for Christ as the Spirit-inspired Son of God.

In summary then, the cherubim are part of the manifestation of divine glory, and appear to mark or emphasise the separation of the divine and eternal from the worldly and temporal. They may have a more particular role of symbolising the role of Christ as the mediator between man and God.

Crystal Sea

This symbol is not easy to interpret with any certainty as it only occurs a few times in the Bible. We can quickly discard ideas based on possible similarities with the ocean or salt sea. We took that to be a symbol of nations in spiritual darkness (see *Sea* below), particularly when it is in turmoil and becomes opaque with disturbed sediment, but the crystal sea is shown in sharp contrast to this, as being pure, peacefully still, and suffused with light or fire.

A more promising approach opens up when we consider that the crystal sea only occurs in visions of heavenly glory. Such visions represent the spiritual realities that lie behind many of the details of the structure and furnishings of the tabernacle and the temple that were at the focus of the Jewish worship of God. As the letter to the Hebrews points out "Christ has not entered a sanctuary made by human hands which is only a pointer to the reality; he has entered heaven itself" (Heb. 9 v. 24). In both of the Jewish sanctuaries there was a large container for water used for ritual cleansing of the priests. In the accounts of the construction of this item (e.g. Ex. 30 v. 18 and 2 Chron. 4 v. 6) it is called a "basin" or "laver" (KJV), but in other references (e.g. 2 Kings 25 v. 13; 1 Chron. 18 v. 8) it is called a bronze "sea". So in this context, "sea" conveys ideas of the ritual cleansing and purification of priests.

Now the faithful believers are to have a role as a royal priesthood in God's kingdom (e.g. 1 Pet. 2 v. 9). Before they enter fully into this role they will have to undergo a final consecration or cleansing when "this perishable body must be clothed with the imperishable, and what is mortal with immortality" (1 Cor. 15 v. 53). So, like the bronze sea for purifying the Levitical priests, the crystal sea seems to represent the wellspring of immortal life or the process of conferring immortality that allows the faithful to enter their new roles in the Kingdom.

As a further point we can note that at a time when glass making was in its infancy, quantities were small and quality was variable. So a huge sheet of pure, translucent crystal was unheard of, and would be perceived as being immensely valuable. This makes it an apt symbol for the promise of eternal life, which is offered to God's faithful people as part of their great reward.

Dragon

The word "dragon", or in some translations "sea monster", is used as a symbol for major world powers in the Old Testament, e.g. for Babylon (in Jer. 51 v. 34) and for Egypt (in Ez. 29 v. 3). A related pictorial image is used to portray Rome (in Dan. 7 v. 7, 19-20) as a strange animal that is said to be "different from other beasts". As it is depicted with iron teeth and ten horns it obviously has no counterpart in the real animal kingdom, and so, like the dragon, it is a mythical beast. The common features of these Old Testament mythical "dragons" is that they are used as symbols for major powers in the earth that have pagan religions and who, for significant periods of their history, worshipped their rulers as gods. In other words they represent powers that contend with God by trying to dominate the world and by raising up man into God's place.

It is interesting to note that in Revelation chapter 12 the dragon power is related to the "ancient serpent" (Rev. 12 v. 9). This makes a link with the scriptural use of the serpent as a symbol of individual sin (see ***Serpent*** below). The use of the serpent as an analogy is drawn from the account of the fall of man in Genesis (Gen. 3) and there are direct references to this in the New Testament (such as 2 Cor. 11 v. 3). The symbolic use is extended by such events as Israel's punishment by venomous snakes during the exodus and the making of the bronze serpent as a focus for their pleas for forgiveness (Num. 21 v. 9). This lifting up of the bronze serpent is in turn taken as an image of Christ's victory on the cross over the power of sin (e.g. John 3 v. 14). Thus while the symbol of the serpent represents sin that puts individuals into conflict with the will of God, the dragon symbol seems to move this conflict up to a larger scale, raising it up from a personal level to a national level to represent a national spirit of man replacing, or contending with, God.

Further evidence of the ideas of "dragon" and "serpent" being linked come from Babylonian religion. Although extra-Biblical sources should normally be treated with great caution, there is powerful evidence of the strong influence that Babylonian ideas had on Jewish culture because of the period of Babylonian domination and Jewish exile in Babylon. Indeed Babylon is the context of the book of Daniel.

The primary god of the Babylonians was Bel. So in the Bible, the prophesied overthrow of Babylon is linked to the confounding of Bel (e.g. Jer. 50 v. 2) and the last Babylonian king is called "Belshazzar" (Dan. 5 v. 1) which means "Bel's leader". The Babylonians believed that Bel was manifested through a subordinate deity, or "familiar", called Marduk who was particularly involved with the city of Babylon. German archaeologists in the early 20th century excavated a magnificent ceremonial gateway, the Ishtar gate, in the walls of Babylon. The gateway was faced with thousands of colourful ceramic tiles bearing an inscription by Nebuchadnezzar and repeated images of lions and dragons. The lion is used in the book of Daniel as a symbol of Babylon while the dragon is known to have been used as a representation of Marduk. The tiles from the Ishtar gate were removed and have been re-assembled on a life-sized replica of the gateway in the Pergamon museum in Berlin. There the image of the dragon can be clearly seen to be a mythical beast with a composite body. Apart from having hind legs like a lion's, forelegs like an eagle's legs, a single, unicorn-like horn, and a scorpion's sting, most of the dragon is formed of the head, body and tail of a snake. So, Marduk's dragon is predominantly a serpent.

There is further confirmation that Babylon was closely associated with the idea of a snake-like dragon-god in the minds of the Jews in the inter-testamental period. This is found in a book in the Apocrypha called "Daniel, Bel, and the Snake" which purports to be an addition to the book of Daniel. It describes how Daniel, while in exile in Babylon, destroyed a pagan image of Bel and an apparently living giant snake that the Babylonians worshipped. The latter was almost certainly linked to the worship of Marduk. While few, if any, would claim inspired authority for this book, which in style is much like a folk-tale, it does show a clear familiarity, in Jewish thinking of the time, with Babylon being represented by a serpent-like image.

Right from its counterpart in the earlier city of Babel, Babylon is used in several places in the Bible to portray man's opposition to God and his people, and this symbolism continues in the Revelation (e.g. Rev. Chs. 17 & 18). Representing this kind of opposition to God by the symbol of a dragon, or snake-like creature, would be quite understandable to anyone familiar with the Jewish history and culture of the classical period.

Eagle

The eagle, together with some other birds of prey, has the sharpest eyesight in the animal kingdom. Humans have very good sight and in the most sensitive part of the retina, the fovea, each square millimetre contains some 200,000 light-sensitive cells, called "rods and cones" because of their shapes. However the fovea of the eagle contains around one million such cells per square millimetre, accounting for its superlative vision. By having so much sharper vision than humans, the eagle comes to be used as a symbol for spiritual insight and omniscience; this can be seen as a metaphor for any message or messenger originating from God, including Christ as the Spirit-inspired Son of God.

Earth
In Biblical use "the earth" is often coupled with "the heavens" to represent the whole of creation (e.g. Gen. 1 v. 1; Ps. 69 v. 34; Ps. 115 v. 15), but when these ideas are used as symbols they are often contrasted. So in the creation account the heavenly bodies are said to rule the day and the night (Gen. 1 v. 16-18). Since to our normal senses the heavenly bodies are above the earth, then if they "rule" it is a natural inference that it is the earth that is "ruled over" or subject to their power. So if in symbolic terms the heavenly bodies represent ruling powers (see also **Heavenly Bodies**), then the earth represents the peoples and organizations of the kingdoms being ruled. So for example in a prophecy about the downfall of Babylon in Isaiah Ch. 13 we are told not only that "the earth will be shaken" (v. 13), but also that human beings will be scarce (v. 12) and that God will "reduce the earth to desolation" (v. 9). This passage obviously does not apply to the whole planet or even just the geographical area controlled by the empire, but rather it is talking about the fate of the people and structures of the kingdom. Note that the sea is also used as a complementary symbol for the peoples of kingdoms (see *Sea* below).

The earth is used as a symbol in this way in many other passages, but in particular there is one Old Testament use that has both a local explanation and a later New Testament explanation that confirms this meaning. So in Hag. Ch. 2 God says twice that he will "shake the heavens and the earth" (v. 6 and v. 21), and using the parallelism of Hebrew poetry this is complemented by saying that "I shall shake all the nations" (v. 7) and "overthrow the thrones of kings, break the power of heathen realms" (v. 22). Then Heb. 12 v. 26-28 quotes this passage and says that it points to "the removal of …. all that is shaken", that is the earth, or rather the kingdoms of men that this symbolizes, "so that what cannot be shaken may remain", which is then confirmed as being Christ's kingdom by saying "the kingdom we are given is unshakeable".

The earth is also used as a symbol for mortality, as for example in the phrase "the dust of the ground" (Gen 2 v. 7) which uses the Hebrew word *adamah* for "ground" or "earth", and from which the name *Adam* is taken as a kind of Hebrew pun.

Glory

While "glory" is not itself a symbol, it is a concept which is often portrayed symbolically in the Bible. Glory is associated with things or beings that have attributes of beauty, honour, or majesty and which are therefore praiseworthy. Dictionaries define glory as exalted renown, honourable fame, or deserved praise. The word also has associated or derived connotations of splendour and radiance. Glory can thus be an intrinsic property of some glorious thing, but it can also refer to the honour and praise rendered to the glorious thing by those who perceive its glory. So, for example, during Israel's exodus wanderings the glory of God rested on Mount Sinai (Ex. 24 v. 16), but also worshippers are called to "ascribe to the Lord the glory due to his name" (Ps. 96 v. 8).

Both of these aspects of glory are reflected in symbolic representations of glory. For example when Daniel is given a vision of a glorious being, the description we are given conveys a powerful sense of radiant light and energy (Dan. 10 v. 5-7). Although the radiant being is only described as a "man", the similarities with John's vision of Christ among the lamp-stands (Rev. 1 v. 12-16) suggests that Daniel was also allowed to see a vision of Christ in his future glory.

An example of ascribed glory occurs when Isaiah is given a vision of the glory of God, in which the divine being on the throne is accompanied by seraphim who cry out "holy, holy, holy is the Lord of Hosts, the whole earth is full of his glory" (Is. 6 v. 2-3). Again this has close similarities with John's vision of God on his throne where the four living creatures round the throne sing, "holy, holy, holy is God the sovereign Lord of all" (Rev. 4 v. 8); see also **Cherubim** above.

Gold

From ancient times gold has been valued for its chemical stability, which can only be compromised by the most powerful reagents. Under normal conditions gold does not easily tarnish or corrode, and this allows it to keep its lustre without repeated polishing. This leads to it being classed as a "noble" metal and to its use as a symbol for purity and incorruptibility. In scriptural usage, gold is often taken as a symbol for faith; and the smelting process, by which the pure metal is separated from the impurities in the ore, is used as a symbol for strengthening faith by undergoing trials. Perhaps the clearest statements of this are "even gold passes through the assayer's fire, and much more precious than perishable gold is faith which stands the test" (1 Pet. 1 v. 7), and "I shall refine them as silver is refined and assay them as gold is assayed. They will invoke me by my name, and I myself shall answer them; I shall say 'These are my people'" (Zech. 13 v. 9).

Following this symbolism, the interior furnishings of the tabernacle, and then the temple, were made of, or clothed in, pure gold. This was to indicate that in order to come into the presence of God and to serve him acceptably, it was necessary to have a pure, tried faith.

Harlot

There are several clear examples of the use of an adulterous wife or a harlot as a symbol in the Bible (also see ***Woman*** below). A common use is as a symbol of the people of Israel as a group turning from God to the world, in order to find political or military power, or to embrace some form of false religion.

A good example of this is found in Ezekiel chapter 23 in the parable of the two women Oholah and Oholibah. The first woman, whose name means "her own tabernacle", is a symbol for Ephraim, who after the separation into two kingdoms set up her own religious sites with two calf idols. The second woman, whose name means "my tabernacle is in her", represents Judah who retained God's temple in Jerusalem. Both groups largely departed from the true worship of God by adopting various forms of idolatry, and this is clearly portrayed in the chapter under the guise of the two women promiscuously taking several foreign lovers.

Another graphic example is found in Hosea chapters 1 to 3 where the prophet is told to take a harlot as his wife. This is an enacted parable in which Hosea represents God, and the harlot he takes to wife represents Israel, who because of her idolatries has been an unfaithful "wife" to God.

Thus, in general, the harlot symbol represents some nation or group of people who have had the chance to be God's people, as God's "wife" in the Old Testament or Christ's "bride" in the New Testament, but have then turned their back on God to follow worldly pursuits or false religions (also see *Wife* below).

Heaven

The idea of heaven is closely related to the concept of "high" or "above". The plural form "heavens" is applied in scripture both to the earth's atmosphere, in which birds fly and clouds float, and to space in which we see the stars and planets. In the Old Testament, the original word used for "heaven(s)" is the Hebrew *shamayim*, which means raised up, or heaped up, things, and thus carries the idea of elevation or superiority. This does not necessarily apply to things which are literally above us in some vertical, spatial plane, but rather carries associations relating to higher qualities or higher powers, as in the contrast between God's way and man's in Is. 55 v. 8-9. These concepts of "above" or "raised up" convey ideas of power and rule that are often used to depict God's supremacy over humankind, but can also be used of human powers and rulers having relative superiority over others. This concept also has the related idea of *Heavenly Bodies* (see below).

Heavenly Bodies (Sun, Moon, and Stars)

The attributes of being elevated or superior that are associated with the concept of *Heaven* (see above) are also applied to the heavenly bodies such as the sun, moon, and stars. For example in the account of the creation of the sun, moon, etc. (Gen. 1 v. 14-18) the idea is repeatedly presented of these bodies *ruling* or *governing* the day or night. Then in Joseph's dream of the power he would be given in Egypt (Gen. 37 v. 9-10) he sees the sun, moon, and stars bowing down to him. Jacob seems to readily understand the symbolism and interprets it as the sun being himself, the moon being Joseph's mother, and the stars being his brothers; these all to be revered later as the founding fathers or princes of the tribes of Israel. Further, the fall of Babylon from power and its ruler's loss of regal power are portrayed in Is. 14 v. 12 through the picture of the morning star falling from heaven.

Putting these clues together with the physical properties of these bodies, we can begin to see some underlying meanings. Thus the sun, which radiates its own energy and supports life on earth, can represent a ruler who exercises absolute power, and controls the lives of men. So the sun is an image of a primary secular power such as a king, emperor, or president. The moon, which reflects light from another source, and is only bright enough to be seen clearly during the night, relates to a derived or secondary power. Thus the moon can represent a dependent secular power, such as a prince or minister; or sometimes, because the moon gives light in darkness, it may represent a religious power such as a prophet or bishop, responsible for bringing spiritual enlightenment. Finally, the stars are "lesser suns", to us seeming much less bright, and so can represent minor rulers, typically subject to some higher authority such as an emperor.

Horns

Horns in scripture are used as symbols of power and strength, often representing the power of a king or of God himself. In the Old Testament the divinely revealed designs for the altars for the tabernacle and the temple included horns on their corners. This was probably intended as a reminder of the power of the God that was being worshipped. It may be this that David is alluding to when he calls God his "sure defender" (Ps. 18 v. 2); more literally "the horn of my salvation" (KJV).

Also, Psalm 132 v. 17 says, "I shall make a king of David's line appear" (REB), which is also translated as "I will make the horn of David to bud" (KJV), or "I will make the horn of David to grow" (NKJV). So there are obvious connotations of kingship, either as an individual king, or as a royal line or dynasty. Also in Luke 1 v. 69 we read of Zechariah, speaking of Christ, saying that God "has raised for us a strong deliverer" (REB), or "hath raised up an horn of salvation for us" (KJV).

Thus horns are typically used as a symbol for a source or holder of power, often in the form of a king or a royal dynasty.

Horses

The scriptural evidence for the meaning of this symbol is not emphatically clear, but there is some guidance that we can use. In the introduction to the seven seals (Section 7.1) we took evidence from Zechariah to suggest that horses represent forces or influences that are under God's control and assist in the fulfilment of God's declared purpose. In Zechariah's time, that purpose was for the Jews to return to Jerusalem and to rebuild the temple as the centre of the true worship of God.

In the general usage of ancient times the horse was too expensive for employing as a common beast of burden, for which donkeys or oxen were commonly used. Rather the horse was used as a weapon of war, to mount cavalry and pull chariots (e.g. Ps. 20 v. 6, 7). This conveys images of conflict and of meeting and overcoming opposition. The horse was also used as a carrier of imperial mail (e.g. Esther 8 v. 10), conveying a meaning of message bearing. Both of these usages reinforce the ideas we have taken from Zechariah, i.e. that horses are a symbol of the power that typically originates from a king, and can convey and carry out the royal will even at long distances from the throne. Where the royal being is God, that power can be his Spirit and / or his angelic forces.

Islands

Islands are not generally used on their own as symbols but tend to be included with other geographic features in passages which describe events that cannot creditably be taken as literal. So for example, in a chapter portraying the establishment of Christ's kingdom (Is. 42) the wilderness is to rejoice (v. 11) while the islands ascribe glory to the Lord and sing his praise (v. 12). Similarly in Psalm 97, the earth is to be glad while the islands all rejoice (v. 1). We have already seen that the earth is used as a symbol for nations and peoples (see *Earth* above), but the sea is also used as a similar symbol for less advanced peoples and tribes (see *Sea* below). Since islands are to be found in the sea it would be natural to think that islands as symbols have something to do with such peoples. A related symbol to the earth was mountains (see *Mountains* below). Mountains are raised up above the earth and so were taken to represent powerful nations or empires that dominate their neighbours. So by similar reasoning, since islands rise out of the sea, we can take them to represent the more dominant and powerful peoples and tribes in the less advanced areas of the world.

Lamb

Under the Law of Moses a lamb was one of the ritually clean animals most used for sacrifices. Many details of these sacrifices point forwards, symbolically to the sacrificial role of Jesus. So, the complete combustion of the burnt offering points to Christ's complete dedication to his Father's will; the sin or guilt offering relates to his role in bringing us grace and forgiveness; and the peace or fellowship offering speaks of the fellowship we can have with God through the reconciliation effected by Christ. Finally the way the Israelites were saved from the angel of death by the sprinkled blood of the Passover lamb speaks of the hope of resurrection for those who have accepted Christ's saving grace. With this wealth of symbolism it is not surprising that John the Baptist calls Jesus the Lamb of God (John 1 v. 29, 36); and Paul refers to him as "Christ our Passover" (1 Cor. 5 v. 7). Altogether in the Revelation there are 28 references to "lamb", occurring mainly in chapters 5, 6, 7, 19, and 21, and all the occurrences are symbolic references to Christ.

Lamp-stand

A lamp-stand (translated in the KJV as "candlestick") is usually assumed to be complete with its lamp sitting on top, and is used to help the lamp cast its light more widely. In biblical times the most common form of artificial light was an oil lamp burning olive oil with the help of a wick. As olive oil is a symbol for the word of God, particularly for the gospel, and light is a symbol for spiritual enlightenment, the lamp-stand makes a good symbol for a believing individual or community that spreads God's word into the world around them to try to enlighten its spiritual darkness (see *Light* below).

In Israel under the Mosaic Law the centre of their worship was the tabernacle and later the temple. Both were illuminated with lamps on lamp-stands (e.g. Ex. Ch. 25, and 2 Chron. Ch. 4). The lamps and stands were all made of pure gold, a symbol for faith (see **Gold** above). We thus have an image of God's word (oil) being retained in faithful hearts (gold) to produce a light by which God's servants (the priests) can see to do their work.

This symbol of the lamp-stand is thus very fitting to represent the seven churches to which John was to send the Revelation (e.g. Rev. 1 v. 12, 20).

Light

Light is used as a powerful symbol for a source of spiritual enlightenment. So when Jesus comes into the world to show us God's love and to preach the gospel of salvation, he is described as "the true light which gives light to everyone" (John 1 v. 9). Jesus called his disciples "light for all the world" (Matt. 5 v. 14). Paul exhorts the Ephesian believers "as Christians you are light.... for where light is, there is a harvest of goodness, righteousness, and truth" (Eph. 5 v. 8-9).

In contrast, darkness is used for a symbol of an environment in which there is an absence of knowledge about God and in which sin flourishes. So Jesus, talking about his own mission, tells Nicodemus "The light has come into the world, but people preferred darkness to light because their deeds were evil. Wrongdoers hate the light and avoid it, for fear their misdeeds should be exposed." (John 3 v. 19-20). Preaching God's truth in a world of darkness is often spoken of as lighting a lamp (see **Lamp-stand** above).

Michael

Michael is the name given in a few places in the Bible to an archangel or divinely appointed leader of God's people. The name means, "Who is like God?", so it obviously refers to someone acting as God's representative. In Daniel the name is given to a being, not specifically identified as an angel, who is described as a "chief prince" or "the great captain who stands guarding your fellow-countrymen" (Dan. 10 v. 13, 21; 12 v. 1). That being uses his power to support and defend God's people, the Jews.

The only other reference to Michael outside the Revelation is when he is referred to as an archangel in Jude (v. 9). On examination this turns out to be a clear reference back to Zechariah chapter 3, which needs to be put in context to be fully understood. In the passage an unnamed angel rebukes Satan who is opposing the high priest of the returned Jewish exiles. They had come back from Babylon to Jerusalem and were trying to rebuild God's temple but were being hindered by the opposition of local non-Jewish peoples (as in Ezra Ch. 4 and Neh. Ch. 4). Given that *satan* means "adversary" (see **Satan** below), it would seem likely that the "satan" in this passage indicates the Jews' political adversaries. In due course the Persian Emperor intervened by commanding the Jews' adversaries to cease their opposition and to actually support the Jews' effort. With the additional encouragement of the prophets Zechariah and Haggai, the work then proceeded successfully (e.g. Ezra Ch 6). The Jews obviously saw this as a rebuke to their enemies, brought about by God's intervention on their behalf. With these events put in their proper context, it can be seen how this divine intervention could be symbolized as a "satan" being rebuked by the angel, Michael.

The references above support an interpretation of "Michael" being a symbol or personification of divine power that is exercised through or for God's people when no divinely appointed king is physically present. In the struggle of good against evil in Revelation chapter 12, Michael is supported by "angels". This can be translated as "messengers", and so be taken to represent the faithful Christians who contended against the powers of pagan darkness to spread the gospel through their witness. In other words, Michael's angels represent the growing body of the early church who carry on their Master's work after he has physically departed from them by ascending to heaven, and who still are being supported by the exercise of the Master's power.

Mountains

Mountains are often used as an extension of the earth symbol (see ***Earth***), together with the "raised up" concept associated with the idea of heaven (see ***Heaven***). So when a kingdom becomes powerful and is able to dominate the nations around and possibly form an empire, it can be thought of as being elevated above its neighbours. So in symbolic terms, a section of earth has been raised up, and has become a mountain. Conversely, when a major nation loses its power then, symbolically, a mountain is thrown down or levelled.

For example, in talking about the conditions in God's Kingdom, Isaiah says "let every valley be raised, every mountain and hill brought low" (Is. 40 v. 4). In other words, no human kingdom is dominant (symbolically the mountains are levelled), and neither is any human kingdom to be oppressed (symbolically the valleys will be filled).

Again, speaking of God's kingdom on earth, Isaiah says "the mountain of the Lord's house will be set over all other mountains, raised high above the hills" (Is. 2 v. 2). So the centre of power in the new kingdom, which will be based in Christ's capital city, Jerusalem, is depicted as being the highest of all mountains. If this were literal then Jerusalem would become higher than Mount Everest, which seems very unlikely and impracticable. However, if seen symbolically, it clearly indicates that as Christ's kingdom grows to become a world-wide empire, it will be more elevated, symbolically, or literally more powerful, than all other nations on earth.

Oil

Oil in the Bible typically refers to olive oil. This was widely used in cooking and as lamp fuel. Thus in food it was a source of energy to the eater, and in lamps it was a source of illumination that allowed the user to see and make sense of his environment once the sun had gone down. Oil is thus a very good metaphor for the inspiring and enlightening power of the word of God in a world of spiritual darkness. Oil was also used to protect and moisturize the skin as an aid to maintaining good health. So a Psalm praising God for his blessings mentions "oil to make their faces shine" (Ps. 104 v. 15). This is not just a picture of physical health but also recalls the way Moses face shone when he had been in the presence of God (Ex. 34 v. 29-35), so highlighting oil as a symbol for the word of God as a means of bringing the faithful into harmony with God and conferring spiritual health. In a similar way oil, along with sweet-smelling spices, was an important constituent of the ritual anointing oil that was used to consecrate kings and high priests under the Mosaic Law. It thereby indicated that these important offices should be held by men whose minds were enlightened by God's laws and teachings. The symbolic meaning of oil also underlies other symbols; see *Lamp-stand* and *Light* elsewhere in the glossary.

Satan

In the Old Testament *satan* is the untranslated Hebrew word for "adversary". In the KJV the verb form is always translated as being an adversary or resisting something. In its noun form it is translated as "adversary" 7 times, but left untranslated 19 times. The word "satan" is usually left untranslated when the opposition is directed against God or those who follow God, but could always be translated as "adversary" without loss of meaning. The word does not always relate to an evil force, and is used for good opposing evil as well as the opposite. So when an angel appears to the prophet Balaam to resist his intention to curse the people of Israel, the angel is described as standing as "an adversary" (Hebrew *satan*) against him.

In the New Testament the Greek word used, *satanas,* is a direct transliteration of the Hebrew word *satan*, but it tends to be used in a more abstract way to convey a spirit of opposition to the ways and thinking of God.

Sea

We have taken the earth to be a symbol of the people and organizations of worldly kingdoms (see *Earth* above), and as in nature the sea is a complementary concept, so it is in scriptural symbolism. For example Isaiah uses the sea (Is. 57 v. 20) as a symbol of wicked peoples, those in spiritual darkness. In differentiating between the use of earth and sea as symbols for peoples we can take a lot of guidance from their natural properties. While the earth has a relatively fixed form and structure, the sea is formless and constantly changing.

Carrying these differences over to their use as symbols, the earth is used for peoples of structured (i.e. organised, civilised) kingdoms, while the sea is used for peoples of relatively formless groupings (i.e. local tribal or nomadic peoples). The more civilised "earth" peoples, with better communication and technology may possibly have some access to enlightenment from God's word – though they may often not avail themselves fully of it. The less stable "sea" peoples, with poorer records and communications, are less likely to have access to the word and so are more typically "in darkness".

Both "earth" and "sea" peoples can be the basis for the emergence of more powerful, or "elevated", groupings in the form of mightier kingdoms or empires. These are represented as "mountains" (raised above the earth), or as "islands" (raised above the sea) – see *Islands* and *Mountains* above.

To give some supporting examples, one key passage is found in Christ's own words about the last days (Lk. 21 v. 25) where "the roar and surge of the sea" is used as a poetic parallel of the more literal "nations will stand helpless, not knowing which way to turn". Similar poetic parallels link the sea to peoples in a Psalm foretelling the setting up of Christ's Kingdom (Ps. 98 v. 7-9). This understanding of the symbolic use of "sea" helps to explain a reference later in the Revelation when Christ's established Kingdom is being described (Rev. 21 v. 1). Here the phrase "there was no longer ant sea" is very difficult to understand literally, but when seen symbolically, as meaning that there will be no more peoples in darkness once Christ rules, the difficulty falls away.

Serpent

The serpent is used in the Bible as a symbol for human behaviour that is contrary to the will of God, i.e. sin. The idea is introduced in the account of the fall of man in Genesis (Gen. 3) where the serpent acts as the tempter that triggers mankind's fall from grace. This is directly referred to in the New Testament where Paul likens the forces threatening the faith of the Corinthian believers to the serpent's cunning that deceived Eve (2 Cor. 11 v. 3). The account of the fall also describes the struggle of mankind against sin as a lasting enmity between the woman's offspring and the serpent

(Gen. 3 v. 15). Special mention is made of a particular descendant of the woman who would be wounded by the serpent, but who would in return be able to defeat the serpent by inflicting a mortal wound on it. This refers to Christ whose sinless life meant that his death on the cross could be turned into the victory of the resurrection.

The symbolic use of the serpent is extended by the events associated with Israel's punishment by venomous snakes during the Exodus. There they were instructed to make a bronze serpent and raise it up on a pole as a focus for their pleas to God for forgiveness (Num. 21 v. 9). This act of looking directly at a symbol of their sins was meant to indicate their acknowledgement of their guilt and their recognition that only God could grant them forgiveness and healing. This lifting up of the bronze serpent is in turn taken as an image of Christ's victory on the cross over the power of sin (e.g. John 3 v. 14).

Seven (number)

The first instance of the number seven in the Bible is in the creation account of there being six days of creation, with the seventh day being a day of rest (Gen. Ch. 1). This is then taken as the basis for there being six days in the working week, completed by a Sabbath (derived from the Hebrew word for "seventh") day of rest (Ex. 20 v. 8-11). On a larger scale of time there were to be six years of farming, followed by a seventh year in which the land was to lie fallow (Lev. 25 v. 1-7). Beyond that, a group of 7 x 7 years of farming cycles was to be followed by a 50th year of Jubilee (Lev. 25 v. 8 ff.) in which purchased or, more correctly, leased land was to be released to the legal heirs. Finally, in the religious calendar, the last religious rituals of the year were to be carried out in the seventh month whose focus was the Day of Atonement.

In consequence, the number seven can be seen as a number of divine completeness, carrying connotations of bringing to rest, of making one, and of making complete. This can relate to a single period or set of events, as in creation. However, the number seven can also be a cyclic number, in which each end or completion is followed by a new start. This conveys the ideas of circularity and repetition. Further, from the use of seven on different scales, such as the days in the week, the 7-year cycle, and the 7 x 7 year cycle to Jubilee, we can see that cycles of seven's may be going on within other cycles, concurrently.

Ten (number)

The use of the number ten in scripture can be associated with assessing or measuring human actions; possibly derived from the hand being used as a metaphor for action and the hands having ten digits. For example, in the OT the standards for assessing human actions are summarised in the Ten Commandments, and in the NT the ten virgins represent the body of believers being tested for fitness to enter their Lord's wedding feast.

Trees

Trees are sometimes used in the Bible as symbols of nations or kingdoms. For example king Jehoash used a parable of the thistle and the cedar to compare the weakness of king Amaziah of Judah with his own strength in Israel (2 Kings 14 v 8-10). Also when David praises God for his power and majesty he describes God's power over the nations poetically as a force that can shatter trees (Ps. 29 v 5, 9). Jesus, in his Olivet prophecy, uses the symbol of trees blossoming to represent states gaining, or regaining, their national independence, and uses the fig tree as a particular symbol for Israel (Lk. 21 v. 29-31).

Warfare

While there are many accounts of war and human conflict in the Bible, the idea of warfare is also used as a metaphor or symbol for the spiritual struggle between good and evil. So Paul urges Timothy to "take your share of hardship, like a good soldier of Christ" (2 Tim. 2 v. 3). He also tells the Corinthians that, "the weapons we wield are not merely human; … we demolish sophistries and all that rears its proud head against the knowledge of God" (2 Cor. 10 v. 4-5). Similarly he tells the Ephesians, "Put on the full armour provided by God, … for our struggle is not against human foes, but against cosmic powers, against the authorities and potentates of this dark age" (Eph. 6 v. 11-12), or again, "throw off the deeds of darkness and put on the armour of light" (Rom. 13 v.

12). Thus, since we have seen that "heaven" refers to the spiritual dimension (see *Heaven* above), it follows that "war in heaven" (e.g. Rev. 12 v. 7) refers to just this sort of conflict between the forces of darkness and light in the struggle for spiritual authority over the hearts and minds of men.

Water (fresh)

Fresh water has considerable natural significance in the hot, dry lands of the Middle East that form the backdrop to so much of the Bible message. For example, when Israel were wandering in the wilderness they became very anxious or even rebellious when there was no obvious source of water available. On two such occasions God directed Moses to provide water miraculously from a rock to meet the people's needs and save them from dying of thirst (Ex. 17 v. 5-6; Num. 20 v. 8). Paul takes this as a type of the promise of salvation and life that is offered to us through Christ (1 Cor. 10 v. 1-4). The symbolism is particularly apt when the water is from a spring as it then appears, almost miraculously, without human effort.

Thus as a biblical symbol, fresh water can be taken to represent the influence of the Spirit or the Spirit-inspired Word that brings life where otherwise death reigns. Indeed, Jesus makes a major play on this parallel between fresh water and his offer of salvation in his discourse with the woman at the well at Sychar (John 4 v. 7-15). The use of fresh water as a symbol for the influence of the Spirit can be generalised a little to see it as representing the whole realm of spiritual life or true religion.

White

White is a common symbol in the Bible for purity and righteousness. So when the Revelation speaks of Christ's bride, the believers, being made ready for him it says "she has been given fine linen, shining and clean, to wear. (The fine linen signifies the righteous deeds of God's people.)" (Rev. 19 v. 6-9). This carries echoes of the priesthood under the Mosaic Law who were clothed in fine linen (e.g. Ex Ch. 28), which would probably have been bleached white. Also angels are typically described as being clothed in white (e.g. Matt. 28 v. 3; Acts 1 v. 10). Further, when

David prays for forgiveness and cleansing over his sin with Bathsheba, he asks to be washed so as to become "whiter than snow" (Ps. 51 v. 7). Thus white is a symbol for spiritual cleanness, and can be thought of as the colour of heaven.

Wife

In the Bible marriage is often used as a symbol of the relationship between God, or Christ, and his people, with the people being represented as a woman (see ***Woman*** below) in the role of wife or bride. So in the New Testament Paul talks about marriage being a symbol or living parable of the relationship between Christ and his church, meaning the full body of believers including men and women (Eph. 5 v. 21-33). Also Jesus in his parables uses the idea of the wedding feast to represent his union with the believers at his return to the earth (Matt. 22 v. 2-14). This has echoes in the Revelation where the union is described as the marriage supper of the Lamb for which "his bride has made herself ready, and she has been given fine linen, shining and clean, to wear. (The fine linen signifies the righteous deeds of God's people.)" (Rev. 19 v. 6-9).

In the Old Testament we find several uses of the same symbol, for example "Your husband is your Maker; his name is the Lord of Hosts" (Is. 54 v. 4-8), and "As a bridegroom rejoices over the bride, so will your God rejoice over you" (Is. 62 v. 5).

Woman

The very first woman we meet in Genesis is Eve whose name means "life" or "life-giving" and who is called "the mother of all living beings" (Gen. 3 v.20). Together with her husband Adam she was given the divine commandment to be fruitful, to increase, and to fill the earth (Gen. 1 v.28). Thus, in God's spiritual creation, woman is a natural symbol for that part of mankind that is spiritually fruitful through responding to God's instructions and so bringing the hope of eternal life to themselves and, by their witness, to others. Thus woman represents a group of people that has the opportunity of receiving seed (the word of salvation) from God and bearing fruit for him by allowing the word to have its full effect in their lives. Those that persevere in this calling are referred to as God's "wife" or as the (multitudinous) "bride" of Christ (see ***Wife*** above). On the other hand, those who have this opportunity but become unfaithful or apostate, by turning away and making liaisons with the world, are represented by the symbol of an adulteress or harlot (see *Harlot* above).

APPENDIX B: ALTERNATIVE WAYS TO APPROACH THE REVELATION

The complexity of the imagery used in the Revelation has led to it being interpreted in many different ways over the centuries since it was first revealed. The nub of the problem lies in trying to find a reliable way of mapping the narrative flow of the book, with all its different symbols, on to recognizable events in world affairs. In general the approaches taken fall into four main groups that are outlined below.

One style of approach maps the narrative of the Revelation on to the history of the early years of the Christian Era. It stresses the references to things that "must soon take place" and to Jesus "coming quickly", which lead it to pay particular attention to the events surrounding the Roman oppression of the Jews in AD 70 and AD100, and the persecution of the early church. This is known as the preterist approach.

A contrasting style stresses the book's repeated references to Christ's return and the establishment of his kingdom on earth. This sees John's visions predominantly as predictions of the events of the end-times at the close of the Christian Era. This is known as the futurist approach.

A third method of interpretation takes the Revelation to have a wider scope than the first two, to the extent that it covers all the Christian Era. It sees the visions as revealing a chronological progression of events spanning the whole of the period from John's day to the return of Christ and the setting up of his kingdom on earth. This is known as the historicist approach.

The remaining interpretive approach sees the imagery of the Revelation as conveying more general truths about the human condition. While treating the book as being relevant to the whole Christian Era, it does not generally expect the narrative to relate to specific events in the course of history. Rather it interprets the various visions and symbols as illustrating different aspects of the Christian life that could be experienced at many points in history, rather like Christ's teachings in his parables. This is known as the idealist approach.

One or other of these four approaches can be detected in virtually all of the attempts to interpret the Revelation, though in some cases a mixture of more than one of the approaches can be seen. For example some writers have taken a preterist view of the first part of the Revelation and then taken the rest of the book from a futurist standpoint. Indeed, applying these "labels" to the interpretation presented here, we could be said, in broad terms, to be applying an idealist approach to Revelation chapters 1 to 11, a historicist approach to chapters 12 to 14, and a futurist approach to chapters 15 to 22. However, as was stated in the preface, no elements of the approach were chosen beforehand, apart from the principle of letting scripture interpret scripture wherever possible. Rather the shape of the interpretation has developed gradually as the understanding of each section has emerged from a study of its Biblical precedents.

Whatever approach is taken there are a number of images and events in the Revelation that might seem to have fairly obvious associations or meanings. If so, these should lead the open-minded student to ask questions about why those things are introduced at that particular point in the narrative and how they fit into the surrounding context. Some of the key questions to arise from such an approach might include the following:
- Chapter 1 – John's attention is specifically drawn to the seven churches in Asia Minor. Also Christ is represented as standing amongst them and they are all to receive copies of the whole book (v. 11), not just the letter addressed to them.
    - What does this imply about the Jewish or Gentile relevance of the Revelation?
- Chapters 2, 3 – the messages in the letters to the churches are also addressed to "he who has an ear".
    - Does this indicate that the messages have some more general relevance, applying to believers beyond the membership of the specific church being addressed?

- Chapters 5, 6 – the sealed scroll that can only be opened by Christ seems to relate closely to the gospel of salvation by faith. This was alluded to by shadows and types in the Old Testament, but was only fully revealed by Christ.
    - If opening the seals is associated with revealing the gospel, how do any events predicted in chapter 6 relate to the Christian experience of preaching?
- Chapters 7, 11, 14 – these all carry strong references, in the present tense, to Christ meeting the glorified believers and / or judging the nations at his return.
    - Why are such strong references to the end-times introduced in these places when the main reference to Christ's return is not made until chapter 19?
- Chapter 12 – the account of the man-child who is "destined to rule all nations with a rod of iron" (v. 5 and Ps. 2) is an obvious reference to the birth, death, and ascension of Jesus.
    - Why is such a strong reference to these events made at the very middle of the book, and what does this tell us about the book's structure?
- Chapter 15 – the seven plagues in the seven bowls are described as "the last plagues of all" with which "the wrath of God was completed" (v. 1).
    - Can this refer to any other period than that immediately leading up to the return of Christ?
- Chapter 19 – the forces of evil and rebellion are defeated by one called "Faithful and true", "the Word of God", and "King of kings and Lord of lords", who will rule the nations "with a rod of iron" and will "tread the winepress of the fierce wrath of God", and who is accompanied by "the armies of heaven".
    - Can this refer to anything other than Christ returning to the earth in glory and with divine power?

Some of the key challenges that have to be met in approaching the Revelation are to answer these questions in a way that makes coherent sense across the whole of the interpretation being presented, while at the same time fitting in well with the predictions, clues, and precedents to be found elsewhere in the Bible.

I have tried to address these issues myself as I encountered them in the course of writing this book but I must leave it to the reader to judge how well I have succeeded.